The Catholic Heart
Day by Day

Uplifting Stories for Courageous Living

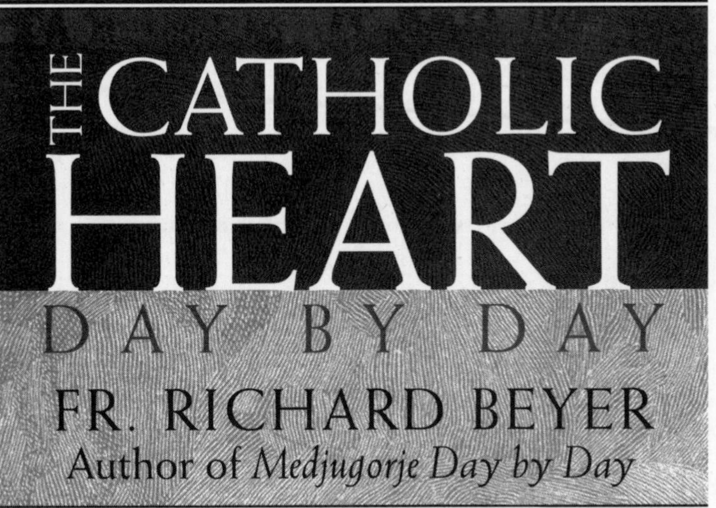

PARACLETE PRESS
BREWSTER, MASSACHUSETTS

The Catholic Heart Day by Day: Uplifting Stories for Courageous Living

2008 First Printing

ISBN: 978-1-55725-600-3

Scripture quotations designated VULGATE are from the Douay-Rheims version of the Bible.

Library of Congress Cataloging-in-Publication Data

Beyer, Richard J.
The Catholic heart day by day: uplifting stories for courageous living / by Richard Beyer.
p. cm.
Includes bibliographical references.
ISBN 978-1-55725-600-3
1. Devotional calendars—Catholic Church. 2. Christian life—Catholic authors. I. Title.
BX2182.3.B49 2008
242'.2–dc22 2008030877

10 9 8 7 6 5 4 3 2 1

Published by Paraclete Press
Brewster, Massachusetts
www.paracletepress.com
Printed in the United States of America

Contents

Introduction

When the followers of Jesus founded the first Christian communities and conveyed the gospel by word of mouth, through story and personal experience, they resonated the enthusiasm and joy of the first Pentecost. It took three and a half centuries for the selected writings of the church finally to be compiled, canonized, and reproduced as a new testament by Emperor Constantine's scribes. Through three long centuries of persecution, the church relied on storytellers who were on fire with the Holy Spirit, traveling throughout the known world, to tell the story of Christ over campfires and in marketplaces. To be sure, the church eventually developed doctrinal divisions, theologies, and philosophical categories to articulate its experience of the Risen Christ, but even today the first thing a convert is told is a story.

By their nature, stories address the heart as well as the mind. A personal experience, story, or image can "sing" the truth and not just tell it, invoking in the hearer an intellectual response, but also a personal and emotive one. As John Henry Newman taught, universals can delight and inform the mind, but only particulars can move the heart to action and commitment.

The Catholic Heart Day by Day is a kaleidoscope of stories, images, allegories, and portraits that seeks to complement our faith, not so much in theology or doctrine, but in living love, living action, living heroism. The settings will change from Nazi Germany to the American heartland to the Jordan River; from Pearl Harbor to the beaches at Normandy to the Japanese hell ships; from ancient

Israel to the reported apparitions of the Blessed Virgin in Bosnia-Herzegovina. But most important, as we spend this year exploring the heart of Catholicism, we will be exploring at the same time the deepest and most beautiful aspects of our own humanity and its limitless potential. So it is my hope that this will be a book of encouragement as well as inspiration.

JANUARY

January 1

Solemnity of Mary, Mother of God

The Word became flesh and made his dwelling among us. . . .
(John 1:14)

The title "Mother of God" (from the Greek *Theotokos*, or "God-bearer") has great significance in the church not only because of its connotations for Mary, but also for the whole mystery of God made man, the Incarnation.

To begin with, the Virgin Mary conceived and brought forth, in his human nature, the One who is God from all eternity. She did not, of course, conceive the divine nature of her Son, but is Mother of God in the sense that from her own flesh and blood she gave to God a human nature like hers. And this human *nature* was more than flesh; it included the very personhood or "humanness" of our God, Jesus Christ.

When we reflect that from Jesus' earthly birth his divine nature was integrated and united completely to his human nature, we begin to see the full import of the title *Theotokos*. It speaks of the mystical union of the human and divine that formed the God-man, and it actually says more about Jesus than it does about Mary.

In the early church there were many false teachings about Christ, especially Arianism, which taught that Jesus was not co-eternal with the Father, but was created by him. The title *"Mother of God"* was declared a dogma of the faith by the Council of Chalcedon in 451 as a clear statement of the true nature of Jesus Christ. It is also the most ancient title of Our Lady, used by fathers of the church as early as AD 200.

January 2
Christmas Dilemma

We have seen his glory, the glory of the One and Only, who came from the Father, full of grace and truth. (John 1:14)

One evening a man sat in reflective silence after reading St. Luke's account of the Incarnation. "There's no point to God becoming a man," he mused. "Why would an all-powerful God want to share even one of his divine moments with the likes of us? Even if he did, why would he choose to be born in an animal stable? The whole thing is *crazy*. Surely, if God wanted to come down to earth, he would have chosen some other way."

Suddenly, he was roused from his reverie by a strange sound outside. He went to the window and saw a small gaggle of blue geese frantically honking and aimlessly flopping about in the snow. They seemed dazed and confused. Apparently, they had been left behind in the flight formations of a larger flock on its way from the arctic islands to the warmer climate of the Gulf of Mexico. Moved to compassion, the man tried to shoo the poor geese into his warm garage, but the more he shooed, the more they panicked. *If they only realized I'm just trying to do what's best for them*, he thought to himself. *How can I make them understand that I want to help them?*

Then a thought crossed his mind. *If for just a minute I could become one of them, an ordinary goose, and communicate with them in their own language, they would know what I'm trying to do.* Suddenly, he remembered Christmas, and a smile came over his face. He pictured that ordinary-looking infant, lying in that stable in Bethlehem, and he knew the answer to his Christmas problem: God had become one of us to direct us to our homeland, to affirm his love for us by the only means possible—by becoming one of us.

January 3

Temple Lambs

And there were shepherds living out in the fields nearby, keeping watch over their flocks at night. An angel of the Lord appeared to them, and the glory of the Lord shone around them, and they were terrified. But the angel said to them, "Do not be afraid. I bring you good news of great joy that will be for all the people." (Luke 2:8–10)

It's interesting that the story of Christ's birth came first to shepherds. They were despised by the orthodox Jews of their day since they were unable to keep the details of the ceremonial law and could not observe all the meticulous hand-washings and rules and regulations. Their flocks made far too constant demands on them, and so the orthodox looked down on them. But it was to simple men of the fields that God's message first came.

However, these were probably very special shepherds. In the temple, morning and evening, an unblemished lamb was offered as a sacrifice to God. To see that the supply of perfect offerings was always available, the temple authorities had their own private flocks of sheep, and we know that these flocks were pastured near Bethlehem. It's quite possible that these shepherds were in charge of the flocks from which the temple offerings were chosen. Perhaps it was no coincidence that the shepherds who looked after the temple lambs were the first to adore the final and perfect Lamb of God who was to take away the sin of the world.

January 4

Feast of St. Elizabeth Ann Seton

Therefore I am sending you prophets and wise men and teachers. (Matthew 23:34a)

Two years before the signing of the Declaration of Independence, a remarkable woman named Elizabeth Bayley was born in New York City. At the age of twenty, she married a businessman named William Seton. Neither she nor William was Catholic. In time the couple had five children.

Then tragedy struck: William contracted tuberculosis. He moved his family to Italy, hoping that the climate would help him, but his illness proved terminal and he died a few years later.

With the help of a generous Italian family, the Setons moved back to the United States. The goodness of that Italian family led the young widow to investigate the Catholic Church, and two years later she embraced the Catholic faith herself. Her relatives and friends were shocked and virtually disowned her; she was forced to get a teaching job to support her five children.

When the children came of age, Elizabeth entered religious life and founded the American branch of the Sisters of Charity. This order established the great Catholic school system in America.

Elizabeth Seton died at the age of forty-six. She wasn't a mystic. She wasn't a martyr. She was simply a widow who gave what she had to God. She was a single parent who turned tragedy in her life—the loss of her husband and the rejection of her family—into a spectacular gift to God and his people.

How fitting it was, then, that in 1975 Elizabeth was the first American-born saint to be canonized.

■

January 5

Case Dismissed

And the prayer offered in faith will make the sick person well; the Lord will raise him up. If he has sinned, he will be forgiven. Therefore confess your sins to each other. . . . (James 5:15–16)

One of the beautiful results of confession is that, as we joyfully accept the Lord's forgiveness, we are then moved to forgive others. There was a Catholic physician in Scotland who was very lenient with his poor patients, and when he found that it was difficult for them to pay his fees, he wrote in red ink across the record of their indebtedness the one word—forgiven. This happened so frequently that his ledger had few pages where those red letters did not appear.

After his death, his executors thought the doctor's estate would be greatly enhanced if some of the "forgiven" debts could be collected. After unsuccessful attempts to collect from the poor patients, they went to court to recover the money. But when the judge examined the ledger and saw the word "forgiven" canceling the entries, he said, "There's no court in the land that could enforce payment of these accounts marked 'forgiven.' The case is dismissed."

In just such a way, the sins forgiven through the blood of Christ are canceled and disappear from existence, unless we allow them to haunt us. It's important, then, to counter the memories of old sins with a phrase such as this: "Lord, just as you have forgiven and forgotten, help me to do the same." This will allow us to become his joyful, not gloomy, witnesses. In this sense, clinging to guilt is a selfish project. Releasing it is the best way to thank God, to truly accept his gift.

January 6

Self-Will Run Riot

So he got up and went to his father. But while he was still a long way off, his father saw him and was filled with compassion for him; he ran to his son, threw his arms around him and kissed him. The son said to him, "Father, I have sinned against heaven and against you. I am no longer worthy to be called your son." (Luke 15:20–21)

Unfortunately, some of us need to hit bottom before we awaken to the real meaning and purpose of life. The prodigal son's errant attitude was based on a desire to live as selfishly as he pleased. A great many people in our society live that same way today. It may take great sorrow and tragedy to cause them to look to God for true fulfillment and peace.

In Alcoholics Anonymous, one of the chief characteristics of the addictive personality is described as "self-will run riot." Unless you can surrender to a "higher power," and exchange your will for God's will, the addictive disease will kill you. Alcoholism is far more than a physical addiction to alcohol; it is a degenerative disease of the mind and spirit as well as the body. A new way of living and thinking must replace the old, or there can be no recovery. In the same way, your own spiritual survival is dependent upon your surrender to the loving will of God. Like the prodigal son, you will find only acceptance and love at the hand of our Father.

January 7

Those Blessed Depths

"Quiet! Be still!" . . . and it was completely calm. (Mark 4:39)

At the foot of a cliff, under the windows of Castle Miramar, eighty feet below the surface of the Adriatic years ago, there was a kind of cage fashioned by divers in the face of the rock. In that cage were some of the most magnificent pearls in existence. They belonged to the Archduchess Rainer.

Not having been worn for a long time, the gems had lost their color, and the experts were unanimous in declaring that the only means by which they could be restored to their original brilliancy was by submitting them to a prolonged immersion in the depths of the sea. Over a period of several years, as they were kept lying in the crystal depths, they gradually regained their unrivalled beauty and splendor.

In the words of St. Robert Bellarmine, "The only secret of regaining the lost luster of the inner life, of spirituality and faith, is to get back again to those blessed depths from which the soul first received its bright touch of the divine and holy."

January 8

A Buzzing Mosquito

In the same way, the Spirit helps us in our weakness. We do not know what we ought to pray for, but the Spirit himself intercedes for us with groans that words cannot express. And he who searches our hearts knows the mind of the Spirit, because the Spirit intercedes for the saints in accordance with God's will. (Romans 8:26–27)

Fr. Albert Shamon tells a unique story of the rosary, and of Dr. Carlos Finlay, the Cuban physician who discovered that yellow fever and malaria are carried by mosquitoes. Returning home one night, exhausted after a long day's work, Dr. Finlay remembered that he had not yet said his rosary, which was his daily devotion. So he began to pray, sleepy though he was. But he was distracted by a buzzing mosquito flying persistently around his head. At that moment, as if by inspiration, the idea occurred to him that it may be the mosquito that transmits malaria and yellow fever. He began to experiment with this theory and proved that it was indeed correct, ending a century of research into the cause of these dreaded diseases.

Prayer, if we allow it to become a habit and it is thus woven into our lives, can effect more than we can dream of, for we can then draw on the power of God himself.

January 9

Christ of the Andes

He will judge between the nations and will settle disputes for many peoples. They will beat their swords into plowshares and their spears into pruning hooks. Nation will not take up sword against nation, nor will they train for war anymore. (Isaiah 2:4)

In 1897 Chile and Argentina disputed over their frontier, which ran along the mountains of the Andes. Both countries prepared for war. On Easter Sunday the archbishop of Buenos Aires preached a sermon urging a peaceful resolution for Christ's sake, and the bishops of Chile concurred. The people listened. The dispute was submitted to arbitration under the English king, Edward VII, and war was averted.

In thanksgiving, and to symbolize the new peace between the two countries, heavy guns from the fortresses of both countries were melted down and formed into a gigantic statue of the Sacred Heart of Jesus. It was erected on a fourteen-thousand-foot mountain on the frontier. It was of such massive weight that mules could not traverse the steep terrain. So men of both countries hauled it by ropes to the summit. There, between the two nations, stands the Christ of the Andes, high on a mountaintop, forever reminding both countries of their new covenant. The inscription on pedestal reads, "He is our peace who hath made both one."

Peace in our own relationships begins with listening and good will. When we invite the Spirit of Peace to help us, his bright light will dispel the darkness of conflict and anger.

January 10

The Great Hope

Guide me in your truth and teach me, for you are God my Savior, and my hope is in you all day long. (Psalm 25:5)

London was bombed mercilessly during World War II. One night an elderly man was standing outside St. Andrew's Church, located on the edge of London and overlooking the city. As he looked down on the fire and on the smoke rising from the city, he began to weep. "Is there no hope at all?" he sobbed. Just then a gust of wind cleared the smoke long enough for him to see the cross atop the dome of St. Paul's Cathedral. The instant he saw it, he felt a surge of hope soar through his body. He stopped being "troubled and afraid," for he suddenly realized that there was a power greater than the evil at work in the world.

Speaking of hope in his encyclical *Spe Salvi* (November 30, 2007), Pope Benedict XVI writes, "We need the greater and lesser hopes that keep us going day by day. But these are not enough without the great hope, which must surpass everything else. This great hope can only be God, who encompasses the whole of reality and who can bestow upon us what we, by ourselves, cannot attain." The virtue of hope is a great gift, saving us from the apathy and despair that lies just beneath the surface of our culture. The surest way to experience a deeper hope is to ask for it in prayer, for it is the gift our Lord died to give us.

January 11

Prayer for Our Children

"The promise is for you and your children and for all who are far off—for all whom the Lord our God will call." (Acts 2:39)

By an anonymous author, the following prayer reflects the deepest desires of all parents and grandparents, who seek protection, health, and faith for their children and grandchildren:

Holy Mother Mary,
who by virtue of your divine motherhood
have become Mother of us all,
I place the children which God has given me
under your loving protection.
Be a protecting Mother to them.
Guard their bodies and keep them in health and
strength.
Guard their minds
and keep their thoughts ever healthy and holy in the
sight of their Creator and God.
Guard their hearts
and keep them strong and happy and pure
in the love of God.
Guard always their souls
and ever preserve them in faith
and in the glorious image of God they received
in holy baptism.
Always, Mother, protect them and keep them
under your motherly care.
Supply in your all-wise motherhood
for their human deficiencies,
and protect them from all evil.
Amen.

January 12

Grand Old Building

Consequently, you are no longer foreigners and aliens, but fellow citizens with God's people and members of God's household, built on the foundation of the apostles and prophets, with Christ Jesus himself as the chief cornerstone. In him the whole building is joined together and rises to become a holy temple in the Lord. And in him you too are being built together to become a dwelling in which God lives by his Spirit. (Ephesians 2:19–22)

It could happen only in Texas. Someone bought the famous Fairmount Hotel in San Antonio and moved it to a new location. Before the move many people doubted whether the eighty-year-old brick structure would be able to make the journey safely. But the grand old building held up beautifully. "It didn't creak, groan, or budge an inch," said the relieved mover.

Paul uses the image of a building to describe the church in today's reading. The church is a noble structure that has held up sturdily in its journey across the centuries. The reason? Through Christ "the whole building is joined together." When our own lives become shaky and disoriented, it is faith in God's firm strength that will always see us through.

■

January 13

A Special Mission

Hope deferred makes the heart sick, but a longing fulfilled is a tree of life. (Proverbs 13:12)

For Christmas of 1987, news reporter Steven Barrie wrote a beautiful story about Tony Melendez of Chino, California, who was born without arms. Tony received national attention by playing the guitar with his feet for Pope John Paul II during the Pope's visit to Los Angeles.

The Pope was so moved by Tony's faith and courage that he left the stage, wrapped his arms around his armless body, and kissed him.

Ever since that moment, Tony's life has changed drastically. He has been invited to play for audiences across the country, has appeared on national television, and is now recording his music.

Tony's victory over his handicap and his new celebrity status have cast him into the role of being a spokesman for the handicapped. "It's scary, very scary," he says. "It's something I have to pray over. I figure God's doing this for a reason. He seems to have a special mission for me and I will do my very best to carry it out."

We all have handicaps of one sort or another, and Tony's example of faith and courage brings into focus the promise of Christ to lighten every burden given to him, to the point of bringing extraordinary meaning and good out of them.

January 14

Authentic Teaching

Therefore, dear friends, since you already know this, be on your guard so that you may not be carried away by the error of lawless men and fall from your secure position. (2 *Peter* 3:17)

There has been some confusion since the Second Vatican Council concerning the authentic teachings of Catholicism, as related in this story by Mother Teresa:

> A newly ordained priest was sent to give an instruction to the Sisters. I was present. The priest laughed at a number of our traditional beliefs. He said there was no need to genuflect before the Blessed Sacrament when you come to the chapel outside the time of Mass, for the presence of Christ was limited to the time of Mass and Communion. He also attacked the idea of religious obedience and ridiculed our traditional devotions. He spoke in that vein for a whole hour.

When he had finished, I led him to the door, thanked him and told him he need not come here any more. Then I returned to the hall and told the sisters, "You have just heard what a young priest without experience said. They are his ideas and those of a small group. Now I shall tell you what is the traditional teaching of the Church."

Unfortunately some priests and catechists teach their own opinions rather than the legitimate teaching of the Church. But with the new Catechism of the Catholic Church, written to accurately inform Catholics on doctrinal and dogmatic issues, as well as websites such as EWTN.com and Catholicity.com, we are able to check the validity of any teaching that we feel may be inaccurate. Another source, of course, is a letter or phone call to the local diocesan offices. Needless to say, there is always room in the Church for opinions, theories, and conjecture, but we must first be grounded on the bedrock of authentic teaching.

January 15

The Priest Who Discovered the Big Bang

For wisdom will enter your heart, and knowledge will be pleasant to your soul. (Proverbs 2:10)

In January 1933, the Belgian mathematician and Catholic priest Georges Lemaitre traveled with Albert Einstein to California for a series of seminars. After the priest detailed his Big Bang theory, Einstein stood up and applauded, saying, "This is the most beautiful and satisfactory explanation of creation to which I have ever listened."

Then in the winter of 1998, two separate teams of astronomers in Berkeley, California, confirmed the discovery. They were both observing supernovae—exploding stars visible over great distances—to see how fast the universe is expanding. In accordance with prevailing scientific wisdom, the astronomers expected to find the rate of expansion to be decreasing. Instead they found it to be *increasing*—a discovery that has since "shaken astronomy to its core" (*Astronomy*, October 1999).

This discovery was no surprise to Fr. Lemaitre (1894–1966), who had described the beginning of the universe as a burst of fireworks, and compared galaxies to the burning embers spreading out in a growing sphere from the center of the burst. He believed this burst of fireworks was the beginning of time itself, taking place on "a day without yesterday."

After decades of struggle, other scientists came to accept the Big Bang as fact. But while most scientists—including the mathematician Stephen Hawking—predicted that gravity would eventually slow down the expansion of the universe and make the universe fall back toward its center, Lemaitre believed that the universe would keep *expanding*. He argued that the Big Bang was a once-only, unique event, while other scientists believed that the universe would shrink to the point of another Big Bang, and so on. The observations made in Berkeley proved Lemaitre's contention that the Big Bang was in fact "a day without yesterday."

Such astounding discoveries put us in mind of the awesome splendor of God, of whom the psalmist writes:

> When I consider your heavens,
> the work of your fingers,
> the moon and the stars,
> which you have set in place,
> what is man that you are mindful of him,
> the son of man that you care for him?
> (Psalm 8:3–4)

Yet, in the end, creation is a gratuitous gift from God to the children he loves so much.

January 16

"Don't Be Afraid of Misfortune..."

Then he said to them, "Watch out! Be on your guard against all kinds of greed; a man's life does not consist in the abundance of his possessions." (Luke 12:15)

Aleksandr Solzhenitsyn, the Russian novelist, dramatist, and historian, brought the world's attention to the brutal conditions in the Soviet labor camps, and was awarded the Nobel Prize in Literature in 1970. While living in exile, he spoke not only against Communism, but against Western materialism. The following is from his book *The Gulag Archipelago*:

> Don't be afraid of misfortune and do not yearn after happiness. It is, after all, all the same. The bitter doesn't last forever, and the sweet never fills the cup to overflowing. It is enough if you don't freeze in the cold and if hunger and thirst don't claw at your sides. If your back isn't broken, if your feet can walk, if both arms work, if both eyes can see, and if both ears can hear, then whom should you envy? And why? Our envy of others devours us most of all. Rub your eyes and purify your heart and prize above all else in the world your faith and those who love you and wish you well. . . .

■

January 17

A Pope's Prayer to Mary

But Mary treasured up all these things and pondered them in her heart. (Luke 2:19)

Pope John XXIII was well known for his devotion to the Blessed Virgin Mary, whom he invoked in every major speech and at every papal audience. The following is a spontaneous prayer he offered to her at the end of one of those audiences, on May 4, 1962:

This welcoming of the Mother of Jesus as our Mother is characteristic of the moving and glorious history of the Church's continual devotion to Mary. Every altar, every chapel, every church built in honor of the Mother of God anywhere in the world, testifies to the historic fidelity of the Church's children to the example of the beloved disciple, "who took her into his home."

> Holy Immaculate Mary, help all who are in trouble. Give courage to the faint-hearted, console the sad, heal the infirm, pray for your people, intercede for the clergy, have a special care for nuns; may all feel and rejoice in your kind and powerful assistance, all who now and will always render you honor, and offer you their petitions. . . . Hear all our prayers, O Mother, and grant them all, for we are your children. Amen.

January 18

To See Christ

"The King will reply, 'I tell you the truth, whatever you did for one of the least of these brothers of mine, you did for me.' " (*Matthew* 25:40)

When Mother Teresa accepted the Nobel Peace Prize in Oslo in 1979, she said, "If now we have no peace, it is because we have forgotten how to see God in one another. If each person saw God in his neighbor, do you think we would need guns and bombs?" Seeing Christ in others, especially the worker, the poor, and the suffering, means thinking in a new way, putting on a new mind, letting our brains be washed with the gospel. In the words of an anonymous poet:

> I saw Christ in a ditch with cursing men
> with a shovel in his hand like any one of them;
> and the dirt weighed heavy in the midday sweat,
> and, working by the side of them,
> his brow was wet.

I saw Christ on a girder with a crew
that toiled bee-like the whole day through,
and the riveter in his hands jarred
his holy frame.
but they didn't know that Lord was his name.

I saw Christ in a gale before the mast
when the men were swearing this voyage was their last,
when the waves rolled high and the sailors' mouths were vile
and Christ was there in oilskins—all the while.

I've seen Christ in every road where man has left his tread,
and I've seen Christ drink even with the worst, and break his bread
even with sinners—and the devil was there,
but never have I seen—the Christ who didn't care.

■

January 19
Abba

For you did not receive a spirit that makes you a slave again to fear, but you received the Spirit of sonship. And by him we cry, "Abba, Father." *(Romans 8:15)*

One hot afternoon Dorothy Dawes was standing by the Sea of Galilee. She was watching swarms of Israeli children splashing in the water. Suddenly one of the children shouted, "Abba!" This word caught her by surprise and moved her deeply, for it was the same ancient word that Jesus used to address his Father.

Occasionally the Old Testament prophets referred to God as "Father." But they never used the word "Abba." Abba was an affectionate title, like Daddy or Poppa. Yet this is the word Jesus used. It is also the word he taught us to use when we address the Father in prayer. It speaks profoundly of the intimate relationship he wishes to have with us. As he told the French mystic Gabrielle Bossis: "Everything that affects you touches me personally. My friends, you are part of me and I, your Christ, am part of you." If we haven't experienced our Lord's intimacy, perhaps we can begin today by speaking to him as we would to the most beloved person in our lives.

January 20

To Console and Heal

For great is your love, higher than the heavens; your faithfulness reaches to the skies. (Psalm 108:4)

When divine love enters our hearts we feel a great desire to love as God loves, universally and indiscriminately. We desire to console and heal, to embrace the whole of humanity. It is a special grace, sometimes given in prayer, sometimes given as a permanent gift, as with Mother Teresa. One poet spoke of it in this way:

Embracing Love

Break my heart into a
thousand pieces, O Lord.
Make it ache
with the suffering and sins
of a thousand generations.
From the eternal reservoir
of infinite love
bind my life
to the desperate souls
of a million years—
every hurt
every malice
every wound—
bind them my love.
That I can embrace
the massive suffering world
like You,
holding it to my heart
consoling, healing, forgiving.
Amen.

January 21

Joy

I have told you this so that my joy may be in you and that your joy may be complete. (John 15:11)

Many years ago a group of prospectors set out from Bannock, Montana, in search of gold. They went through many hardships and several of their small company died en route. Finally they were overtaken by Native Americans who took their good horses, leaving them with a couple of limping old ponies. They were ordered to go back to Bannock and stay there, or the Native Americans would scalp the lot of them.

Defeated, discouraged, and downhearted, the prospectors sought to make their way back to Bannock. On one occasion when they made camp near a creek, one of the men casually picked up a small stone from the creek bed. He called to his friends for a hammer, and after cracking the rock, he said, "It looks like there might be gold here."

They then panned gold the rest of the afternoon and came up with twelve dollars' worth. The next day they panned fifty dollars' worth, a huge amount in those days. They said to each another: "We've struck it!"

They continued on to Bannock and vowed not to breathe a word concerning the gold strike. They secretively set about re-equipping themselves with supplies for the trip back. But as they started out, they found they were being followed by a hundred other prospectors. Who had let the secret out? Apparently no one. Their beaming faces had betrayed them.

Our joy in Christ is also impossible to hide—and is the best way to draw others to him.

January 22

For the Family

Be devoted to one another in brotherly love. Honor one another above yourselves. (Romans 12:10)

The following prayer can be offered by parents, children, grandparents, or any member of a family, invoking the protection of the Mother of God and consecrating our families to her:

Prayer for Our Family to Mary

Most blessed Virgin Mary,
I kneel before you with thoughts of my family,
and choose you
as my Mother and Advocate before God.
I consecrate myself and all of my family
to your service now and forever.
Take us under your protection.
Bless this family that reveres you.
In every temptation defend us.
Protect us from every danger.
Provide for us the necessities of life.
Comfort us in every sorrow, in every sickness,
and especially at the hour of our death.
Grant that we may all enter into heaven
to thank you and, in your company,
to praise and love Christ our Redeemer
for all eternity.
Amen.

January 23

The Little Flower

But eagerly desire the greater gifts. . . . And now these three remain: faith, hope and love. But the greatest of these is love.
(1 Corinthians 12:30; 13:13)

St. Therese was a Carmelite nun in Lisieux, France. She died on September 30, 1897, at the age of twenty-four, and was later honored with the rare title "Doctor of the Church" by Pope John Paul II. Among her writings was a passage in which she talks about her search for the calling God had given to her to better serve the Church.

She turned to Paul's letters and read that not everyone was called upon to be an apostle, a prophet, or a teacher. This left her more confused than ever. She continued reading Paul until she came to the words in today's reading: "Set your hearts, then, on the more important gifts. . . . The greatest of these is love." Then, she writes: "Nearly ecstatic with supreme joy in my soul, I proclaimed: 'Jesus . . . At last I have found my calling: my calling is love.'"

■

January 24

John Paul II on the Meaning of Suffering

When he heard this, Jesus said, "This sickness will not end in death. No, it is for God's glory so that God's Son may be glorified through it." (John 11:4)

In a message for the World Day of the Sick in 2001, John Paul II wrote, "To discover the fundamental and definitive meaning of suffering, we must look to the revelation of divine love, the ultimate source of the meaning of all that exists. The answer . . . has been given by God to man in the Cross of Jesus Christ. Suffering, the consequence of original sin, takes on new meaning: It becomes a sharing in the saving work of Jesus Christ."

The pope expands on this meaning in his apostolic letter *Salvifici Doloris* (February 11, 1984), in which he states,

> Faith in sharing in the suffering of Christ brings with it the interior certainty that the suffering person "completes what is lacking in Christ's afflictions"; the certainty that in the spiritual dimension of the work of Redemption he is serving, like Christ, the salvation of his brothers and sisters. Therefore he is carrying out an irreplaceable service. In the Body of Christ, which is ceaselessly born of the Cross of the Redeemer, it is precisely suffering permeated by the spirit of Christ's sacrifice that is the irreplaceable mediator and author of the good things which are indispensable for the world's salvation. It is suffering, more than anything else, which clears the way for the grace which transforms human souls. Suffering, more than anything else, makes present in the history of humanity the powers of the Redemption. In that "cosmic" struggle between the spiritual powers of good and evil, spoken of in the Letter to the Ephesians, human sufferings, united to the redemptive suffering of Christ, constitute a special support for the powers of good, and open the way to the victory of these salvific powers."

January 25

The Emperor and His Son

He will turn the hearts of fathers to their children, and the hearts of children to their fathers. . . . (Malachi 4:6)

Jesus Christ calls us to an intimate relationship with God. But the Father is so awesome that we might sometimes fear approaching him. There is a secret here however: it is to approach God as a child.

There is an old Roman story that recalls the triumphal parade of a Roman emperor who had been victorious in battle. He was a majestic and fearful figure indeed, with thousands of troops marching ahead of him, and behind him followed a parade of wagons of booty and prisoners. The streets were lined with cheering people. The legionaries did their best to keep the people in their places.

At one point on the triumphal route there was a platform where the empress and her family were sitting to watch the celebration. On this platform, with his mother, was the emperor's youngest son, a little boy. As the emperor came closer, his son jumped off the platform, burrowed through the crowd, tried to dodge between the legs of a legionary, and was prepared to run out on the road to meet his father's chariot.

The legionary stooped down and stopped him. He swung him up in his arms: "You can't do that, boy," he said. "Don't you know who that is in the chariot? It's the emperor. You can't go running out there." And the little boy laughed from his height and said, "I know he's the emperor, but he's also my poppa!" and off he ran.

Adults can be scared of God. Children simply run to where the love is, like frisky puppies, and are lifted high up in the arms of the beloved. Remember that we are all children in the eyes of God, and running without inhibition into his arms is a delight both to him and to us.

January 26

Acknowledging Goodness

A cheerful look brings joy to the heart, and good news gives health to the bones. (Proverbs 15:30)

The following is a paraphrase of a sermon by the eminent Croatian spiritual writer and psychologist Fr. Slavko Barbaric:

> There is a Slavic expression that states, "Where gratitude ends, sin begins." The circumstances of the first sin certainly bears this out, with Eve becoming blind to the gifts all around her—Paradise itself—and simply focusing on what was forbidden, what she and Adam did not possess. It is the prototype of all sin that occurs when ungrateful eyes do not see the goodness of God and his manifold gifts, thus opening themselves to conflict and sin. Spiritually, there are few dangers greater than an attitude of negativity or indifference.

In rearing children the formation of attitude entails a special, as well as a pleasant, responsibility. We are to avoid the imprudent faultfinding and criticism that is analogous to a schoolteacher underlining in heavy red pencil the mistakes in a student's assignment. Common sense tells us that stressing primarily the faults of a child puts him in constant mind of them, erodes self-esteem and steals inner peace. This can be an almost insurmountable problem when the parents themselves have been raised in such a way, since it normally takes someone who discerns the positive and acknowledges the goodness of others to properly convey it.

Certainly priests who display the opposite attitude soon lose credibility with the young and are avoided. When they attribute this faultfinding and negativity to the Lord himself, no matter how well intentioned, it can destroy any budding faith based on love, leading to an indifference and even antagonism to God.

A sense of love, gratitude and affirmation are the greatest gifts we can give to children.

January 27

He and I by Gabrielle Bossis

Your love, O LORD, reaches to the heavens, your faithfulness to the skies. (Psalm 36:5)

One of my favorite books for meditation is *He and I* by Gabrielle Bossis, a French woman who received locutions (heard the voice of Christ) from 1936 until her death in 1950. The messages she received underwent careful study by the Church and were given the imprimatur of French Archbishop Jean-Marie Fortier in 1969. What is extraordinary about the messages is the breathtaking love and intimacy they convey. In this excerpt Christ speaks of the total acceptance he has of all his children:

> Offer yourself to me just as you are. Don't wait to be pleased with yourself. Be one with me even in your greatest shortcomings.

I will take them and restore you, if you put your trust in me. Have confidence. . . . You worry about not thinking of me enough. You worry about your many shortcomings and are afraid to look at me. You mustn't do this. Just give yourself to me as you are. I know all about human nature. I came to help and restore. Transplant yourself in me not because of your worth but because of my yearning. . . .

Give yourself to me as you are. At any moment in your life. Just as you are. . . . Don't drag your past along with you constantly if it burdens you and hinders you from coming close to me. Just as you are, throw yourself into my arms for your joy. . . . Give all your loving attention to each little moment. Think of this all your life through. Nothing of the past. Nothing of the future. Only the present moment of love.

January 28

Life as a Dialogue

Hear my prayer, O God; listen to the words of my mouth. (Psalm 54:2)

To pray does not always mean to think about God in contrast to thinking about other things, or to spend time with God instead of spending time with other people. Rather, it means to think and live in the presence of God. Fr. Henri Nouwen writes, "As soon as we begin to divide our thoughts into thoughts about God and thoughts about people and events, we remove God from our daily life and put him in a pious little niche where we can think pious thoughts and experience pious feelings."

Although it is important and even indispensable for the spiritual life to set apart time for God and God alone, prayer can become unceasing prayer only when all our thoughts—beautiful or ugly, high or low, proud or shameful, sorrowful or joyful—can be thought in the presence of God. Thus, "Converting our unceasing thinking into unceasing prayer moves us from a self-centered monologue to a God-centered dialogue. This requires that we turn all our thoughts into conversation. The main question, therefore, is not so much what we think, but to whom we present our thoughts."

January 29

The Humility to Receive

God is not unjust; he will not forget your work and the love you have shown him as you have helped his people and continue to help them. (Hebrews 6:10)

One spring a terrible flood engulfed a rural area and stranded an old woman in her house. As she stood on the front porch, a man in a boat appeared and said, "I've come to save you." "No thanks," said the woman. "I trust God completely. If worst comes to worst, he'll save me."

The next day the water rose to the second floor. As the woman stood at her bedroom window, another man in a boat shouted up, "I've come to save you." "No thanks," said the woman. "I trust God completely. If worst comes to worst, he'll save me."

The next day the water rose to the roof. As the woman sat there, a helicopter hovered above and the pilot shouted down, "I've come to save you." "No thanks," said the woman. "I trust God completely. If worst comes to worse, he'll save me."

The next day the flood engulfed the house and the woman drowned.

When she got to heaven, she said to St. Peter, "Before I go inside, I want to register a complaint. I trusted that God would save me from the flood, but he let me down." Peter gave the woman a puzzled look and said, "I don't know what more he could have done for you. He sent you two boats and a helicopter."

Needless to say, God often chooses to help us through the love and care of his people. But as with all divine gifts and graces, it is up to us to accept his gift.

January 30

Before I Formed You

"Before I formed you in the womb I knew you, before you were born I set you apart. . . ." (Jeremiah 1:5)

In her speech at the National Prayer Breakfast in Washington, D.C., in 1994, Mother Teresa voiced her conviction that "the greatest destroyer of peace today is abortion, because it is a war against the child, a direct killing of the innocent child, murder by the mother herself." In front of a political audience that included President and Mrs. Clinton and most members of Congress, she continued, "If we accept that a mother can kill even her own child, how can we tell other people not to kill one another? . . . Any country that accepts abortion is not teaching its people to love, but to use any violence to get what they want. This is why the greatest destroyer of love and peace is abortion."

And from Dietrich Bonhoeffer, an educator and theologian imprisoned and subsequently executed by the Nazis in 1945:

> Destruction of the embryo in the mother's womb is a violation of the right to live which God has bestowed upon this budding life. To raise the question whether we are here concerned already with a human being or not is merely to confuse the issue. The simple fact is that God certainly intended to create a human being and that this nascent human being has been deliberately deprived of his life. And that is nothing but murder.

In our own lives we can make a real difference in protecting the lives of the unborn by supporting pregnancy crisis centers such as Birthright and National Life Centers, which rely on us to carry on their work. Volunteers are needed to take crisis calls, and maternity and baby clothing are always needed. Birthright.com has an excellent website, and every diocese has a Life Center that has a variety of resources we can use.

■

January 31

"Till Someone Else Does More..."

They charge like warriors; they scale walls like soldiers. They all march in line, not swerving from their course. (Joel 2:7)

During his sermon at the Mass for Veterans Day in 1983, the words of Fr. Charles Fink, a former sergeant in the 199th Light Infantry Brigade in Vietnam, were etched in the memories of his listeners, many of them veterans. "When I go to my grave," he said, "I can say that my service in Vietnam was the proudest thing I ever did in my life. It was a brave thing just going there. But I was scared every time I heard a shot."

Fr. Charlie, as his friends called him, captured his comrades' pride in his poem "Bury Me with Soldiers", which he shared during his sermon. The last stanza was particularly poignant:

> So bury me with soldiers, please,
> though much maligned they be.
> Yes, bury me with soldiers
> for I miss their company.
> We'll not soon see their like again,
> we've had our fill of war.
> But bury me with men like them
> 'til someone else does more.

When we think of the sacrifices veterans have made to ensure our freedom, perhaps the finest way to express our gratitude is through prayer. Even one Hail Mary each day for deceased and disabled veterans is a precious gift, something we can give in return for all they have done for us.

FEBRUARY

February 1

Christ and Buddha

For we are God's workmanship, created in Christ Jesus to do good works, which God prepared in advance for us to do. (*Ephesians* 2:10)

Compassion, charity, and self-giving love are the foundations of Christ's teaching, but of course there are other religions and creeds that differ markedly.

In his book *Now and Then*, Frederick Buechner includes a section that compares the teachings of Buddha and of Jesus Christ, a topic he wrestled with when he was teaching at Phillips Exeter Academy: "Finally, lest students of comparative religion be tempted to believe that to compare them is to discover that at their hearts all religions are finally one, and that it thus makes little difference which one you choose, you have only to place side by side Buddha and Christ themselves." He continues:

Buddha sits enthroned beneath the Bo tree in the lotus position. His lips are faintly parted in the smile of one who has passed beyond every power in earth or heaven to touch him. "He who loves fifty has fifty woes, he who loves ten has ten woes, he who loves none has no woes," he has said. His eyes are closed.

Christ, on the other hand, stands in the garden of Gethsemane, angular, beleaguered. His face is lost in shadows so that you can't even see his lips, and before all the powers in earth or heaven he is powerless. "This is my commandment, that you love one another as I have loved you," he has said. His eyes are also closed.

The difference seems to me this. The suffering that Buddha's eyes close out is the suffering of the world that Christ's eyes open to and embrace. It is an extreme difference, and even in a bare classroom in Exeter, New Hampshire, I think it was as apparent to everyone as it was to me that before you're done, you have to make a crucial and extraordinary choice.

February 2

"This is Your Hour, O Mary..."

The smoke of the incense, together with the prayers of the saints, went up before God from the angel's hand. (Revelation 8:4)

In the midst of the Cold War between the Soviet Union and the West, Pope John XXIII wrote a special prayer to Our Lady pleading for peace. Today, in the midst of an ongoing struggle against terrorism sparked by the events of 9/11, this timeless prayer is as important as ever.

For Peace

We turn to you, O Blessed Virgin Mary,
Mother of Jesus and our Mother too.
How could we, with trembling hearts,
concern ourselves with the greatest problem
of all,

that of life and death, now overshadowing
all mankind,
without trusting ourselves to your intercession
to preserve us from all dangers?

This is your hour, O Mary.
Our blessed Jesus entrusted us to you in the final
hour of his bloody sacrifice.
We are confident that you will intervene.

And now indeed,
we implore you for peace,
O most sweet Mother and Queen of the world.
The world does not need victorious wars
or defeated peoples,
but renewed and strengthened health of mind,
and peace which brings prosperity and
tranquility;
this is what it needs and what it is crying out for,
the beginning of salvation and lasting peace.
Amen.

February 3

Sweet Music

But let all who take refuge in you be glad; let them ever sing for joy. Spread your protection over them, that those who love your name may rejoice in you. (Psalm 5:11)

Writers and poets throughout the ages have sought to convey the joy and protection they have felt in the presence of the Blessed Mother. One of these is Pope Leo XIII (d. 1903), who wrote no less than nine encyclicals regarding devotion to the Blessed Virgin and to the Rosary. The following is an especially poignant prayer offered to her in his old age:

It Is Sweet Music

It is sweet music to the ear to say:
I honor you, O Mother!
It is a sweet song to repeat:
I honor you, O holy Mother!

You are my delight, dear hope, and chaste love,
my strength in all adversities.

If my spirit
that is troubled
and stricken by passions
suffers from the painful burden
of sadness and weeping,
if you see your child overwhelmed by misfortune,
O gracious Virgin Mary,
let me find rest in your motherly embrace.

But alas,
already the last day is quickly approaching.
Banish the demon to the infernal depths,
and stay closer, dear Mother,
to your aged and erring child.
With a gentle touch,
cover the weary pupils
and kindly consign to God
the soul that is returning to him.
Amen.

February 4

"Humility is Nothing but Truth..."

When pride comes, then comes disgrace, but with humility comes wisdom. (Proverbs 11:2)

In Boston a parish priest noticed a group of boys standing around a small stray dog. "What are you doing, boys?"

"Telling lies," said one of the boys. "The one who tells the biggest lie gets the dog."

"Why, when I was your age," the priest said, "I never ever thought of telling a lie."

The boys looked at one another, a little crestfallen. Finally one of them shrugged and said, "I guess he wins the dog."

St. Vincent de Paul tells us that God is such a great lover of humility because he is such a great lover of truth. "Humility is nothing but truth," he writes, "while pride is nothing but falsehood." This is also true of spirituality, belying those who would boast of spiritual favors or graces. In the words of St. John of the Cross: "All visions, revelations, heavenly feelings—and whatever is greater than these—are not worth the smallest act of humility, which is the fruit of that love which neither values nor seeks itself, which thinks well, not of oneself, but of others. Many souls, to whom visions have never come, are incomparably more advanced in the way of perfection than others to whom many have been given."

Humility is truth, acknowledging God for who he is and ourselves for who we are, which is literally nothing. Created from nothing, we remain in and of ourselves nothing—except for the grace of God, which has made us everything, a sharer in his own divine life. Recognition of this truth should not depress us, but lead us to the most profound gratitude.

February 5

The Power of Example

"I have set you an example that you should do as I have done for you." (*John* 13:15)

Tom Brown's *School Days* was a famous British novel that was later made into a popular movie. Tom Brown was a popular boy who attended a boarding school in England. He lived with about a dozen other boys in one of the dormitories. Whatever Tom said or did always had a big impact on others at the school.

One day a new boy came to the school and, when it came time for bed that night, he innocently knelt down beside his bed to say his prayers. A few of the boys began to snicker; a couple of others began to laugh and joke. One even threw a shoe at the kneeling boy.

That night Tom didn't go to sleep right away. He lay awake thinking about what had happened to the newcomer. He also began to think about his mother and the prayers she taught him to say each night before bed—prayers he had not said since coming to the school.

The next night several of the boys in the dormitory were looking forward to poking fun at the new boy again. When bedtime came, however, something totally unexpected happened. When the boy knelt down to say his night prayers, Tom knelt down also. When the other boys saw this, there was a hush in the dormitory.

Have we ever thought of the power of our own example and its effect on others?

February 6

The Experience of Love

Do not let any unwholesome talk come out of your mouths, but only what is helpful for building others up according to their needs, that it may benefit those who listen. (*Ephesians* 4:29)

In the church of a small village an altar boy serving the priest at Sunday mass accidentally dropped the cruet of wine. The village priest struck the altar boy sharply on the cheek and in a gruff voice shouted: "Leave the altar and don't come back!" That boy became Tito, the Communist leader.

In the cathedral of a large city an altar boy serving the bishop at Sunday Mass also dropped the cruet of wine. With a warm twinkle in his eyes the bishop gently whispered: "Someday you will be a priest." That boy grew up to become Archbishop Fulton Sheen.

Psychologists tell us that it takes close to fifty positive comments to offset the effect of just one negative remark. And although we may hear countless words about love in sermons and books, they mean little to someone who has not *experienced* love at the hands of another. This is an integral part of the ministry of priests and religious and all who help form the spirituality of the young. In the words of St. John Bosco to his order of teachers: "Dear brothers, let us always err on the side of love."

February 7

The Diamond

They preached the good news in that city and won a large number of disciples. Then they returned to Lystra, Iconium and Antioch, strengthening the disciples and encouraging them to remain true to the faith. "We must go through many hardships to enter the kingdom of God," they said. (Acts 14:21–22)

Many years ago, the most magnificent diamond in the history of mining was found in an African mine. It was eventually presented to the king of England for the state crown, but was first sent to Amsterdam to be cut by an expert lapidary, who proceeded to cut a notch in it! Then he struck a hard blow with his hammer and the great jewel lay in his hand cleft in two. A terrible mistake? Definitely not. For days and weeks that blow had been studied and planned. Drawings and models had been made of the gem; its quality, its defects, its lines of cleavage had all been studied with minute care.

When he struck the blow, the lapidary did the one thing that would bring the diamond to its most perfect shapeliness, radiance, and jeweled splendor. The blow that seemed to ruin the jewel in the eyes of the untrained was, in fact, its perfect redemption.

Sometimes, God lets a stinging blow fall upon our lives. Our nerves wince and the soul cries out in agony. The blow seems to be an appalling mistake. But it isn't, for we are the most priceless jewels in the world to our Lord, who is the most skilled lapidary of all, shaping us for eternal life.

February 8

Taking Time

But seek first his kingdom and his righteousness, and all these things will be given to you as well. (Matthew 6:33)

A nervous husband left his wife behind when rushing to the hospital recently in Tulsa, Oklahoma. The father had called police to ask for help in getting his expectant wife to the hospital in a hurry. A patrol car was dispatched to meet the emergency. But after speeding through the city, with police clearing the way, the overanxious husband suddenly discovered that he had left his wife at home. Together with the officer he wheeled around and sped back to the starting point, picked up his wife, and resumed the race to the hospital.

In the rush of daily living it's easy to get caught up in the incidentals and overlook the essentials. Taking time simply to reflect on our use of time—work, meals, family time, prayer, recreation, TV—can help us to see how our time is used and whether we are prioritizing what is truly important. Then we will be better able to hear the voice of the Holy Spirit reminding us of important things we are forgetting.

February 9

Look Fear in the Face

There is no fear in love. But perfect love drives out fear, because fear has to do with punishment. The one who fears is not made perfect in love. (*1 John 4:18*)

In this passage from John's first letter, we are assured that "there is no fear in love." This is illustrated in a story set in Nazi Germany. An order had gone out that incurables and the insane were no longer to be a burden on the Reich.

Three high officials descended upon the Bethel Institution in Berlin, a Christian hospital for epileptics and the mentally ill. "Herr Pastor," they said, "the Fuehrer has decided that these patients must be eliminated." Dr. von Bodelschwingh, the administrator, looked at them calmly. "Well, you can put me in a concentration camp if you choose. I have no power over that. But as long as I am free, you will not touch one of my patients. I cannot change to fit the times or the wishes of the Fuehrer. I stand under orders from our Lord Jesus Christ."

Eleanor Roosevelt, perhaps America's most respected First Lady, said with great insight, "You gain strength, courage, and confidence by every experience in which you really stop to look fear in the face. You must do the thing which you think you cannot do."

■

February 10

Instruments of God

The LORD *will save me, and we will sing with stringed instruments all the days of our lives in the temple of the* LORD. (*Isaiah 38:20*)

It's human nature to feel useless to God at times. But he wants us to understand that we are all he has to complete his work on earth—and all we really need is willingness, since he will provide the rest. The following story illustrates this point:

One Saturday afternoon an auction was being held to benefit a local charity. At one point the auctioneer held up an old, battered violin. "Any bids?" A smile went around. It was such a shabby-looking thing. Then one man shouted out: "Two cents!" There was general laughter and shouts of "Let him have it!"

Then the auctioneer said, "Hey, it can't be that bad. Anybody out there want to play it?" At which point an old man stepped up onto the platform, raised the violin to his chin, and began to play softly. He drew from the old instrument such an exquisite melody that his listeners were enraptured.

The auctioneer picked up the violin again. "Any bids?" "Ten dollars!" "Twenty dollars." The violin was finally sold for $200. What had happened? It was the same violin as before, but now they had heard it under the touch of a master's hand.

In those times when we feel useless and helpless, we can be encouraged that under the touch of the master's hand anything is possible.

February 11

The Feast of Our Lady of Lourdes

And Mary said:
"My soul glorifies the Lord
and my spirit rejoices in God my Savior . . .
for the Mighty One has done great things for me—
holy is his name."
(Luke 1:46–49)

When Bernadette had seen Our Lady several times at the Grotto of Lourdes, she was told to give a message to the priests, asking them to build a chapel at the Grotto. She did so, in fear and trembling. The pastor (who did not then believe in the apparitions) said they would build the chapel, but first, the Lady should reveal her name.

Bernadette had asked her name already, but she had only smiled. On the feast of the Annunciation, when she saw the Lady again, she said during her ecstasy, "Madame, will you have the kindness to tell me who you are?" At first the Lady smiled again, but after Bernadette had asked three times, she let her arms fall to her side (in the attitude of the Miraculous Medal) and joined them again on her breast. Then she raised her eyes and said, "I am the Immaculate Conception."

When her ecstasy was over, Bernadette went home with her friend Ursule, and could not help telling her about the name, because it made her so happy. She did not know what the words "Immaculate Conception" meant, and she kept repeating them all the way home so as not to forget them.

Perhaps we may guess from this how grateful Our Lady is for this gift, to be the only woman since Eve to be conceived without original sin, as she chose this particular title to confirm her identity at Lourdes.

February 12

Locked In

Tongues, then, are a sign, not for believers but for unbelievers; prophecy, however, is for believers, not for unbelievers. (1 Corinthians 14:22)

Harry Houdini used to issue challenges wherever he went. He could be locked in any jail cell in the country, he claimed, and set himself free in a short time. Always he kept his promise, but one time something went wrong. Houdini entered the jail in his street clothes; the heavy, metal doors clanged shut behind him. He took from his belt a concealed piece of metal, strong and flexible. He set to work immediately, but something seemed to be unusual about this lock. For thirty minutes he worked and got nowhere. An hour passed, and still he hadn't opened the door. By now he was sweating and exhausted, but he still couldn't pick the lock. Finally, as evening drew on, Houdini collapsed in frustration and failure against the door he couldn't unlock. But when he fell against the door, it swung open!

It had never been locked at all. But in his mind it was locked, and that was all it took to keep him from opening the door and walking out.

Christianity is a countercultural movement that directly opposes nihilism and its primary expression of narcissism and self-gratification at any expense. Because we are constantly bombarded by the media, entertainment, and merchants to lock ourselves into this prison, we must fight to keep the perspective of faith. It is our focus on the eternal Christ and his gospel of life that will keep us free.

February 13

The Warmth of God

Do not be anxious about anything, but in everything, by prayer and petition, with thanksgiving, present your requests to God. (*Philippians* 4:6)

In the kingdom of heaven there is no worry or fear because God is in full control, protecting us in a loving intimacy much like a mother with her child in her arms. The following prayer is a plea for that reassurance:

In Time of Worry

Dear Blessed Mother,
many times I worry and am anxious,
for the world and its problems are
always around me.
Please take these
anxieties from me,
so that, at peace, I may feel
the warmth of God
and his eternal protection.
You are the advocate of the most troubled and
abandoned;

you are the special friend of those in need.
Help me.
Come to my assistance
as I commend myself to you,
and place in your hands all of my worries and
fears,
confident of your powerful help,
O Mother of Consolation,
O Queen of Peace!
Amen.

■

February 14

The Eucharist in Siberia

Jesus said to them, "I tell you the truth, unless you eat the flesh of the Son of Man and drink his blood, you have no life in you. Whoever eats my flesh and drinks my blood has eternal life, and I will raise him up at the last day. For my flesh is real food and my blood is real drink." (John 6:53–55)

The Western church has often taken the Mass for granted; we have been spared the persecutions that once tormented Eastern Europe and the former Soviet Union under Communism. There is a story that may help change our perspective:

In 1956, news came to us about one of Stalin's forced-labor camps in Siberia, by way of Dr. Joseph Scholmer, who had been a prisoner there. He said that 4 bishops, 700 priests, and 900 monks and nuns had been deported from Lithuania, as well as many lay Catholics. They worked in mines 600 feet below the ground, and Mass was often said down there by some priest dressed in his usual overalls. The altar hosts came by mail from Lithuania, allowed through as "Lithuanian bread," and the wine was from the Crimea. The miners had made a tiny silver chalice only one and one-quarter inches high. At Easter, over 400 of the Lithuanian miners received Easter Communion hidden in tins of cigarettes that were being distributed. Each host, wrapped in a small piece of linen, was hidden under a top layer of cigarettes, and broken up for four communicants. If a miner was caught, the penalty for such subversive action was death.

Prayer

Lord, help us to understand that your body and blood is the most precious gift in the universe, for it is your own divine life that infuses our human life, making us one. May our love and reverence for the Eucharist grow ever deeper. Amen.

February 15
Twenty-Five Years Later

For whoever wants to save his life will lose it, but whoever loses his life for me will find it. What good will it be for a man if he gains the whole world, yet forfeits his soul? Or what can a man give in exchange for his soul?
(Matthew 16:25–27)

In 1923 a high-level business meeting was held in Chicago's old Edgewater Beach Hotel. Present at the meeting were nine of the most powerful men in America. They included such people as the presidents of the nation's largest steel company, the nation's largest oil company, and the nation's largest utility company.

Twenty-five years later, where were these nine powerful men? Three had died penniless, three had committed suicide, two were in prison, and one had gone insane. Their fate helps illustrate Jesus' point in today's reading: "Does a person gain anything if he wins the whole world but loses his soul?"

February 16

Congressional Medal of Honor

"Have I not commanded you? Be strong and courageous. Do not be terrified; do not be discouraged, for the LORD *your God will be with you wherever you go." (Joshua 1:9)*

In the wake of the terrible scandals that have involved some priests in recent times, it's important to realize that the great majority of priests are dedicated and honorable men who take very seriously the promises made at their ordination. Since we have been exposed to the worst, maybe it's time to hear a little bit about our best priests. The following is the official citation for the Congressional Medal of Honor awarded during World War II to Lieutenant Commander (Chaplain) Joseph O'Callahan:

> Citation: For conspicuous gallantry and intrepidity at the risk of his life above and beyond the call of duty while serving as chaplain on board the U.S.S. Franklin when that vessel was fiercely attacked by enemy Japanese aircraft during offensive operations near Kobe, Japan, on 19 March 1945.
>
> A valiant and forceful leader, calmly braving the perilous barriers of flame and twisted metal to aid his men and his ship, Fr. O'Callahan groped his way through smoke-filled corridors to the open flight deck into the midst of violently exploding bombs, shells, rockets, and other armament. With the ship rocked by incessant explosions, with debris and fragments raining down and fires raging in ever-increasing fury, he ministered to the wounded and dying, comforting and encouraging men of all faiths; he organized and led firefighting crews into the blazing inferno on the flight deck; he directed the jettisoning of live ammunition and the flooding of the magazine; he manned a hose to cool hot, armed bombs rolling dangerously on the listing deck, continuing his efforts, despite searing, suffocating smoke which forced men to fall back gasping and imperiled others who replaced them. Serving with courage, fortitude, and deep spiritual strength, Lt. Comdr. O'Callahan inspired the gallant officers and men of the Franklin to fight heroically and with profound faith in the face of almost certain death and to return their stricken ship to port.

February 17

The Lighthouse

This is the message we have heard from him and declare to you: God is light; in him there is no darkness at all. (1 John 1:5)

One of the most fascinating sights at sea are the tall lighthouses of old that threw their beams bright and far, guiding ships to safety in a storm, and pointing people to their destined ports. Day and night, in all kinds of weather, those perpetual lights used to guide the great ships away from shoals and danger spots, guiding them along the channels of safety into the harbor.

A lighthouse must be a strong structure. There is one, for example, at McNutt's Island off the coast of Nova Scotia, built in 1784, with walls six feet thick. All along the Eastern coast we find these massive structures.

On the sea of life we find another lighthouse—the presence of Christ in the Tabernacle of every Catholic church. Nearby shines the altar light, day and night, through storm and calm, beaconing the faithful not only to safe harbor, but to the Harbormaster himself. He will warn us of shoals and rocks and joyfully bring peace and hope to those who are already sinking, their spirits going under.

February 18

He Needed a Son

Even in darkness light dawns for the upright, for the gracious and compassionate and righteous man. (Psalm 112:4)

Fr. Mark Link tells the story of an old man who collapsed on a busy street corner in downtown Brooklyn. Within minutes an ambulance rushed him to Kings County Hospital. There he kept calling for his son.

A nurse found a dog-eared letter in the man's wallet. From it she learned that his son was a marine stationed in North Carolina. That night a marine showed up at the hospital, and immediately the nurse took him to the old man's bedside.

The old man was heavily sedated, so the nurse had to tell him several times, "Your son is here! Your son is here!" Finally, the old man opened his eyes. He could barely make out his son, but he recognized his marine uniform. At that point, the son took his father's hand and held it lovingly.

For the rest of that night, the marine sat at the old man's bedside. Occasionally he patted the man's hand and spoke to him tenderly. Several times the nurse urged the marine to take a break and get something to eat or drink, but he refused. Toward dawn, the elderly man died.

When the nurse extended her sympathy to the young marine, he asked, "Who was that man?" "Wasn't he your father?" the nurse asked. "No, he wasn't," said the marine. "I'm afraid I never saw him before." "Why didn't you say something?" said the nurse.

"I would have," said the marine. "But I could see that he was too sick to realize I wasn't his son. I could also see that he was slipping away and needed him. I felt I needed to become that son."

Our impulses to charity and compassion are always the work of the Holy Spirit, and so it is important to flow with them, even when they interfere with our time and plans. One of the major reasons we were placed on earth was to help one another. And to help one another is to help Christ himself.

February 19
Where Your Treasure Is

Then he said to them, "Watch out! Be on your guard against all kinds of greed; a man's life does not consist in the abundance of his possessions." (Luke 12:15)

On the triple doorway of the cathedral of Milan, there are three inscriptions spanning the towering arches. Over one arch is carved a beautiful wreath of roses, and underneath is the inscription, "All that pleases is but for a moment." Over the other is sculptured a cross, and these are the words beneath: "All that troubles is but for a moment." But underneath the great central entrance in the main aisle is the legend, "That only is important which is eternal."

This is one of the ageless teachings of Catholicism, which urges us to focus our lives on what is truly important, and not on the passing and the material. The so-called "gospel of prosperity," preached by some fundamentalist groups, is simply a convenient lie. Nothing could be further from the spirit and teachings of Jesus Christ: "Therefore I tell you, do not worry about your life, what you will eat; or about your body, what you will wear. . . . Provide purses for yourselves that will not wear out, a treasure in heaven that will not be exhausted. . . . For where your treasure is, there your heart will be also" (Luke 12:22, 33–34).

February 20
Mary and Pope Pius XII

Yet give attention to your servant's prayer and his plea for mercy, O LORD my God. Hear the cry and the prayer that your servant is praying in your presence. (2 Chronicles 6:19)

A man of deep prayer, Pope Pius XII was deeply devoted to the Blessed Mother, writing the encyclical *Ad caeli Reginam* (1954), dealing with the dignity of Mary, and the apostolic constitution *Munificentissimus Deus* (1950), defining the Assumption. He wrote the following prayer in her honor:

Mary Our Strength

O Virgin, fair as the moon,
delight of the angels and saints in heaven,
grant that we may become like you
and that our souls may receive a ray of your beauty,
which does not decline with the years
but shines forth into eternity.
O Mary, sun of heaven,
restore life where there is death
and enlighten spirits where there is darkness.
Turn your countenance to your children
and radiate on us your light and your fervor.
O Mary, powerful as an army,
grant victory to our ranks.
We are very weak
and our enemy rages with uttermost conceit.
But under your banner
we are confident of overcoming him. . . .

Save us, O Mary,
fair as the moon,
bright as the sun,
awe-inspiring as an army set in battle array
and sustained not by hatred
but by the ardor of love.

Amen.

February 21
The Helpless Christ
You give me your shield of victory, and your right hand sustains me; you stoop down to make me great. (Psalm 18:35)

Within the Mass there are deep currents of divine love that can be penetrated only by a quiet, prayerful heart. Carol Houselander (d. 1954), a Catholic writer and poet of the last century, reflects on one of these in *The Reed of God*:

> By his own will Jesus Christ was dependent on Mary before she bore him on Christmas day: he was absolutely helpless; he could go nowhere but where she chose to take him; he could not speak; his breathing was her breath; his heart beat in the beating of her heart.
>
> Today Christ is dependent upon us. In the sacred Host he is literally put into our hands. We must carry him to the dying, must take him into the prisons, workhouses, and hospitals, must carry him to soldiers on the field of battle, must give him to little children and "lay him by in his leaflight house of gold," the Tabernacle.
>
> The modern world's feverish struggle for unbridled, often unlicensed, freedom is answered by the bound, enclosed helplessness and dependence of Christ—Christ in the womb, Christ in the Host, Christ in the tomb.

February 22
Accepting Forgiveness
Blessed is he whose transgressions are forgiven, whose sins are covered. (Psalm 32:1)

Mother Angelica, founder of the Eternal Word television and radio ministry, relates a story about forgiveness in her own life. It seems that between talks at a conference, she went to the Pacific seashore to enjoy the sunshine and the ocean, with its waves that at the time she playfully dared to get bigger and come in closer.

After a while one particular wave seemed to take up her dare, getting bigger and bigger. Mother could tell that it was going to swamp her if she stayed where she was, but for some odd reason she couldn't move. The wave did come in and covered her up to the waist and then gently receded. Afterward she noticed a droplet of seawater on her wrist, dazzling in the sunlight like a jewel, somehow unearthly in its beauty. Instinctively thinking that she was unworthy of such a gift, she shook the droplet from her hand.

It was then that she heard Christ's voice saying, "That drop represented all of your sins, all the shame and guilt from the past. The vast sea before you represents my merciful love, where you have thrown the droplet. Can you go out there now and find it?"

Mother said, "No, it would be impossible."

"Then you must stop retrieving the sinful past from your memory. It is forgiven and forgotten, lost forever in my ocean of love."

Afterward Mother Angelica commented, "It seems the greatest gift we can give Our Lord is to accept his merciful forgiveness. He forgives and forgets, and so must we, for this is the source of our Christian joy."

■

February 23
Rattlesnakes

Then the LORD sent venomous snakes among them; they bit the people and many Israelites died. The people came to Moses and said, "We sinned when we spoke against the LORD and against you. Pray that the LORD will take the snakes away from us." So Moses prayed for the people. (Numbers 21:6–7)

At the turn of the nineteenth century there was a farmer who had three sons: Jim, John, and Sam. No one in the family ever attended church or practiced their religion. The pastor of the local parish church had tried for years to interest the family in the faith, but to no avail. Then one day Sam was bitten by a rattlesnake. The doctor was called and did all he could to help Sam, but the outlook for his recovery was very dim. So the pastor was called and appraised the situation, and then commenced to pray as follows:

"O wise and righteous Father, we thank thee that in thy wisdom thou didst send this rattlesnake to bite Sam. He has never been inside the church and it is doubtful that he has, in all this time, ever prayed or even acknowledged thy existence. Now we trust that this experience will be a valuable lesson to him and will lead to his genuine repentance.

"And now, O Father, wilt thou send another rattlesnake to bite Jim, and another to bite John, and another really big one to bite the old man. For years we have done everything we know to get them to turn to thee, but all in vain. It seems, therefore, that what all our combined efforts could not do, this rattlesnake has done. We thus conclude that the only thing that will do this family any real good is rattlesnakes; so, Lord, send us bigger and better rattlesnakes. Amen."

February 24

Like New Snow

But I have stilled and quieted my soul; like a weaned child with its mother, like a weaned child is my soul within me. (*Psalm 131:2*)

Prayer is the means to great love and peace, but it often requires solitude and quiet so that the tranquil presence of God's Spirit can be felt. This is the theme of a beautiful a poem by James Dillet Freeman:

> Prayer is a state of being, like snowfall
> at night. As in the silence of yourself you pray,
> all things particular, familiar, small
> or large, dissolve and slowly melt away.

Only the white perfection of your prayer
is there, enveloping all things, until
the oneness of the One is everywhere.
Nothing remains the same—only the still,
only the peace of being, not so much
filling space as obliterating space,
an emptiness and allness, like the touch
of snowfall in the night upon your face.
But when your prayer ends and you rise and go,
your world shines new around you, like
  new snow.

■

February 25

Never Alone

So in Christ we who are many form one body, and each member belongs to all the others. (*Romans 12:5*)

The Church, of course, is not confined to the earth. Most of it is invisible or supernatural, comprised as it is not only of the members of the Church on earth but also of all the souls in heaven and those in purification. And we are all linked in Christ forever in a oneness or communion we call (inadequately) the Communion of the Saints (although not all of us are saints yet).

The souls in heaven and purgatory are directed to one goal: pushing those of us who are alive into heaven, so to speak—for their ultimate fulfillment is dependent on the final union of all people in the mystical, glorious body of Christ, which we call Paradise. We are, then, not so much beside each other as within each other.

And so it is helpful to pray in union with the whole Church, that our prayer will be taken up by the other dimensions of the Church that we cannot see, but that constantly hold us up to God. This is the theology behind praying to the saints, and most especially to the Queen of Heaven.

■

February 26

Jade Garments

The angel said to the women, "Do not be afraid, for I know that you are looking for Jesus, who was crucified. He is not here; he has risen, just as he said. Come and see the place where he lay." (*Matthew* 28:5–6)

The Chinese princess Tou Wan, who died about 104 BC, was buried in a jade suit. Her husband, who had died nine years earlier, was given a similar suit. The pair was laid to rest in vast tombs hollowed out of a rocky hillside.

In 1969, when their tombs were discovered, they created a sensation because of the staggering wealth of the 2,800 funeral offerings. Most spectacular of all were the jade suits, each made up of more than 2,000 tiny plates of thin jade, sewn together with gold thread. Nobles of the period believed gold and jade would stand the ravages of time and so would confer immortality.

St. John Chrysostom wrote, "After the royal throne comes death; but after the dunghill comes the kingdom of Heaven." Despite failure, mankind has been undeterred in its attempts to conquer death. But the message of Christ is one of sure hope and eternal life. We have no need, then, of jade garments, for we have the promise of the Son of God.

■

February 27

Science and Religion

For the L*ORD gives wisdom, and from his mouth come knowledge and understanding.* (*Proverbs* 2:6)

Over a century ago, in 1880, two men were on a train in France. The older man was reading the story of the multiplication of the loaves. Noting this, the younger man said, "Pardon me, sir, but do you really believe what you're reading?" "Yes," said the older man, "Don't you believe it?"

"No," said the younger man. "I'm a scientist, and that story flies in the face of all scientific laws."

At this point the train slowed down. "This is my station," said the young man. "Nice talking to you, Mr. . . ."

"Pasteur," said the older man, "Louis Pasteur."

In an address to the Pontifical Academy of Sciences, John Paul II stated, "Science can purify religion from error and superstition; religion can purify science from idolatry and false absolutes." In the end, science is a tool of discovery, allowing us to probe and utilize the mysteries of creation for the benefit of humanity. Rather than direct us away from God, reason is one of the greatest means of finding him, as we see in the writings great intellects from Aquinas to Copernicus to Einstein. And on a personal level, the more reasonable and understanding we are, the more we will resemble our Creator.

February 28
The Image of Orpheus

Cast all your anxiety on him because he cares for you. (1 Peter 5:7)

In the earliest Christian art, that of the Catacombs, Christ is represented as the Greek Orpheus, with the lyre in his hand, drawing everything to him by his magic spell. These early Christians, standing near to Greek civilization, chose this out of all the figures of Greek mythology to express their ideas of the Lord whom they loved and worshiped. This story of Orpheus is one of the noblest that has come down to us from the ancient land of Greece.

Orpheus was the greatest of all musicians, for Apollo had bestowed upon him the lyre, which Hermes had invented. So wonderfully did he play that when his fingers touched the instrument, the beasts of the field drew near, and the birds were arrested in their flight, and even the things of nature gathered spellbound around him. He could make the strings wail so pitiful a lament that tears trickled down the scarred cheeks of the rocks. When he sang of love, the world was filled with sudden sunlight, and even the wildest beast became tame and gentle.

The early Christians thought of Christ in this way. They felt his drawing-power, the strange spell that he had over everything. Possessed in their hearts, he transfigured nature, but most of all he transfigured them. His music banished anxieties, doubts, and suffering. In his presence there could only be hope and peace.

■

March

March 1

Transforming Kindness

I led them with cords of human kindness, with ties of love; I lifted the yoke from their neck and bent down to feed them. (Hosea 11:4)

A century ago, in a mental institution outside Boston, a young girl known as "little Annie" was locked in a dungeon. It was the only place, said the doctors, for those who were hopelessly insane. In little Annie's case, they saw no hope for her, so she was consigned to a living death in that small cage that received little light and even less hope. About that time, an elderly nurse was nearing retirement. She felt there was hope for every child, so she started taking her lunch into the dungeon and eating outside Annie's cage. She felt perhaps she should communicate some love and hope to the little girl.

In many ways, little Annie was like an animal. On occasions, she would violently attack people who came into her cage. At other times, she would completely ignore them. When the elderly nurse started visiting her, Annie gave no indication that she was even aware of her presence. One day, the nurse brought some brownies to the dungeon and left them outside the cage. Annie gave no hint she knew they were there, but when the nurse returned the next day, the brownies were gone. From that time on, the nurse would bring brownies when she made her Thursday visit. Soon after, the doctors in the institution noticed a change was taking place. After a period of time they decided to move her upstairs. Finally, the day came when the "hopeless case" was told she could return home. But Annie did not wish to leave. She chose to stay, to help others. She was the one who cared for, taught, and nurtured Helen Keller, for little Annie's full name was Anne Sullivan.

March 2

Kindness

Carry each other's burdens, and in this way you will fulfill the law of Christ. (*Galatians* 6:2)

In his autobiography, *Up from Slavery*, Booker T. Washington recalled a beautiful incident of an older brother's love. He said the shirts worn by the slaves on the plantation were made of a rough, bristly, inexpensive flax fiber. As a young boy, he found that the garment was so abrasive to his tender, sensitive skin that it caused him a great deal of pain and discomfort. His older brother, moved by his brother's suffering, would wear Booker's new shirts until they were broken in and smoother on his skin. Booker said it was an act of kindness he remembered for the rest of his life.

"You may be sure of this," our Lord said to the French mystic Gabrielle Bossis, "although I am no longer on earth, your neighbor is there. And your desire to love me, to receive me, to serve me, and to give me rest, may be realized in what you do for others. . . . [I]t is I myself who receive it all."

March 3
Held Aloft

But I have stilled and quieted my soul; like a weaned child with its mother, like a weaned child is my soul within me. (Psalm 131:2)

About 6:00 AM on a Wednesday morning James Lawson left home to apply for a job. About an hour later his thirty-six-year-old wife, Patsy, left for her fifth-grade teaching job down the mountain in Riverside, California. In the car were her two children, five-year-old Susan and two-year-old Gerald, who were to be dropped off at the babysitter's. But they never got that far.

Eight hours later, James found his wife and daughter dead in their wrecked car, turned upside down in a cold mountain stream. His two-year-old son was just barely alive in the forty-eight-degree water. But in her death the character of the mother was revealed in a dramatic and heartrending way. For when the father scrambled down the cliff to what he thought were the cries of his dying wife, he found her locked in death, holding her little boy's head just above water in the submerged car. For eight hours Patsy Lawson had held her beloved child afloat and had finally died, her body almost frozen in death in that position of self-giving love, holding her baby up to breathe. She died that another might live, the very essence of divine love.

William Thackeray once wrote, "*Mother* is the name of God in the lips and hearts of little children." May we always trust in the self-giving love of Christ, who has promised to hold us aloft from every danger.

March 4

A Miracle of Freedom

And will not God bring about justice for his chosen ones, who cry out to him day and night? Will he keep putting them off? (Luke 18:7)

There is a little-known story of Austria's great Rosary crusade that liberated the country from Communist control. At the end of World War II, the victorious allies partitioned Austria into four sections, with Vienna and the eastern area in Soviet hands. After several attempts by the Soviets to take complete control of the country, Fr. Petrus Pavlicek, a Capuchin priest, initiated a Rosary crusade to save the tottering nation. By April 1955, the crusade had 500,000 members.

At one point the chancellor of Austria was summoned to Moscow and was received on May 13th, the anniversary of the first Fatima apparition. He wrote: "Today, a day of Fatima, the Russians are still hardened. Pray to the Mother of God that she aid the Austrian people." It seemed all was lost, but then a miracle occurred. Without any notice the Russians suddenly granted independence to Austria.

During the subsequent thanksgiving ceremony in Vienna, each speech attributed the victory to Our Lady of the Rosary. Much has been written of the power of prayer, but the surest way to discover this power in our own lives is simply by praying. It is then that we open ourselves to receive the infinite grace and power of God.

March 5
A Typical Day

Then Jesus told his disciples a parable to show them that they should always pray and not give up. (*Luke* 18:1)

In *My Life for the Poor*, Mother Teresa details a typical day in the lives of the Sisters of Charity:

We begin our day with meditation, Mass, and Holy Communion. We begin the day at 4:30 in the morning, with prayer and meditation. Then, since we each have only two saris, we have to wash one every day. By 7:30, some of the sisters go to the Home for the Dying, some go to work with lepers, some go to the little schools that we have in the slums, some go to prepare food, some go to families, some to teach catechism, and so on. We come back at 12:30 and then we have lunch. Then we often do housework. Then, for half an hour every sister goes to rest, because during all of this time they have been on their feet. After lunch, we have an examination of conscience and say the divine office and the Stations of the Cross.

By 2:00 we have spiritual reading for half an hour, then have a cup of tea. By 3:00 the professed sisters go out again. Novices and postulants remain in the house. They have classes of theology and Scripture and other things, like constitutions. Between 6:15 and 6:30 everybody comes back home. From 6:30 to 7:30 we have adoration with the Blessed Sacrament exposed. To be able to have this hour of adoration, we have not had to cut down the work.

At 7:30 we have dinner. After dinner, for about twenty minutes, we prepare the work for the next morning. From 8:30 until 9:00 we have recreation. (Everybody talks at the top of her voice because all day we have been working.) At 9:00 we go for night prayers and preparation of meditation for next morning.

It is unmistakable that the motivation and ability of the Missionaries of Charity to do their work arises from their prayer and meditation, which punctuates each part of their day. It is an example we can follow by praying, even briefly, at morning, noon, and night. We will then find that we can do even the most difficult tasks with attentiveness and peace.

March 6

Just a Little Prayer

I will extol the LORD at all times; his praise will always be on my lips. (Psalm 34:1)

The English journalist William Aitken tells the story of a parish priest who was suspicious of a shabby old man who used to go into his church at noon every day and spend a few minutes and then leave. What could he be doing? He asked the caretaker to question the old man. After all, the place contained valuable furnishings and sacred vessels.

"I go to pray," the old man said in reply to the caretaker's questioning.

"Come on," he replied, "you're never in church long enough to pray."

"Well, you see," the shabby old man went on, "I can't pray a long prayer, but every day at twelve o'clock, I just comes and says, 'Jesus, it's Jim,' and waits a minute and then comes away. It's just a little prayer, but I guess he hears me."

When Jim was injured some time later and taken to the hospital, he had a wonderful influence on others in the ward. Grumbling patients became cheerful, and often the ward would ring with laughter.

"Well, Jim," said the sister to him one day, "the men say you're responsible for this change in the ward. They say you are always happy."

"Aye, sister, that I am. I can't help being happy. You see, it's my visitor. Every day he makes me happy."

"Your visitor?" The sister was puzzled. She always noticed that Jim's chair was empty on visiting days, that he was a lonely old man, with no relatives.

"But when does he come?"

"Every day," Jim replied, the light in his eyes growing brighter. "Yes, every day at twelve o'clock he comes and stands at the foot of my bed. I sees him and he smiles and says, 'Jim, it's Jesus.'"

March 7
The Call to Peace

[H]ear from heaven their prayer and their plea, and uphold their cause. (1 Kings 8:45)

The greatest peacemaker of our age was Pope John Paul II. He consecrated his reign to the Blessed Virgin, as revealed in the words on his papal coat of arms, *totus tuus*, or "totally yours." Amid a modern trend to de-emphasize and even ignore Our Lady's role in the Church, John Paul resolutely upheld the importance of Marian devotion not only to the individual Catholic, but to the Church as a whole. The following prayer reflects his abiding love for the Blessed Virgin and her special call to peace:

Our Lady of the Millennium

Mother of the Redeemer,
with great joy we call you blessed.

In order to carry out his plan of salvation,
God the Father chose you before the creation of
the world.
You believed in his love and obeyed his word.
The Son of God desired you for his Mother
when he became man to save the human race.
You received him with ready obedience
and undivided heart.
The Holy Spirit loved you as his mystical spouse
and he filled you with singular gifts.
You allowed yourself to be led
by his hidden and powerful action.
In this third Christian millennium,
we entrust to you the church
which acknowledges you and invokes you as Mother.

To you, Mother of the human family and of the nations,
we confidently entrust the whole of humanity,
with its hopes and fears.
Do not let it lack the light of true wisdom.
Guide its steps in the ways of peace.
Enable all to meet Christ,
the Way and the Truth and the Life.

Sustain us, O Virgin Mary, on our journey of faith
and obtain for us the grace of eternal salvation.
O clement, O loving, O sweet Mother of God
and our Mother, Mary!

■

March 8

Feast of St. John of God

"The King will reply, 'I tell you the truth, whatever you did for one of the least of these brothers of mine, you did for me.' " (*Matthew* 25:40)

It was at the shrine of Our Lady of Guadeloupe in Mexico that the nature of John's vocation was revealed to him by the Blessed Virgin in 1521. Returning to Spain, he gave himself up to the service of the sick and poor, renting a house in which to care for them. After furnishing the house with what was necessary, he searched the city for the most seriously ill, bearing on his shoulders any who were unable to walk.

In one of the many stories of John's charity, he noticed while washing the feet of a beggar that the man's feet bore the marks of the crucified Christ. Without getting excited and with complete simplicity, the saint looked up into the beggar's face and declared, "So it is you, Lord."

St. John of God is patron saint of hospitals, chaplains, nurses, and the sick, and is the founder of the Brothers Hospitallers.

Prayer

Saint John of God, help us to act out of love as soon as we feel the promptings of the Holy Spirit. Help us learn to fight the little voices in our heads and hearts that give us all sorts of practical reasons to wait or delay in our service of God. Amen.

■

March 9

A Lenten Objective

We know that the law is spiritual; but I am unspiritual, sold as a slave to sin. I do not understand what I do. For what I want to do I do not do, but what I hate I do. (Romans 7:14–15)

Two hunters flew deep into a remote part of Canada to hunt elk. Their pilot, seeing that they had bagged six elk, told them the plane could only carry four out. "But the plane that carried us out last year was exactly like this one," one of the hunters protested. "The horsepower was the same, the weather was similar, and we had six elk then."

Hearing this, the pilot reluctantly agreed to try. They loaded up and took off, but sure enough there was insufficient power to climb out of the valley with all that weight, and they crashed. As they stumbled from the wreckage, one hunter asked the other if he knew where they were. "Well, I'm not sure," replied the second, "but I think we're about two miles from where we crashed last year."

Like the hunters, we may find that it might be time for us to break some dangerous habits—and that is the primary objective of Lent. The first step is to identify any sinful patterns we have acquired and then regularly pray to seek God's help and grace. Then we acknowledge them in the Sacrament of Reconciliation, where we may receive spiritual counsel and, of course, God's forgiveness. We should also be patient and persevering with ourselves, for it often takes time to be healed of a habit that may have taken years to acquire.

■

March 10

The Love of God

Jews demand miraculous signs and Greeks look for wisdom, but we preach Christ crucified: a stumbling block to Jews and foolishness to Gentiles, but to those whom God has called, both Jews and Greeks, Christ the power of God and the wisdom of God. (1 Corinthians 1:22–24)

In the Middle Ages, a very popular preaching monk announced that he was going to speak on the love of God. On the appointed Sunday, the cathedral was filled to overflowing with worshipers. But instead of going into the pulpit, the preacher simply sat down. The setting sun was shining through the stained glass and flooding the cathedral with glorious color and warmth. Still the preacher just sat in silence. Finally, as the cathedral grew darker, he went to the altar and lit a candle. Then he walked over to a statue of Christ on the cross. In silence, he held up the candle to the wounded hands, illuminating them for several minutes. Then he moved the candle down to the feet, which, like the hands, had felt the sharp nails tearing into the flesh. Then up to the crown of thorns. Having done this, the old monk pronounced the benediction. And everyone left the cathedral knowing that they had heard an unforgettable sermon on the love of God, even though the preacher had spoken not a word.

March 11
Fathomless Love

Then he released Barabbas to them. But he had Jesus flogged, and handed him over to be crucified. (Matthew 27:26)

We sometimes hear that we should not dwell on the physical aspects of the crucifixion; in fact most non-Catholics display the cross without the crucified body of Jesus on it. But the Catholic tradition holds that the crucifixion speaks of the fathomless love of God like nothing else.

Yosef Klauzner, the noted Jewish scholar, wrote, "Crucifixion is the most terrible and cruel death which man has ever devised for taking vengeance on his fellowmen." Cicero called it "the most cruel and the most horrible torture." Tacitus called it "a torture only fit for slaves."

It originated in Persia; its origin came from the fact that the earth was considered to be sacred to the god Ormuzd, and the criminal was lifted up so that he might not defile the earth, which was the god's property. From Persia, crucifixion passed to Carthage in North Africa, and it was from Carthage that Rome learned of it, although they reserved it for rebels, runaway slaves, and the worst type of criminal.

Klausner writes that the criminal was fastened to the cross, already a bleeding mass from a vicious scourging. There he hung to die of hunger, thirst, and exposure, unable even to defend himself from the torture of the gnats and flies that settled on his naked body and on his bleeding wounds.

The more we dwell upon the Love that would endure such torture for us, the more we will be filled with the profound gratitude and grace that motivates us to love and serve God and one another. What else can we do in the face of such overwhelming love?

March 12

This Is Your Mother

Near the cross of Jesus stood his mother, his mother's sister, Mary the wife of Clopas, and Mary Magdalene. (John 19:25)

Jesus met his mother as he was being led to his execution. She did not faint or scream in rage or despair; she did not try to prevent the soldiers from torturing him. She looked him in the eyes and knew that this was his hour. In Cana, when she had asked his help, he had put some distance between them and said, "Dear woman . . . my time has not yet come" (John 2:4). But now his sorrow and her sorrow merged in a deep knowledge of the hour in which God's plan of salvation was being fulfilled. Soon Mary will stand under the cross and Jesus will give her to John, his beloved disciple, with the words: "Here is your mother" (John 19:27).

Mary's sorrow has made her not only the mother of Jesus, but also the mother of all her children who suffer. She stood under the cross; she stands there still and looks into the eyes of those who are tempted to respond to their pain with revenge, retaliation, or despair. Her sorrow has made her heart a heart that embraces all her children, wherever they may be, and offers them the consolation and comfort of a true mother. May we remember this whenever suffering enters our lives.

■

March 13

Arranging Deck Chairs

The LORD your God will circumcise your hearts and the hearts of your descendants, so that you may love him with all your heart and with all your soul, and live. (Deuteronomy 30:6)

When the Titanic hit an iceberg in the North Atlantic and sank, over 1,500 people lost their lives in one of the worst maritime disasters in history. Recently a magazine recalled the tragedy and asked its readers this seemingly bizarre question: "If you had been on the Titanic when it sank, would you have walked around arranging the deck chairs?"

At first we say to ourselves, "What a ridiculous question! No one in his right mind would ignore wailing sirens on a sinking ship and rearrange its deck chairs." But as we continue to read the article, we see the reason for the strange question. And suddenly we ask ourselves, "Are we, perhaps, rearranging deck chairs on a sinking ship?" For example, are we so caught up with material things in life that we are giving a backseat to the spiritual? Are we so busy making a living that we are forgetting the purpose of life? Are we so taken up with life that we are forgetting why God gave us life?

There is an urgency to the gospel that echoes these questions. Again and again it speaks of the urgency of following Christ, not only for our own salvation but also that of others. But have we listened? Has the routine of our daily lives been changed at all? Or are we still arranging deck chairs? Lent is the special time to reflect on such questions.

March 14

The Hand Surgeon

Then he said to Thomas, "Put your finger here; see my hands. Reach out your hand and put it into my side. Stop doubting and believe." (John 20:27)

A physician who specializes in hand surgery wrote in a national publication that at some point in every operation he says, "My Lord and my God!"

The story behind this unusual practice dates back to when he was in Vietnam. One night, fresh out of medical school, the surgeon was called upon to remove a bullet from a soldier's hand. Moreover, he had to do it by flashlight. That operation moved him so deeply that after the war he decided to specialize in hand surgery.

Because of his specialty, the surgeon has a deep appreciation of the terrible pain caused by something, such as a bullet, ripping through the bones, muscles, and nerves of the human hand. He says he winces every time he thinks about the excruciating pain that Jesus endured when his hands were nailed to the cross.

Referring to today's Scripture reading, the surgeon writes that Thomas' cry, "My Lord and my God!" was more than a profession of faith. He feels it was also a cry of shock at seeing how torn and mangled the hands of Christ were. Only then did Thomas fully realize what he had suffered on the cross. And that discovery, says the surgeon, "was almost more than Thomas could bear."

March 15

The Way of the Cross

So the soldiers took charge of Jesus. Carrying his own cross, he went out to the place of the Skull (which in Aramaic is called Golgotha). (John 19:17)

The origin of the stations of the cross is shrouded in mystery. Legend tells us that after the Ascension, the Blessed Mother went out daily on the Sorrowful Way from Pilate's palace to Calvary in order to deeply reflect on her Son's passion. The apostles emulated the Blessed Mother, and the early Christians followed their lead. As a result, the stations were carefully marked as Jerusalem's Via Dolorosa, the Sorrowful Way.

By the fourth century, the time of St. Helena and the Emperor Constantine, the devotion was firmly established by pilgrims. The Muslims later suppressed the practice, and in time the actual route was obscured by subsequent conquerors and their destructive wars.

In the Middle Ages, people longed to visit the Holy Land to walk the footsteps of Christ, but like many of us today, they could not make the journey. So the practice of the observing the stations outside of Jerusalem sprang up after the wave of Crusades, but there was little uniformity in the devotion. The number of stations varied from five to thirty-six.

The fourteen stations as we know them today were introduced by the Franciscans after they took custody of the Holy Land's shrines.

March 16
The Rat

"Therefore I tell you, do not worry about your life, what you will eat or drink; or about your body, what you will wear. Is not life more important than food, and the body more important than clothes?" (Matthew 6:25)

In the pioneer days of aviation, a pilot was making a flight around the world. After he had been gone for some two hours from his last landing field, he heard a noise in his plane, which he recognized as the gnawing of a rat. Apparently, while his plane had been on the ground, a rat had crawled onboard. For all he knew it could be gnawing through a vital cable or control, so the situation was very serious. He became anxious and didn't know what to do. It was two hours back to the landing field from which he had taken off and more than two hours to the next field ahead.

Then he remembered that the rat is a rodent. It's not made for the heights; it's made to live on the ground and under the ground. Therefore the pilot began to climb. He flew up a thousand feet, then another thousand and another until he was more than twenty thousand feet up. The gnawing finally ceased; the rat was dead. He could not survive in the atmosphere of those heights. More than two hours later the pilot brought the plane safely to the next landing field and later found the dead rat.

Worry is a rodent. It cannot live in the secret place of the Most High. It cannot breathe in an atmosphere of trust and peace. Worry dies when we ascend to Christ through quiet prayer.

March 17

The Prayer of Quiet

O Lord, I call to you; come quickly to me. Hear my voice when I call to you. May my prayer be set before you like incense; may the lifting up of my hands be like the evening sacrifice. (Psalm 141:1–2)

The highest form of prayer is beyond words, found in the silence that is God's first language. The "prayer of quiet" or "centering prayer," in which we experience God in the very depths of our being, is not difficult but it does take perseverance. The following guidelines will be helpful:

- Choose a place where you can be alone without distraction. Take a comfortable bodily position, close your eyes, and put everything out of your mind.
- Physically relax and let all tensions leave you. Deep, deliberate breathing will aid this process. Let your total being, mind and body, arrive at a gentle silence.
- Center all your attention on God and let a word or phrase form in your consciousness. Suggestions might be "Jesus," or "peace," or "Mary," or whatever word has meaning for you.
  The word is used only to bring you back when your mind wanders away. Distractions always come but they should be accepted quietly and then you should move on.
- Twenty minutes twice a day, morning and evening, will allow God to deeply penetrate your soul and begin the healing and transformation of your spirit.
- Your prayer should end slowly and quietly, perhaps with the slow recitation of the Our Father.

The great master of centering prayer is Fr. Thomas Keating, author of many books, including *Open Mind, Open Heart; Invitation to Love;* and *The Mystery of Christ,* all of which would make excellent Lenten reading.

March 18

Image and Meditation

By day the L*ORD directs his love, at night his song is with me—a prayer to the God of my life. (Psalm 42:8)*

The sunset at the beach was extraordinary. Beautiful lavenders and pinks were streaked across the sky, and the setting sun was an orb of pulsating fire and life, gently sinking from view on the horizon.

I was only four years old, sitting alone on the beach and watching the spectacle of light, when suddenly I remembered that Jesus said he would meet me on the path to the beach at sunset. The thought of him filled me with happiness and I began to run to the path to meet him, so he wouldn't have to look for me.

But then I saw him running toward *me* on the beach. He was early. When we met he drew me up in his arms and kissed me on the forehead and held me close in his arms, my head resting on his chest as he sat down facing the beauty of the sunset. I don't know why I was tearful, but all I could say to him was, "But Jesus, I wanted to meet *you* on the path. I wanted to run to you. But you came running to me."

He kissed me again on the forehead and said, "Be still for now. Look at the sunset and the stars coming out. They are all for you. Now be one with me, safe in my arms, now and forever, for I love you more than you will ever know."

When I was a child, this is one way that I imagined an encounter with Jesus. Today, in a quiet place, close your eyes and think of the most beautiful place on earth. See yourself encountering Jesus there. What does he look like? He lifts you up, for you are a child in his eyes, and he speaks to you. What does he say? What do you say back to him?

This form of meditation using images can be powerful in bringing a new dimension and depth to our prayer. As we ask the Holy Spirit to guide our imagination, he will choose the images that will touch us most deeply.

March 19

Feast of St. Joseph

All spoke well of him and were amazed at the gracious words that came from his lips. "Isn't this Joseph's son?" they asked. (Luke 4:22)

During Vatican II, an aged bishop from Yugoslavia shuffled up to the podium and appealed to the assembled bishops to include the name of St. Joseph in the First Eucharistic Prayer, or traditional Canon, of the Mass. To the majority present this seemed unimportant at the moment. They were concerned with major changes and expressed their disapproval in the routine fashion of slapping the bench in unison to the chant, "*Non ad rem!* (not to the point!)."

The old bishop then left the podium and tottered back to his place. But in the papal apartments, Pope John XXIII (who watched all the proceedings on closed-circuit TV) was not amused. He knew that this old bishop had been imprisoned for nine years in a Communist jail, and that his captors had broken both his legs and simply left him in his pain. During this ordeal the agonizing bishop had prayed to St. Joseph.

The very next day, Pope John made the first change in the Canon of the Mass in centuries: he ordered the inclusion of the name of Joseph. Upon further inquiry, the bishops found out that twenty-six among them still bore on their bodies the scars of Communism. The incident turned out to be the most moving of the long Council.

March 20
Christ in China

"I am the living bread that came down from heaven. If anyone eats of this bread, he will live forever. This bread is my flesh, which I will give for the life of the world." (John 6:51)

Stories continue to come out of China of the heroic efforts of the few remaining bishops and priests to keep the faith alive and nourish the underground church. One such story tells of a priest who lives and works as a coolie. By means of prearranged sign language, he gets messages around of where he is to be found—usually at the corner of a local market selling soap. Customers who, like the early Christians, give a secret sign, are given a piece of soap, between the wrappings of which is hidden a small consecrated host.

The Chinese Catholic takes his purchase home and usually, after a short family service, receives Communion. Clearly the most exalted gift of Christ is his very body and blood in the Eucharist. St. Ambrose wrote of the miracle: "Christ is food for me; Christ is drink for me; the flesh of God is food for me, the blood of God is drink for me. Christ becomes one with me daily. Alleluia."

■

March 21
The Fall

For in his own eyes he flatters himself too much to detect or hate his sin. (Psalm 36:2)

Sin is not only what we actively do that is wrong, but also with what we neglect to do that is right—sometimes called the sin of omission. In Albert Camus' novel *The Fall*, there's a devastating line that expresses the truth of how ingrained and terrible these sins can be.

A respectable lawyer, walking in the streets of Amsterdam, hears a cry in the night. He realizes that a woman has fallen or has been pushed into the canal and is crying for help. Then the thoughts come rushing through his mind. Of course he must help, but . . . a respected lawyer getting involved in this way, what would the implications be; what about the physical danger . . . after all, who knows what has been going on?

By the time he has thought it through, it is too late. He moves on, making all kinds of excuses to justify his failure to act. Camus writes, "He did not answer the cry for help because that was the kind of man he was."

Prayer

Lord Jesus Christ, in the Letter of James we read that faith not expressed in good works is dead (2:20). Help us to put into action the faith we profess and, like the Good Samaritan, go out of our way to help those in need. Amen.

March 22

Spiritual Freedom

Then I acknowledged my sin to you and did not cover up my iniquity. I said, "I will confess my transgressions to the LORD"—and you forgave the guilt of my sin. (Psalm 32:5)

Emilie Griffin was a New York advertising executive when she felt herself drawn to Catholicism. In her book *Turning: Reflections on the Experience of Conversion*, she describes her first reaction to the Sacrament of Confession: "The notion of confessing my sins was hateful to me. It was not a question of unwillingness to confess my sins before another human being; it was in fact an unwillingness to confess my sins at all. I could not admit myself to be a sinner. Yet in some part of me I knew I was flawed . . . and I was profoundly ashamed."

When Emilie decided to become Catholic, therefore, she found herself confronted, for the first time, with admitting that she was a sinner. Finally, the hour came for her to receive the sacrament. It was an experience she would never forget. She said she experienced a spiritual freedom that caused her great joy. And to her surprise, she found that confessing her sins to a priest was not confessing to a priest at all. She says in her book: "I had begun to see priests not as men but as Christ himself; and I remember with what tenderness he dealt with the tax collectors and the adulteress."

March 23
Impossible Love

This is love: not that we loved God, but that he loved us and sent his Son as an atoning sacrifice for our sins. Dear friends, since God so loved us, we also ought to love one another. (1 John 4:10–11)

Love can do the impossible. The *New York Times* once ran a story of a crippled woman leaving her crutches and running up a flight of stairs to rescue her three-year-old daughter, when fire threatened to trap the child in an upstairs bedroom. The mother, injured in a car crash two years previously, had been unable to walk without crutches ever since the accident. Realizing that the life of her little daughter was at stake, she momentarily overcame her own physical handicap. She rushed to the upper floor, grabbed the sleeping child, and carried her to safety.

For most of us, there are times when our capacity to love is obstructed by self-concern, worry, or a flagging faith. In such a case, we are encouraged to surrender these obstacles to the Son of God, who will again infuse us with his peaceful love.

March 24

Daughter of the Poor

Yet give attention to your servant's prayer and his plea for mercy, O LORD my God. Hear the cry and the prayer that your servant is praying in your presence. (*2 Chronicles 6:19*)

Among the great poets of Our Lady was James of Sarug (d. 521), the author of many poems and hymns to the Virgin. The following comes down to us over the course of fifteen centuries:

Blessed are you, O Mary,
and blessed is your holy soul,
for your beatitude
surpasses that of all the blessed.

Blessed are you who have borne, embraced,
and caressed as a baby
the one who upholds the ages
with his secret word.
Blessed are you, from whom the Savior
appeared on this exile earth,
subjugating the seducer
and bringing peace to the world.

Blessed are you, because the whole universe
resounds with your memory,
and the angels and human beings celebrate your feast.

Daughter of the poor,
she became the Mother of the King of Kings.
She gave to the poor world
the riches that can make it live.

She is the ark laden with the goodness
and the treasures of the Father,
who sent his riches once again
into our empty home.
Amen.

March 25
G.K. Chesterton

"If you forgive anyone his sins, they are forgiven; if you do not forgive them, they are not forgiven." (John 20:23)

One of the most brilliant of the twentieth-century converts to Catholicism was G.K. Chesterton. For many years his keen intellect and powerful pen were devoted to the service of the faith he had so completely embraced. His command of language and quick wit, his clear thinking, and his deep knowledge of the faith made him one of its great defenders in Anglican England.

As people often ask converts, so they asked Chesterton: "What brought you to the faith?" One would expect some profound intellectual reason from a man with the mind and ability of Chesterton, something unusual or exceptional. Yet he always answered with the simple statement, "I just wanted to get rid of my sins." However, the whole theology of redemption lies hidden in his words, including the rebirth to innocence that is the gift of the Sacrament of Confession. "It sets me back to my childhood," he said.

Prayer

Lord Jesus, through your cross you have freed us from sin and restored the innocence of our childhood. Help us to truly accept this greatest of all gifts, so that gratitude and joy may permeate our lives. Amen.

March 26

The Divine Nature

Rejoice in the Lord always. I will say it again: Rejoice! Let your gentleness be evident to all. The Lord is near. Do not be anxious about anything, but in everything, by prayer and petition, with thanksgiving, present your requests to God. (Philippians 4:4–6)

Prayerful encounters with our Lord are often joyous, for that is the essence of the divine nature. The spiritual writer Samuel Gordon (d. 1936) wrote that joy is a distinctly Christian word and a Christian experience. "It is the reverse of happiness," he says. "Happiness is the result of what happens of an agreeable sort. Joy has its spring deep down inside, and that spring never runs dry, no matter what happens. Only Christ gives that joy. He had joy, singing its music within, even under the shadow of the cross."

Joy is the echo of God's life within us. In the words of St. Augustine, "There is a joy which is not given to the ungodly, but to those who love you for your own sake, whose joy you yourself are. And this is a happy life, to rejoice to you, of you, for you; this is it, and there is no other."

Are we aware of the "spring deep down inside" us, the conviction that, in the end, everything is all right? Sometimes reflecting on the very fact of our salvation, of being the eternal sons and daughters of God, can stir the divine joy deep within.

March 27

Germany and America

For you have spent enough time in the past doing what pagans choose to do—living in debauchery, lust, drunkenness, orgies, carousing and detestable idolatry. (*1 Peter 4:3*)

During the first part of the twentieth century, Germany was considered not only a great industrial power, but also highly cultured and educated. By 1933, an incredible change had occurred, as we see in this excerpt from *Time* magazine dated July 10, 1933:

> Thus incited, Nazi police raided in Berlin six Catholic organizations whose headquarters they padlocked: the Catholic Peace League; Catholic Scouts; Windhorst League; Flock of the Cross; Peoples Union of Catholic Germany and Catholic Young Men's Association.
>
> With religious frenzy mounting, half-naked Nazis appeared in Berlin wearing strips of animal skins and ancient Teutonic horned caps. Loudly touting a return to the worship of Thor and Wodan they celebrated in a Berlin stadium the "Festival of the Swastika," and seemed to consider their acts religious. Sunday found banners with the pagan swastika or Hakenkreuz ("hooked cross") stuck up beside the cross of Christ in a majority of Berlin churches. . . .

Americans must realize that our great history does not insure us against a similar future. As the culture war rages and a new paganism presses in from all sides, we must be vigilant and courageous in standing up for the ethical and spiritual heritage that was clearly in the minds of the founders of our nation—especially in any national crisis when the call to radicalism and intolerance can be overwhelming.

March 28

A Gentle Breeze

But I have stilled and quieted my soul; like a weaned child with its mother, like a weaned child is my soul within me. (Psalm 131:2)

One summer a young woman had been rehearsing some songs, leaving her harp before an open window. Suddenly she heard the sound of distant and very lovely music. It lasted only a few seconds and left her very puzzled. When it happened again she noticed that the sound came from the instrument and was caused by the gentle breeze from the open window playing on the harp strings.

At times of prayer we can be like that harp, by allowing sufficient calm to gather around us so that the Holy Spirit, the Breath of God, may play his music in us. But remember, it was a gentle breeze, and the music could be heard only because of the surrounding stillness.

■

March 29

Do This Alone and It Is Enough

Dear friends, let us love one another, for love comes from God. Everyone who loves has been born of God and knows God. (1 John 4:7)

There is an ancient tradition about the last days of St. John, the author of the fourth Gospel, two Letters, and the book of Revelation. He lived to a great age and became so feeble that he had to be carried to the meetings of the faithful. There, because of his weakness, he was unable to deliver a long discourse; so at each gathering he simply repeated the words, "Little children, love one another." The disciples, weary of hearing the same words over and over, asked him why he never said anything else. And John gave this answer: "Do this alone and it is enough."

■

March 30

Captain George Grant

He brought me out into a spacious place; he rescued me because he delighted in me. (*2 Samuel 22:20*)

Captain George Grant gives us a unique example of love in action. Several years ago he was given an extraordinary award for saving 106 lives during his fifty years at sea. His rescues included two men on a sinking fishing boat in the Gulf Stream, three others on a raft off the west coast of Mexico, seventeen sailors from a navel vessel that sank outside of San Francisco harbor, as well as eighty-three survivors of a collision between a tanker and an icebreaker.

The most unique rescue involved one of his sailors who fell overboard and was not missed until several hours later. The captain immediately turned his ship around and retraced the exact course. After a careful search the seaman was eventually picked up unharmed.

Few of us can duplicate such dramatic feats of love, but in our own lives we have countless opportunities to love others by showing a Christlike concern and alertness for those in distress.

March 31

The Old Grandmother

After David had finished talking with Saul, Jonathan became one in spirit with David, and he loved him as himself. (*1 Samuel 18:1*)

As a part of an assignment for a doctoral thesis, a graduate student spent a year with a group of Navajos on a reservation in the Southwest. As he did his research he lived with one family, sleeping in their hut, eating their food, working with them, and generally living the life of a twentieth-century Native American. The old grandmother of the family spoke no English at all, yet a very close friendship formed between the two.

They spent a great deal of time sharing a friendship that was meaningful for each of them, yet unexplainable to anyone else. In spite of the language difference, they shared the common language of love and understood each other. Over the months he learned a few phrases of Navajo, and she picked up a little English. When it was time for him to return to the campus and write his thesis, the tribe held a going-away celebration. It was marked by sadness since the young man had become close to the whole village. As he prepared to get up into the pickup truck and leave, the old grandmother came to tell him good-bye. With tears in her eyes, she placed her hands on either side of his face, looked directly into his eyes and said, "I like me best when I'm with you."

That's the way we should feel in the presence of our closest friends, who are always a gift from God. They bring out the best in us. We learn to see ourselves as worthy and valuable when we're in their presence.

APRIL

April 1

"Unfasten the chains..."

For God did not give us a spirit of timidity, but a spirit of power, of love and of self-discipline. (2 Timothy 1:7)

Fr. Michael Shaw, a physician as well as a priest, was deeply moved at the sight of the three men before him. He was a Franciscan missionary who, having just arrived in India, asked to be assigned to one of the leper settlements. Three men had manacles and fetters binding their hands and feet, cutting their diseased flesh. Fr. Shaw turned to the guard and said, "You can unfasten the chains." "It isn't safe," the guard replied. "These men are criminals as well as lepers!" "I'll be responsible. They're suffering enough, I think," Fr. Shaw said, as he put out his hand and took the keys, kneeling to remove the shackles. He then treated their bleeding ankles and wrists.

About two weeks later the priest had his first misgivings about freeing the criminals; he had to make an overnight trip and was anxious about leaving two missionary sisters alone in the settlement, but they insisted they weren't afraid.

The next morning when they went to the front door, they were startled to see the three men lying on the front steps. But in broken English one of them explained, "We know the doctor go. We stay here all night so no harm come to you."

It's hard to comprehend the effects of kindness, even the smallest kind word or gesture. It seems that the grace of God magnifies it a thousandfold, and only in heaven will we see the astonishing effect of our efforts. This should encourage us to be even more persistent in showing compassion and kindness to others today.

April 2
The Path

Jesus answered, "I am the way and the truth and the life. No one comes to the Father except through me." (John 14:6)

Missionary and educator Stanley Jones (d. 1973) was the author of some thirty books. He is especially remembered for the thousands of ecumenical lectures he presented to the educated classes in India and his friendship and support of Mahatma Gandi.

He once spoke of the experience of a missionary priest who got lost in an African jungle with nothing around him but bush and vines. He found a native and asked if he could lead him out. The native said he could. "All right," said the missionary, "show me the way." The native said, "Walk." So they walked and hacked their way through unmarked jungle for more than an hour. But the priest got worried. "Are you sure this is the way? Where is the path?" The native said, "Friend, in this place there is no path. I am the path."

Sometimes in our journey through life we experience uncertainty, confusion, and a nearsightedness that keeps us from seeing what is really important. Knowing this, Christ offers us himself as an infallible guide, asking only that we keep our hearts open and our eyes fixed on him, who is himself the path and the way.

April 3

The Spontaneity of Love

Let love and faithfulness never leave you; bind them around your neck, write them on the tablet of your heart. (*Proverbs* 3:3)

I remember a Sunday afternoon when I stopped by a local restaurant for dinner. As I sat in one of the booths, I casually looked about to see if there was anyone I knew. My eye landed on a booth where three boys, somewhere between the ages of seven and twelve, were sitting with their father, who was speaking and laughing with them. It looked as though they had finished dinner and were waiting for their mother to reappear. While the boys talked among themselves, Dad leaned back and simply gazed at his children.

And then, spontaneously, the father turned toward his youngest son, took his head in his hands, and kissed him on the forehead. I remember the boy's surprise and delight. It was a blessing and affirmation—a spontaneous act of love.

This small, fleeting incident struck an inner chord within me. Part of it may have been a flashback to my own childhood, but there was also a certain power in this joyous love that I could feel even from across the room. No one else seemed to notice. But later on, as I went through the remainder of the day, I found that the image kept coming back to mind. A week, a month, a year later, the memory came back, often when I was in prayer. It's a powerful image of the Father and his longed-for relationship with us—one without fear or doubt but filled with total acceptance, delight, and the spontaneity of love.

April 4
G. Gordon Liddy

All that the Father gives me will come to me, and whoever comes to me I will never drive away. For I have come down from heaven not to do my will but to do the will of him who sent me. (*John* 6:37–38)

One of the men convicted in the Watergate affair that forced President Nixon to resign in 1973 was G. Gordon Liddy. After his release from prison in 1977, Liddy wrote an autobiography entitled *Will*. It was a fitting title, for since childhood Liddy has been a man of tremendous willpower.

In his book he describes how he used to perform painful and distasteful acts in order to strengthen his will. For example, as a youngster he ate part of a rat. On other occasions he held his hand steady in a burning flame.

In the 1960s, Liddy abandoned his Catholic faith. But twenty years later, in the 1980s, he underwent a religious conversion. It came about as a result of attending Scripture study meetings with his former FBI colleagues. Commenting on the experience, Liddy says that he resolved to spend the rest of his life seeking and doing God's will rather than his own. "The hardest thing I have to do now, each day, is to decide what is God's will rather than what is my will. So the prayer I say most often is, first of all, 'God, please tell me what you want.' And second, 'Give me the strength to do your will.' "

April 5
I'm Counting on You

Therefore go and make disciples of all nations. (*Matthew* 28:19a)

There is a story that after Jesus returned to heaven he and Gabriel the Archangel were conversing. Even in heaven Christ bore the marks of the crucifixion. Looking at Jesus' wounds, Gabriel said, "Lord, you have suffered so much. But now, do people know and understand the extent of what you did for them, how you must love them?" Jesus replied, "Oh, no; not yet. Right now only a few people in Palestine know."

The Archangel was perplexed and said, "Then what have you done to assure that all the rest will know?"

The Lord answered, "I've have asked Peter, James, John, and a few others to tell them. Those who are told will tell others, who in turn will tell still others, until the last man and woman in the farthest corner of the earth will have heard the story of my profound love and shared it with others."

Gabriel frowned and looked rather skeptical. "Yes, but what if Peter and the others get tired? What if the people who come after them forget? Surely you've made some contingency plans."

Jesus replied, "Gabriel, I haven't made any other plans. I'm counting on them."

April 6

Chaplain Eugene O'Grady

"Do not be afraid, O man highly esteemed," he said. "Peace! Be strong now; be strong." When he spoke to me, I was strengthened and said, "Speak, my lord, since you have given me strength." (Daniel 10:19)

Father Eugene P. O'Grady was killed instantly on November 29, 1944, when a mortar shell burst near him. He had enlisted in the Army three years earlier in 1941, when the 29th Division of the National Guard was called up. In the official citation, his battalion commander wrote this of him:

> It may be said without exaggeration that the greatest single contribution to the morale of the personnel of this battalion has been the work of Chaplain O'Grady.

He was seen as a man of God, and a few words from Father O'Grady have, on untold occasions, when the going was rough, changed the entire outlook of individuals, buoyed them up and spurred them on to greater efforts.

He seemed mindless of the danger that often surrounded him. For this and other qualities he is admired and respected by all as an ideal combat chaplain. This priest landed on the beach early on D-Day with a rifle company, and he has been at or near the front lines ever since. Aiding the wounded, comforting the dying under heavy enemy fire were just part of his daily tasks. He worked on tirelessly day and night.

Speaking of his last day, Fr. O'Grady's colleague, Fr. Harold Donovan, stated: "He had spent the preceding twenty-four hours at our division clearing station where we have a priest on duty at all times when engaged. His unit was moving into the line, and he was joining them when he was killed. I received the news when I returned to my office that evening, and immediately made arrangements for the funeral. I blessed the body and placed my stole around Gene's shoulders, and carried him to the Army cemetery in Holland, where we had six priests for pallbearers, and I offered Mass for Gene's soul before burying him. It was a sad group leaving the cemetery, for Gene was well loved among the priests."

When we hear stories of heroic and good priests, we see the grace of God working in ordinary lives to achieve extraordinary ends. At their best, they are truly *alter Christus*, or other Christs. I have met many of them in clergy conferences of the Archdiocese for Military Affairs. They tell me the one thing they need most, and that we can each give them, is our heartfelt prayers.

■

April 7

Repairing the Broken

Praise be to the God and Father of our Lord Jesus Christ! In his great mercy he has given us new birth into a living hope through the resurrection of Jesus Christ from the dead. (1 Peter 1:3)

In 1981 Peter Cropper, the British violinist, was invited to Finland to play a special concert. As a personal favor to Peter, the Royal Academy of Music lent him their priceless 285-year-old Stradivarius for use in the concert. This rare instrument takes its name from the Italian violinmaker Antonio Stradivari. It's made of eighty pieces of special wood and covered with thirty coats of special varnish. Its beautiful sound has never been duplicated.

When Peter got to Finland, an incredible nightmare took place. Going on stage, he tripped and fell, and the violin broke into several pieces. Later he flew back to London in a state of shock.

A master craftsman named Charles Beare agreed to try to repair the instrument. He worked endless hours on the project and finally got it back together again. Then came the dreaded moment of truth. What would the violin sound like? The craftsman handed it to Peter. His heart was racing as he picked up the bow and began to play. Those present could scarcely believe their ears. The violin's sound was as excellent as before, but had acquired a new, even more beautiful tone.

In the months ahead Cropper took the violin on a worldwide tour. Night after night the violin that everyone thought was ruined forever drew standing ovations from concert audiences.

Our faults, past sins, and brokenness can also be transformed into something beautiful under the hand of Christ. Indeed, the wounded healer is the most effective of all.

April 8

The Seed of Faith

Therefore I endure everything for the sake of the elect, that they too may obtain the salvation that is in Christ Jesus, with eternal glory. Here is a trustworthy saying: If we died with him, we will also live with him; if we endure, we will also reign with him. (2 *Timothy* 2:10–12)

Many years ago two men were on board a sailing ship, going back to their home on a far-off Pacific island, when one of them noticed a little grain of corn at his feet. He picked it up and examined it. "It's a grain of corn," he said. "If it were a sack full it might be of some use!" and he threw it away again carelessly.

But the other man picked it up, put it in his pocket, and treasured it until they reached their island home. Then he sowed it. It grew into a plant, and yielded a tiny crop, so small as to be laughable. But he planted that in turn, and the next time the result was enough to fill a cup. This he sowed again, and there was enough to give a few grains to each of his many friends. So the crop grew, and in the end it yielded an abundant harvest. The little seed was the means of introducing corn to the Pacific islands.

When the seed of faith first comes into our lives with its love and power and we feel its great energy, we treat it with great reverence. As time goes by, however, we may begin to take it for granted and perhaps become careless. But if we are persistent in our prayer, which is the food for our souls, we will find the reverse happening. Our faith and our love will continue to grow, become more enthusiastic, and bear a great harvest.

April 9
The Lamplighter

"You are the light of the world. A city on a hill cannot be hidden. Neither do people light a lamp and put it under a bowl. Instead they put it on its stand, and it gives light to everyone in the house. In the same way, let your light shine before men, that they may see your good deeds and praise your Father in heaven." (Matthew 5:14–16)

John Ruskin, the nineteenth-century English writer and social theorist, once sat with a friend in the dusk of an evening and watched a lamplighter, torch in hand, lighting the streetlights on a distant hill. Very soon the man's form was no longer distinguishable in the distance, but everywhere he went he left a light burning brightly.

"There," said Ruskin, "that is what I mean by a man of faith. You can trace his course by the light he leaves burning."

Drawing others to Christ is often not a matter of words or preaching but the example of our lives. Only in eternity will we be shown the profound effect we have had on others—without our being aware of it.

■

April 10
One Abused Child

Fathers, do not exasperate your children; instead, bring them up in the training and instruction of the Lord. (Ephesians 6:4)

As a ten-year-old boy who had tried to run away from home because of his abusive father, Adolf Hitler was beaten so severely that he went into a coma for days, his family not knowing if he would survive. It was the worst incident in a childhood filled with abuse.

Psychologists have long known that frequent or severe punishment conveys to children that they are evil. Being nearly killed by parents conveys that they are unworthy to live. Thus the boy Adolf began to experience himself as evil and worthless—feelings he would describe in middle age and be haunted by until his death.

Psychologists are also painfully aware that many abused children accept their situation and what it implies about them until they reach a position from which they can abuse others—usually their own children. In Hitler's case, he would become *Führer* and judge millions of his subjects to be *lebensunwurdige Leben*—living things unworthy to live—and have untold numbers beaten, mutilated, and killed.

It can be well argued that the greatest evil in the world, given its continual resonance through generations, is child abuse.

April 11

"I Just Burst with Joy..."

They drove out many demons and anointed many sick people with oil and healed them. (Mark 6:13)

The following is an excerpt from a letter by a Vietnam veteran, written from a hospital bed while recuperating from battlefield injuries. It speaks of the Sacrament of the Sick, which, as any priest can testify, conveys healing that can even border on the miraculous.

> From the split second I was hit, I was completely alone. I've heard it said, but never realized it—when you're dying there's no one but you. You're all alone. I was hurt bad; a 4.2 mortar landed about six feet behind me and took off my left leg, ripped up my left arm, hit me in the back, head, hip, and ankle. Shock was instantaneous, but I fought it knowing that if I went out I'd never wake up again.
>
> After they carried me into the first-aid station, I felt four or five people scrubbing my body in different places. This caused me to

open my eyes, but I could only see about a foot in front of me. Anyway, someone bent over me. It looked like our chaplain, but then I started to fade out. As I was going out, my eyes closed and I heard Father say, "Through this holy anointing may the Lord grant you pardon and peace . . ." Then a split second before I went out, I felt oil on my forehead. And something happened which I'll never forget—something which I never experienced before in life.

All of a sudden, I stopped grasping for every inch of life; I just burst with joy. . . . I was on cloud nine. I felt free of body and mind. After this, I was conscious about three or four times during the next ten-day period; I never worried about dying. In fact, I was almost waiting for it.

As a hospital chaplain, I administer the Sacrament of Anointing frequently and am continually amazed at its healing effects, especially on the spirit. Even in the most trying circumstances, as with the dying, God invariably gives the grace to cope peacefully, if he is asked. May we always ask to receive this great sacrament when the need arises.

April 12

Memo from God

So then, just as you received Christ Jesus as Lord, continue to live in him, rooted and built up in him, strengthened in the faith as you were taught, and overflowing with thankfulness. (Colossians 2:6–7)

Dear child,

I am God. Today I will help you handle all your problems. If life happens to deliver a situation you can't handle, don't try to resolve it alone. I will take care of it if you'll let me.

Once you give the problem to me, don't hold on to it by worrying about it. Instead, focus on all the wonderful things that are present in your life now. If you find yourself stuck in traffic, don't get angry.

There are people in this world for which driving is an unheard-of luxury. Should you have a bad day at work, think of the man who has been out of work for years.

Should you despair over a relationship gone bad, think of the person who has never known what it's like to love and be loved in return. Should you grieve the passing of another weekend, think of the woman in dire straits, working twelve hours a day, seven days a week to feed her children.

Should your car break down, leaving you miles away from assistance, think of the paraplegic who would love the opportunity to take that walk. Should you notice a new gray hair in the mirror, think of the cancer patient in chemo who wishes she had hair to examine. Should you find yourself at a loss and pondering what life is all about, be thankful. There are those who didn't live long enough to get the opportunity.

Be grateful. Be happy. Keep me in your heart.

With great love,
God

April 13

Arrogance

In his pride the wicked does not seek him; in all his thoughts there is no room for God. (Psalm 10:4)

It's interesting that when Napoleon was excommunicated by Pius VII in 1809 (according to the memoirs of Cardinal Bartolommeo Pacca, a Vatican statesman), he made light of it and said, "Does he think it will cause the guns to drop from the hands of my soldiers?"

All the same, he felt uneasy, and told Monsieur de Champagny, his Minister of Foreign Affairs, to draw up a list of all the monarchs that had been excommunicated. The minister didn't think he was serious and did nothing about it, but Napoleon insisted that the list be made up. There were eighty-five cases, not counting the case of Napoleon himself, which was tactfully omitted. In all cases, the excommunication seemed to have detrimental effects.

Three years afterward, Napoleon's decline began with the disastrous retreat from Moscow. Ironically, the guns actually did fall from the frozen hands of the emperor's soldiers, caught in the intense cold of the Russian winter.

The book of Proverbs reminds us that, "When pride comes, then comes disgrace, but with humility comes wisdom" (Proverbs 11:2). In fact, pride is condemned all through the Bible, from Exodus to Revelation, and for good reason. It is, in essence, a denial of God, or the reality that all is grace, all is gift. Humility, on the other hand, is simply truth. Except for God, we are a wisp of air. May we continue to live in the truth, which is far more beautiful than self-delusion.

April 14

With Infinite Yearning

By day the LORD directs his love, at night his song is with me—a prayer to the God of my life. (Psalm 42:8)

In Christ's words to Gabrielle Bossis, the French locutionist, Christ's one great theme is his love for his people. The following is typical of the urgent language he uses to convey this love:

> Picture me as a living being, loving you more than you could ever imagine even in your deepest longing. And keep before you the thought that this living being who gave his life for you is waiting with infinite yearning for the moment of our meeting. . . .
>
> Do you at last believe with all your heart that I created you in order to make you eternally happy? It was out of pure love that I made you—not for my own interest but for yours: to give you infinite bliss. . . .

Write! I don't want people to be afraid of me anymore, but to see my heart full of love and to speak with me as they would with a dearly beloved brother.

For some I am unknown. For others, a stranger, a severe master or an accuser. Few people come to me as to one of a loved family. And yet my love is there, waiting for them. So tell them to come, to enter in, to give themselves up to love just as they are. Just as they are. I'll restore. I'll transform them. And they will know a joy they have never known before. . . .

April 15

Call Evil by Its Name

Be self-controlled and alert. Your enemy the devil prowls around like a roaring lion looking for someone to devour. (1 Peter 5:8)

Although Pope John Paul II admitted it sounds "a bit strange" to speak of the devil during a Mass of Thanksgiving, he stressed that the power of evil in the world should be called by name. The pope celebrated an evening Mass on December 31, 1993, at Rome's St. Ignatius Church to mark the end of that year. "The ending of a year should make Christians think about the end of time and of God's plans for eternal salvation," he said. The pope quoted from the First Letter of St. John: "Children, it is the last hour, and just as you heard that the anti-Christ was coming, so now many 'antichrists' have appeared."

In his book *Crossing the Threshold of Hope*, John Paul II elaborated on this theme: "To save means to liberate from evil. This does not refer only to social evils, such as injustice, coercion, exploitation. Nor does it refer only to disease, catastrophes, natural cataclysms, and everything that has been considered disaster in the history of humanity. To save means to liberate from radical, ultimate evil."

Our greatest defense against all forms of evil is the protective hand of God. In turning to him in times of temptation and fear, we will find not only refuge and safety, but also the courage to actively fight against evil in all its manifestations.

April 16

Giving of Ourselves

For this very reason, make every effort to add to your faith goodness; and to goodness, knowledge; and to knowledge, self-control; and to self-control, perseverance; and to perseverance, godliness. (2 Peter 1:5–6)

Fr. Frank Paovone, national director of Priests for Life, has written, "One should note that *Humanae Vitae*'s message is broader than the rejection of birth control. It is a declaration of the dominion of God over human life, and of the full beauty of human sexuality. The problem of our age is not that it is obsessed with sex, but that it is afraid of it—afraid of the full dimensions of its claim on human commitment, self-sacrifice, and generosity—afraid of the fact that authentic sex does not let us get lost in ourselves and our pleasures, but demands that we give of ourselves for the good of the other, including the children God may give us."

Mother Teresa of Calcutta speaks to this in a story she tells:

A group of lepers, of slum dwellers, of beggars (these are our people!) came to the house one day to thank me for allowing the young sisters, the novices, to teach them family planning. They said, "You people who have a vow of chastity, you are the best people to teach us because it is nothing else but self-control out of love for each other. We thank you for teaching us because our family is united, our family is healthy and we can have a baby whenever we want."

We have heard the government say that in these years that more than 150,000 fewer babies have been born in Calcutta alone, because of this beautiful way among the beggars, among the lepers, among the slum dwellers. It is beautiful to see them: how they help each other to grow in love!

April 17

Amazing Love

In this same way, husbands ought to love their wives as their own bodies. He who loves his wife loves himself. (Ephesians 5:28)

During World War I, Newton D. Baker, the secretary of war, visited a military hospital and found there a desperate case. A young soldier had had both legs shot away. One arm was gone as well. He had been blinded in both eyes, and his face was terribly battered and disfigured. No one expected him to survive.

A few months later the secretary met a friend who worked at the hospital. "Did the young man live?" asked Baker. "Did he live?" said the friend. "Believe it or not, he married his nurse." Baker had to admire the woman's heroism in loving a man in such a desperate condition—no legs, one arm, blind, and disfigured. After several years Baker had almost forgotten the story.

One day, however, as a trustee of Johns Hopkins University, he received a notice that the university was conferring the degree of doctor of philosophy on a man named William H. Craig. The secretary discovered that this young man, despite almost insurmountable handicaps, had performed one of the most brilliant pieces of research ever done at Johns Hopkins.

Baker was dumbfounded when he found out that Craig, the man who was to receive this honor, was none other than the mutilated soldier he had seen years before. When the legless and one-armed veteran was wheeled across the stage to receive the degree, the students and faculty rose to their feet and cheered.

In the back of Secretary Baker's mind was the thought of the nurse and the amazing love that had helped this extraordinary man to survive and flourish. He could not help thinking of the amazing love that had given new hope to his sightless eyes, new strength to a mangled, crippled body.

April 18

The Monument at Verona

"Though the mountains be shaken and the hills be removed, yet my unfailing love for you will not be shaken nor my covenant of peace be removed," says the LORD, *who has compassion on you.* (*Isaiah* 54:10)

Sometimes a story of men living in peace is more valuable than words about peace. F.H. Drinkwater relates such a story, set in Italy during World War II.

In the mountain village of Giazza, north of Verona, German paratroopers were going to execute some villagers, presumably for showing resistance. The parish priest, Fr. Domenico Mercante, offered himself as a hostage. The Germans accepted his offer, and decided to shoot him. When the time came, one of the firing-party refused to obey orders. "I can't shoot a priest," he said. He was placed at the priest's side, and both were shot together. The soldier's name is unknown.

Fifteen years later, the Bishop of Verona unveiled a simple white monument commemorating the two heroes. The German embassy in Rome was represented, and the Italian minister of justice gave an address. He said, "The example of a priest and a soldier dying by the same rifle fire, in order that not only the written law but the unwritten law too should be respected, provides an example of great moral value. It gives rise to the hope that the cause of peace may find its strongest protection in the conscience of humble but heroic spirits."

April 19

The Playground

Whoever would love life and see good days must keep his tongue from evil and his lips from deceitful speech. He must turn from evil and do good; he must seek peace and pursue it. (1 Peter 3:10–11)

There is a great motion picture, a classic in Japan, about an old man's struggle to find meaning in his life after learning that he has a terminal illness. This causes him to reflect on his uneventful life as a minor city hall bureaucrat. He is spiritually troubled because he has made no significant contribution to his fellow man. So despite his weakened condition, he resolves to do something for others before he dies.

With his remaining energy he supports a playground project that has had one obstacle after another thrown in its path by local bureaucrats. As a result of his efforts, the playground is finally completed and the city's children are presented with their new paradise. But the experience has transformed the stuffy old ex-bureaucrat into a warm and compassionate man.

At the end of the film, the old man is seen contentedly seated on one of the new playground swings, slowly moving back and forth and softly humming a tune. There, peacefully, he dies.

Prayer

Lord Jesus Christ, help me to be a channel of your love and peace throughout my life. Help me not to put off the good works that I can do now, for love of you and my neighbor. Amen.

April 20

Contentment

I know what it is to be in need, and I know what it is to have plenty. I have learned the secret of being content in any and every situation, whether well fed or hungry, whether living in plenty or in want. (Philippians 4:12)

A wealthy tourist, complete with dark glasses and camera, went walking along a tropical beach one morning and found a local fisherman sitting alongside his canoe and peacefully praying the Rosary.

"Why aren't you out fishing?" asked the tourist.

"I've caught enough fish for today," he answered.

"But why don't you go out and catch more?"

"Why?"

"You could sell them and get enough money to buy a net."

"What for?"

"So you could catch even more. Then you could buy a motor and go out farther, where there's many more fish."

"But why do that?"

"So you could make a lot of money and then buy a whole fleet of fishing boats."

"And then what?"

"Then you would become rich and you could spend your time taking it easy."

"That's what I'm doing now," he replied.

In sacred Scripture, Our Lord stresses that contentment and inner joy are not found in material goods, but are the natural side effects of following him with faith and commitment. It is difficult for us in our consumer society to hear this message, but so very important to our spiritual lives and our search for peace.

April 21

Marine Corps Chaplain Vincent Capodanno

When they saw the courage of Peter and John and realized that they were unschooled, ordinary men, they were astonished and they took note that these men had been with Jesus. (Acts 4:13)

Father Vincent Capodanno, a chaplain with the Marine Corps, was killed in battle on September 4, 1967, somewhere in the Que Son Valley in Vietnam. The official citation of the Congressional Medal of Honor, awarded posthumously, relates an amazing story:

> Rank and organization: Lieutenant, U.S. Navy, Chaplain Corps, 3d Battalion, 5th Marines, 1st Marine Division (Rein), FMF. Place and date: Quang Tin Province, Republic of Vietnam, 4 September 1967. Citation: For conspicuous gallantry and intrepidity at the risk of his life above and beyond the call of duty as Chaplain of the 3d Battalion, in connection with operations against enemy forces. In response to reports that the 2d Platoon of M Company was in danger of being overrun by a massed enemy assaulting force, Fr. Capodanno left the relative safety of the company command post and ran through an open area raked with fire, directly to the beleaguered platoon.
>
> Disregarding the intense enemy small-arms, automatic-weapons, and mortar fire, he moved about the battlefield administering last rites to the dying and giving medical aid to the wounded. When an exploding mortar round inflicted painful multiple wounds to his arms and legs, and severed a portion of his right hand, he steadfastly refused all medical aid. Instead, he directed the corpsmen to help their wounded comrades and, with calm vigor, continued to move about the battlefield as he provided encouragement by voice and example to the valiant marines.
>
> Upon encountering a wounded corpsman in the direct line of fire of an enemy machine gunner positioned approximately fifteen yards away, Chaplain Capodanno rushed a daring attempt to aid and assist the mortally wounded corpsman. At that instant, only inches from his goal, he was struck down by a burst of machine gun fire.
>
> By his heroic conduct on the battlefield, and his inspiring example, Lt. Capodanno upheld the finest traditions of the U.S. Naval Service. He gallantly gave his life in the cause of freedom.

Father Vincent never thought of himself as a hero, but as a Catholic priest, a missionary of the Maryknoll Order, who was temporarily a Marine Corps chaplain. He was simply living out his vocation.

■

April 22

Communion at Dachau

To all in Rome who are loved by God and called to be saints:
Grace and peace to you from God our Father and from the Lord Jesus Christ.
(Romans 1:7)

The God Delusion by Richard Dawkins, *Atheist Universe*, and other books on atheism fail to answer one interesting question: if faith is the product of self-delusion and ignorance, how could so many of the finest minds and personalities in history be so easily duped? We might begin with Einstein, Pasteur, Newton, and Galileo, to name a few. Without the reality of faith, how can one explain the life of Edith Stein, the brilliant philosopher and Jewish convert to Catholicism who was martyred at Auschwitz? Or the life of Katherine Drexel, who founded dozens of schools for black and Native Americans and a religious order to staff them?

What is to be made of Francis of Assisi, the nobleman who became a beggar and spearheaded the renewal of the Church in the thirteenth century; or Dorothy Day, founder of the Catholic Worker Movement; or Mother Teresa, Maximilian Kolbe, Martin de Porres, or John-Paul II? These aren't delusional personalities but highly intelligent and committed people who were grounded in the real world and solved real problems, often persecuted and sometimes martyred. They are the true thousand points of light that have created a humane civilization at every level. For those who require proof of God's existence, their lives offer the greatest testimony of all.

■

April 23

To Gaze Upon You

And pray in the Spirit on all occasions with all kinds of prayers and requests. With this in mind, be alert and always keep on praying for all the saints. (Ephesians 6:18)

Paul Claudel (d. 1955) possessed the diverse talents that led to his success as one of France's great twentieth-century poets, dramatists, and diplomats. The title of the following prayer, "I Come, O Mother, To Gaze Upon You," reflects Claudel's feeling that our first spiritual relationship with Our Lady is simply a glance. What sustains that glance is not an articulated prayer, but the song of the heart, which is voice given by our love for her:

I Come, O Mother, To Gaze Upon You

It is noon.
I see the church open,
and I must enter.

Mother of Jesus Christ,
I do not come to pray.
I have nothing to offer
and nothing to request.
I come solely to gaze upon you,
O Mother. To gaze upon you,
weep for joy,
and know this:
that I am your child and you are there.
I come only for a moment
while everything is at a standstill,
at noon!
Just to be with you,
O Mary,
in this place where you are.
Not to say anything
but to gaze at your countenance,

and let the heart sing
in its own language;
not to say anything
but solely to sing
because my heart is overflowing.
Amen.

■

April 24

Beyond the Cross

"Don't be alarmed," he said. "You are looking for Jesus the Nazarene, who was crucified. He has risen! He is not here. See the place where they laid him." (Mark 16:6)

Every year thousands of people climb a mountain in the Italian Alps, passing the stations of the cross to stand at an outdoor crucifix. One tourist noticed a little trail that led beyond the cross. He fought through the rough thicket and, to his surprise, came upon another shrine, one that symbolized the empty tomb. It was neglected, and brush and weeds had grown up around it. Almost everyone had gone as far as the cross, but there they stopped.

Far too many have gotten to the cross and have known pain or heartbreak, but we are called to move forward to find the real message of Easter—the empty tomb, life restored, and love triumphant.

Then rose from death's dark gloom,
Unseen by mortal eye,
Triumphant o'er the tomb,
The Lord of earth and sky!

Oh, let your hearts be strong!
For we, like him, shall rise;
To dwell with him ere long
In joy beyond the skies!

Henry Lyte (d.1847)

■

April 25

Easter Blossoms

Then go quickly and tell his disciples: "He has risen from the dead and is going ahead of you into Galilee. There you will see him." Now I have told you. (Matthew 28:7)

There is an old legend of a priest who found a branch of a thorn tree twisted around so that it resembled a crown of thorns. Thinking it was a good symbol of the crucifixion, he placed it on the altar of his parish church on Good Friday. Early on Easter morning he remembered the crown of thorns and, feeling it was not appropriate for Easter Sunday, he hurried into the church to clear it away before his parishioners arrived. But when he went into the Church, he found that the thorn branches had blossomed into white roses.

O Tree of life, in early morn,
You bear the fruit of death reborn
For all who seek the garden closed
Until the Sun of God arose.

O Tree of life, we bow in praise
Before the One to glory raised
In love to reign in majesty
Through your bright wood, O living Tree!

Samuel Crossman (d. 1683)

April 26

Resurrected but Scarred

Then he said to Thomas, "Put your finger here; see my hands. Reach out your hand and put it into my side. Stop doubting and believe." (John 20:27)

Dr. John Vannorsdall, former chaplain at Yale University, brings up a striking paradox of the Resurrection. He writes:

> If God raised Jesus from the dead, why didn't God fix him up? Why scars? Why the print of nails that you could feel with your fingers? Can it be that the gospel is saying: "You will not see Jesus Christ unless you see the wounds"? Somehow we must understand that the resurrected Christ is forever the wounded Christ. Living, but never fixed up. Not bound by death, yet scarred for eternity.
>
> The deaf have a sign for Jesus. Quickly they make this sign many times during their worship: the middle finger of each hand is placed into the palm of the other. Jesus, the one with wounded hands. And when they touch their palm, they remember. They hear the name in their own flesh.

■

April 27

"He Is Risen Indeed!"

Martha answered, "I know he will rise again in the resurrection at the last day." Jesus said to her, "I am the resurrection and the life. He who believes in me will live, even though he dies; and whoever lives and believes in me will never die." (John 11:24–26)

In 1931 Communist leader Nikolai Bukharin journeyed from Moscow to Kiev. His mission was to address a huge assembly on the subject of atheism. For several hours he took aim at Christianity, hurling argument and ridicule at this opiate of the people. At last he finished and viewed what seemed to be the smoldering ashes of people's faith.

"Are there any questions?" Bukharin demanded. A solitary man arose and asked permission to speak. He mounted the platform and stood next to the Communist official. The audience was breathlessly silent as he surveyed them first to the right, then to the left. At last he shouted the ancient Russian Orthodox greeting, "Christ is risen!" The vast assembly rose as one man and the traditional response resounded through the hall, "He is risen indeed!"

■

April 28

Opening the Dawn

When the perishable has been clothed with the imperishable, and the mortal with immortality, then the saying that is written will come true: "Death has been swallowed up in victory."

"Where, O death, is your victory?
Where, O death, is your sting?"

(1 Corinthians 15:54–55)

Victor Hugo (d. 1885), the great French novelist, poet, and statesman, was also a man of deep faith. Toward the end of his life he wrote the following:

> I feel within me that future life. I am like a forest that has been razed; the new shoots are stronger and brighter. I shall most certainly rise toward the heavens. . . . [T]he nearer my approach to the end, the plainer is the sound of immortal symphonies of worlds which invite me.
>
> For half a century I have been translating my thoughts into prose and verse: history, philosophy, drama, romance, tradition, satire, ode, and song; all of these I have tried. But I feel I haven't given utterance to the thousandth part of what lies within me. When I go to the grave I can say, as others have said, "My day's work is done." But I cannot say, "My life is done." My work will recommence next morning. The tomb is not a blind alley; it is a thoroughfare. It closes upon the twilight but opens upon the dawn.

■

April 29

Catherine of Siena

Because of the tender mercy of our God, by which the rising sun will come to us from heaven to shine on those living in darkness and in the shadow of death, to guide our feet into the path of peace. (*Luke* 1:78–79)

Saint Catherine of Siena (d. 1380) once prayed: "O Lord, by reason of your immeasurable love, extend your infinite mercy to all of us." God's unbounded mercy was the great theme of the life and work of St. Catherine. A remarkable woman for any age, not only was she a great scholar and reformer of religious life, but also she brought peace and concord to the feuding city-states of Italy in the fourteenth century. Her many writings include *The Dialogue on Divine Providence*, from which the following is taken:

> Eternal God, eternal Trinity, you have made the Blood of Christ immeasurably precious through his sharing in your divine nature. You are a mystery as deep as the sea; the more I search, the more I find, and the more I find, the more I search for you.
>
> I can never be satisfied; what I receive will ever leave me desiring more. When you fill my soul I have an even greater hunger and I grow more famished for your light. I desire above all else to see you, the true light, as you really are.

April 30

The Empty Tomb

The angel said to the women, "Do not be afraid, for I know that you are looking for Jesus, who was crucified. He is not here; he has risen, just as he said. Come and see the place where he lay. Then go quickly and tell his disciples: 'He has risen from the dead and is going ahead of you into Galilee. There you will see him.' Now I have told you." (Matthew 28:5–7)

While visiting the Holy Land, we were fortunate to have as our guide a Maronite Christian who was raised in the area. One of the highpoints for me was the Church of the Holy Sepulcher, built over the empty tomb of Christ. Our guide explained its history and also informed us that outside the city walls of Jerusalem, in a beautiful garden, there is another sepulcher that a number of Christians believe was the original tomb. With a smile he gave us his own opinion: "I'm not too bothered that there are two tombs claimed to be the burial place of Christ; the important thing is that they are both empty."

May 1

Pope John Paul II on Prayer

They were hungry and thirsty,
and their lives ebbed away.
Then they cried out to the LORD in their trouble,
and he delivered them from their distress.
Let them give thanks to the LORD for his unfailing love
and his wonderful deeds for men,
for he satisfies the thirsty
and fills the hungry with good things.
(Psalm 107:5–6, 8–9)

On April 25, 2001, in a general audience in St. Peter's Square, Pope John Paul II spoke of prayer, using the imagery of Psalm 107:

> Prayer becomes desire, thirst, and hunger, because it involves the soul and body. St. Teresa of Avila once described her need for God as a thirst from which we die if we are deprived of it.

The images of thirst and hunger help us to understand how essential and profound is the need for God; without him breath and life itself come to nothing. The psalmist goes so far as to put physical existence itself in second place, if it means he will be deprived of union with God.

In prayer and the Sacraments, the soul is clasped to God. Indeed, the psalm speaks of an embrace, an almost physical clasping: now God and man are in full communion. Even when undergoing the dark night we feel protected by the wings of God, as the ark of the covenant was covered by the wings of the cherubim. Fear vanishes; the embrace does not clasp the void but God himself.

May 2

Tuscans and Christians

When the perishable has been clothed with the imperishable, and the mortal with immortality, then the saying that is written will come true: "Death has been swallowed up in victory." (1 Corinthians 15:54)

Before Christ's coming the Tuscans made their tombs face the west, for death meant for them the close of life's day and the passing into eternal night. After Christ's coming the tombs face the east, for the Easter day had come with its radiant promise, bringing life and immortality to light. In this changed attitude we find the secret of that overwhelming joy that Christianity brought into the world, throwing a light upon the mountaintops of death.

The same vivid contrast is to be found in the Catacombs. In one chamber that dates back to the time of Julius Caesar, the tombs are marked with the signs of pagan gloom and hopelessness. The inscriptions are either cynical at the expense of the gods, or embittered in their complaints. Nearby is a chamber used for the burial of early Christian martyrs who were burned, crucified, sawn apart, or thrown to the beasts. But here there is no gloom. Lilies and garlands adorn the tombs, expressive of immortality, and the inscriptions express a serene joy. The whole chamber is decked as if for marriage rather than death, and the spirit pervading it is one of resurrection. Today let us rejoice in the hope that is set before us.

May 3

Healing Humor

He jumped to his feet and began to walk. Then he went with them into the temple courts, walking and jumping, and praising God. (Acts 3:8)

I smile whenever I read this verse—the joyous reaction of the lame man after being healed by Peter. Humor relieves stress and can lighten our loads, and I think the God who created the penguin and the kangaroo shares this trait.

One evening a physician, working at the veteran's hospital where I serve as chaplain, related an incident that happened to one of his patients when he first began to practice medicine in a small Texas town.

Apparently a middle-aged woman was sitting in her den when all of a sudden a small black snake crawled across the floor and under the couch. The woman was deathly afraid of snakes, so she immediately ran to the bathroom to get her husband, who was in the bathtub. The man of the house came running from the shower to the den with only a towel around his waist. He took an old broom handle and began poking under the couch to retrieve the snake. At that point the family dog, which had been sleeping, awoke and became excited. In the dog's frenzy over the actions of the husband, the little terrier touched his cold nose to the back of the man's heel. Startled by what had happened, he thought the snake had outmaneuvered him and bitten him on the heel. He fainted dead away.

His wife concluded that her husband, because of the excitement over trying to kill the snake, had had a heart attack, and called 911. The ambulance drivers arrived shortly and placed the man, who was now semiconscious, on a stretcher. As the attendants were carrying him out of the den, the snake emerged from beneath the couch, whereupon one of the medics became so excited that he dropped his end of the stretcher and broke the man's leg.

It took a few weeks before the couple could appreciate the humor of the incident.

If there are times when we find life too intense, the divine gift of humor can bring us back to a lightness of spirit that allows us to again enjoy the world God has given us. The saints knew this refreshment well, including Blessed Teresa of Calcutta, who was rarely seen without a smile.

May 4

The Monument in Taintrux, France

And we, who with unveiled faces all reflect the Lord's glory, are being transformed into his likeness with ever-increasing glory, which comes from the Lord, who is the Spirit. (2 *Corinthians* 3:18)

In August 1941, in the small village of Taintrux, France, a Catholic army chaplain was seriously wounded in battle. While he lay dying, he saw a man in chaplain's uniform passing by. He asked him to hear his confession and give him the Last Rites. This chaplain happened to be a Jewish rabbi. He explained this to the priest and then knelt by the bleeding padre to ask for God's mercy. He even held the crucifix to the dying priest's lips. As he did so, a shell exploded close by and the rabbi was killed instantly, his dead body falling over the body of his dying comrade.

After the war the Catholics of the French village erected a monument to the rabbi and the priest, a powerful reminder that divine Love that bonds all human beings together, and that we are also called to reflect that love in our own lives.

Prayer

Father, today we ask for the spirit of tolerance and fellowship with all people, whether they be Christian, Jewish, Hindu, and any of the myriad faith traditions that are spread across the globe. As Christ approached pagans and Samaritans with benevolence and good faith, may we imitate his charity. Amen.

May 5

The Way to Freedom

"You have heard that it was said, 'Love your neighbor and hate your enemy.' But I tell you: Love your enemies and pray for those who persecute you, that you may be sons of your Father in heaven." (Matthew 5:43–45a)

Needless to say, forgiving is one of the hardest things in life, but the grace of God can do for us what we find to be out of the question. As we pray for our enemies, even if it's initially a matter of the will rather than of the heart, we will eventually be given the grace to genuinely forgive those who have hurt us. The Holy Spirit within us does what for us is impossible.

To forgive another person from the heart is also an act of liberation. We free ourselves from the burden of being a victim. As long as we do not forgive those who have wounded us, we carry them with us or, worse, pull them as a heavy load. The great temptation is to cling in anger to our enemies and continually experience anger, resentment, and depression. Forgiveness, therefore, liberates us from a real form of slavery. It is the way to freedom for the children of God, who will settle all accounts in his own time.

May 6

Unashamed Love

For I tell you that unless your holiness surpasses that of the Pharisees and the teachers of the law, you will certainly not enter the kingdom of heaven. (*Matthew* 5:20)

Holiness fits uniquely into the character of each of us and is expressed through our personalities, our actions, and our words. The following anonymous letter speaks eloquently of how we can enhance the faith of others by simply being ourselves:

> Dear Father,
>
> We have some friends who have a little boy who was born with a severe handicap that causes him to go into very violent seizures without any warning. The father would usually be the one holding him during Mass, and I remember one particular occasion when the little guy started into a seizure. The father got up and with a strong yet gentle love carried the boy to the back of the church where he held him close to his chest and rocked him, whispered to him, and did all he could to help his son through it.
>
> One thing I noticed most of all was that there was no hint of embarrassment or frustration in the father's love for his hurting son. I felt Christ speak to my own heart and in so many words say, "That's just the way I love you through your imperfections. I'm not embarrassed to have people know that you are my son." I have come to know that it's in my times of greatest frustration that my Father draws me close and weathers the storm with me.

May 7
Victory in Christ

"At that time the kingdom of heaven will be like ten virgins who took their lamps and went out to meet the bridegroom." (Matthew 25:1)

During the time of the old Soviet Union, Boris the Russian arrived at the Pearly Gates and was welcomed by St. Peter. Showing him around, the saint said, "You can go anywhere you want with one exception. You cannot go on the pink clouds!"

"Why not?" asked Boris.

"Because," answered St. Peter, "the pink clouds are reserved for people who have done something great."

"But I have done something great," said Boris. "I made a speech at the Kremlin against the Russian officials. Then I urged the people to revolt."

"Just when did this happen?" asked St. Peter.

Boris looked at his watch. "About two minutes ago."

Perhaps the greatest expert on achieving heaven is St. Bernard of Clairvaux, theologian, mystic, and spiritual master. He writes, "Only by desertion can we be defeated. With Christ and for Christ victory is certain. We can lose the victory by flight but not by death. Happy are you if you die in battle, for after death you will be crowned. But woe to you if, by forsaking the battle, you forfeit at once both the victory and the crown."

May 8

Animals or Saints

Dear friends, do not be surprised at the painful trial you are suffering, as though something strange were happening to you. But rejoice that you participate in the sufferings of Christ, so that you may be overjoyed when his glory is revealed. (1 Peter 4:12–13)

Viktor Frankl, one of the great psychotherapists of our time, addresses the meaning of suffering in his best-selling book *Man's Search for Meaning*. Frankl was a prisoner of the Nazis during World War II and experienced firsthand the brutal climate in the concentration camps, which turned some prisoners into animals and others into saints.

He experienced firsthand the evil that drove some prisoners to despair and hatred and others to hope and love. Frankl says the deciding difference was faith. It was faith that gave their lives—and thus their suffering—ultimate meaning. This faith put them in touch with a power that helped them maintain their humanity even in the face of inconceivable inhumanity.

■

May 9

The Morning Offering

But I cry to you for help, O LORD; in the morning my prayer comes before you. (Psalm 88:13)

In Catholic spirituality, the worth of any human action depends on the intention behind it. Anything offered to God has eternal value, for it is mystically united to the life and death of Christ and becomes part of his self-offering to the Father for the salvation of humankind. Thus John Paul II wrote that the Morning Offering is "of fundamental importance in the life of each and every one of the faithful."

In the following prayer I have tried to incorporate the best elements of several offerings that have come down to us through the centuries:

Beloved Lord Jesus Christ,
I thank you for the dawning of this new day,
a day of new life and of possibilities,
and I joyfully abandon myself into your hands.
Let only your loving will be done in me
and in all your children.

I offer you my work, joys, prayers and
sufferings this day, that nothing may be
in vain, but all might be used for the
purpose of my salvation, that of my
loved ones, and of all humanity.

Guide me with your Holy Spirit,
and through the prayers of Mary, our
Mother, bring me safely to the day's
end, and the end for which I was created.
Amen.

■

May 10

Mother Teresa's Prayer to Mary

"My prayer is not for them alone. I pray also for those who will believe in me through their message." (*John* 17:20)

Mother Teresa of Calcutta, founder of the Missionaries of Charity, was awarded the Nobel Peace Prize in 1972 for her work with the poor. Her great devotion to Mary is reflected in the habit of the Missionaries of Charity, which is bordered in blue and includes the Rosary, which hangs from the cincture at the waist. Mother Teresa's lifelong devotion to Mary is expressed in this prayer she wrote for her nuns:

To Mother Mary

Blessed Mary,
you are the Mother of God,
the Mother of Jesus
and our Mother.
We ask this day that you make our hearts
humble, as your Son's was.
For it is so very easy to be proud
and harsh and selfish—so easy;
but we have been created for greater things.
How much we can learn from you!
You were so humble because
you were entirely God's.

Say to your Son: "They have no wine;
they need the wine of humility,
of kindness and compassion."
And you are sure to tell us:
"Do whatever he tells you."
Mother Mary,
the hope of mankind,
come into our lives,
into the life of the world to bring joy and peace;
to lead us back to God.
Amen.

May 11

The Totality of Love

Jesus said to them. "Can you drink the cup I am going to drink?" "We can," they answered. Jesus said to them, "You will indeed drink from my cup. . . ." (Matthew 20:22–23)

It seems inconceivable, even anomalous, that some of the saints used to pray for suffering. What would motivate such a desire? The answer sheds light on one of the great mysteries of our faith—the meaning of suffering.

There is, first of all, the redemptive value of suffering when it is united to Jesus' suffering on the cross, referred to by St. Paul: "Now I rejoice in what was suffered for you, and I fill up in my flesh what is still lacking in regard to Christ's afflictions, for the sake of his body, which is the church" (Colossians 1:24). But beyond this core meaning, there is something else. Fr. Thomas Keating speaks of this in his book *Open Mind, Open Heart*:

> From the point of view of divine love, pain can be joy. It is a way of sacrificing ourselves completely for the sake of the Beloved. It does not cease to be pain, but it has a different quality from ordinary pain. Divine love is the source of that quality. It finds in pain a way of expressing its love with a *totality* that would not be otherwise possible. Jesus crucified is God's way of expressing the immensity of his love for each of us, proof that he loves us infinitely and unconditionally.

When experiencing pain of any sort, we are given the opportunity of not only joining it to the redemptive action of Christ, but also allowing it to express the totality of our love, a prayer of praise beyond all others.

May 12

"We Return Thanks to the Good God"

Praise the LORD from the heavens;
praise him in the heights above.
Praise him, all his angels,
praise him, all his heavenly hosts.
Praise him, sun and moon,
praise him, all you shining stars.
Praise him, highest heavens
and you waters above the skies.
Let them praise the name of the LORD,
for he commanded and they were created.
(Psalm 148:1–5)

Because the goodness of God abides in the hearts of all people, we should not be surprised that this spirit was sometimes present in societies that for centuries never heard of Jesus Christ. The following is a prayer from the Native American tribe of the Iroquois, handed down orally from generation to generation:

We Return Thanks

We return thanks to our mother, the earth, which sustains us. We return thanks to the rivers and streams, which supply us with water. We return thanks to all herbs, which furnish medicines for the cure of our diseases. We return thanks to the corn, and to her sisters, the beans and squashes, which give us life. We return thanks to the bushes and trees, which provide us with fruit. We return thanks to the wind, which, moving the air, has banished diseases. We return thanks to the moon and stars, which have given us their light when the sun was gone. We return thanks to our grandfather He-no, that he has protected his grandchildren from witches and reptiles, and has given us his rain. We return thanks to the sun, that he has looked upon the earth a beneficent eye. Lastly, we return thanks to the Great God, in whom is embodied all goodness, and who directs all things for the good of his children.

As we see in this Native American prayer, spiritual truth is inherent in our nature. Even in the most violent, pagan societies, there was usually a natural love between man and wife, parents and children, elders and the young. The sense of awe and wonder at the natural word seems to be a common phenomenon among peoples everywhere and in every age. Although he has been called by many names, God speaks one truth that has been heard softly or loudly throughout history.

■

May 13

To Light Our Way

When Jesus spoke again to the people, he said, "I am the light of the world. Whoever follows me will never walk in darkness, but will have the light of life." (John 8:12)

A man was flying his single-engine airplane toward a small country airport. It was late in the day, and before he could get the plane into position to land, dusk fell and he could not see the hazy field below. He had no lights on his plane, and there was no one on duty at the airport. He began circling, but the darkness deepened, and for two hours he flew the plane around and around, knowing that he would certainly crash when his fuel was expended.

Then a miracle happened. Someone on the ground heard his engine and realized his plight. A man drove his car back and forth on the runway, to indicate where the airstrip was, and then shone the headlights from the far end of the strip to guide the pilot to a safe landing.

In a similar fashion, Christ lights the way of our lives. There is complete safety in the path he has chosen for us, but we should be aware that darkness lies to the left or the right. Therefore we must keep our eyes on the road.

■

May 14

Loaves of Bread

And he directed the people to sit down on the grass. Taking the five loaves and the two fish and looking up to heaven, he gave thanks and broke the loaves. Then he gave them to the disciples, and the disciples gave them to the people.
(Matthew 14:19)

Mother Teresa tells this story of a remarkable event:

> We deal with thousands of people and yet there has not been one occasion when we have had to say to somebody, "Very sorry, we don't have. . . .' In Calcutta, we cope with more than 20,000 people every day. (The day we don't cook, they don't eat.) I can remember one day a sister came and told me, "Mother, there is no more rice for Friday and Saturday. We will have to tell the people that we don't have it."
>
> I was a little surprised because in all my years I had never heard that before. But on Friday morning at 9:00 a truck full of bread—thousands of loaves of bread arrived! Nobody in Calcutta knew why the government closed the schools, but the schools were closed and all the bread was brought to us and for two days our people ate bread and bread and bread! I knew why God closed the schools: he closed the schools because he wanted our people to know that they are more important than the grass, the birds and the flowers of the fields; they are special to him.

May 15
The Nagasaki Christians

The boundary lines have fallen for me in pleasant places; surely I have a delightful inheritance. (Psalm 16:6)

In his book *The Soul of the Apostolate*, Jean-Baptiste Chautard writes, "Some years ago when I was in Japan I was astonished and deeply moved when I had the joy of encountering some of the Christian families which were discovered years ago near Nagasaki. I have never heard anything so amazing! Surrounded by pagans, forced to conceal their religion, deprived of priests for three centuries, these courageous Catholics inherited from their parents not only faith, but the enthusiasm that goes with deep Christian commitment."

Where are we to find the extraordinary influence that can explain the strength and duration of this beautiful heritage? First, of course, is the family, in which the teachings of the faith were passed down from one generation to the other. The second reason: their ancestors had been educated by the Church's greatest missionary to the East, St. Francis Xavier.

What this says to us is that parents and family are the first and foremost teachers and exemplars of the faith, which, unaided in any other way, can be passed down through the centuries.

May 16

Spiritual Reading

The people read it and were glad for its encouraging message. (Acts 15:31)

Saint Augustine wrote, "He who wishes often to be with God ought to pray frequently and read spiritual works." From the early church onward, this advice has been reaffirmed by spiritual writers who recognized that spiritual reading is normally necessary in leading an interior and supernatural life. Fr. Edwin Leen, a spiritual writer himself, states:

> Such reading provides the foundation on which the work of meditation is to be built up; it both affords an immediate preparation for the prayer and sustains it over time. It is to prayer what oil is to a lamp; it supplies the fuel from which the flame lives and by which it is kept bright and burning. It is for this reason that the religious orders from the beginning have insisted so much on the necessity of spiritual reading, making it a part of their rule.

May 17

The Outlaw Dismas

When they had gone, an angel of the Lord appeared to Joseph in a dream. "Get up," he said, "take the child and his mother and escape to Egypt. Stay there until I tell you, for Herod is going to search for the child to kill him." (Matthew 2:13)

There is a story from antiquity that links Christmas and Good Friday in a surprising way. It seems that during the flight of the Holy Family to Egypt, they were waylaid by a band of robbers. This was the greatest risk of traveling in the ancient world, sometimes ending in murder or enslavement. As Joseph and Mary were surrounded, one of the outlaws, named Dismas, happened to see the Christ child in Mary's arms and was somehow moved beyond words by the child's face. As he recovered his focus he spoke to the other thieves and persuaded them to let the Family pass unharmed, for "they have nothing of value." But before he left, Dismas leaned over the infant and said, "Remember me, child; do not forget this hour."

The story concludes with the revelation that the outlaw turned out to be the good thief who was crucified along with Jesus. It was to him that he said, "This day you will be with me in Paradise."

The human heart is not unchangeable. Throughout our lives God gives us grace upon grace to help guide us in the right direction. We should never give up, for as St. Paul said, "in all things God works for the good of those who love him" (Romans 8:28).

May 18

Both Sides of the Embroidery

"For I know the plans I have for you," declares the LORD, "plans to prosper you and not to harm you, plans to give you hope and a future. Then you will call upon me and come and pray to me, and I will listen to you. You will seek me and find me when you seek me with all your heart." (Jeremiah 29:11–13)

Corrie ten Boom, whose family sheltered Jews during the Holocaust and sacrificed their lives in their mission, often showed a piece of embroidery to her audiences. She would hold up the piece of cloth, first showing the beauty of the embroidered side, with all the threads forming a beautiful picture, which she described as the plan God has for our lives. Then she would flip it over to show the tangled, confused underside, illustrating how we view our lives from a human standpoint.

This is a good image to keep in mind when we are going through a painful or frustrating period in our lives. We know that God does not cause evil, but he will cause good to come out of it if we place it in his hands. This divine skill in drawing good out of evil is called the Providence of God. Everything we experience in life has meaning and purpose when given to Christ. It is transformed into the means of our salvation.

May 19

Legend of the Four Chaplains

I have given them the glory that you gave me, that they may be one as we are one. (*John* 17:22)

The wound was mortal. On February 3, 1943, the USS Dorchester took on water rapidly and began listing to starboard. The men milled around on deck on the ragged edge of panic. Many came up from the hold without life jackets; others, wearing nothing but their underwear, felt the artic blasts and knew they had only minutes to live. On the promenade deck, Second Engineer Grady Clark saw the four ship chaplains—Catholic, Jewish, Protestant—coolly handing out life jackets from the locker until there were no more left. Then he watched in awe as they gave away their own. By now the rail was awash, and Clark slipped into the frigid water. Looking back as he swam away, he saw the chaplains standing—their arms linked and braced against the slanting deck. They were praying. Other men drew close. There were no more outcries, no panic, just words of prayer in Latin, Hebrew, and English, addressed to the same God. Then the stern came high out of the water, and the Dorchester slid down into the sea.

Nearly half a century later, the legend of the Four Chaplains speaks to something deep in our hearts, the yearning for brotherhood and oneness in God.

May 20

Playing Chess with the Devil

Indeed, in our hearts we felt the sentence of death. But this happened that we might not rely on ourselves but on God, who raises the dead. He has delivered us from such a deadly peril, and he will deliver us. On him we have set our hope that he will continue to deliver us. (2 Corinthians 1:9–10)

There is an interesting painting by Moritz Retzsch (d. 1857) in which a young man is playing chess with the Devil. The Devil has just made a decisive move that checkmates the young man's king. Serious chess players who examine the painting immediately feel sympathy for the young man because they understand that the Devil's move has finished him, that he's come to a blind alley from which there's no exit.

Paul Murphy, one of the world's great chess players, once studied the painting for a long time. He saw something that no one else had seen. This excited him, and he cried out to the Devil's opponent in the picture, "Don't give up! You still have a move! You still have a move!"

In the words of St. Paul, "He has delivered us from such a deadly peril, and he will deliver us." For there is no unforgivable sin, and God's mercy is infinite.

May 21

The Blessed Sacrament

Jesus said to them, "I tell you the truth, it is not Moses who has given you the bread from heaven, but it is my Father who gives you the true bread from heaven. For the bread of God is he who comes down from heaven and gives life to the world." (John 6:32–33)

The Church has always urged the faithful to adore the living Christ present in the Tabernacle, or Blessed Sacrament, realizing that through this adoration, extraordinary graces are received.

On this subject, Fr. Albert Shamon tells the story of the Countess of Feria, whose mentor was the great Spanish mystic St. John of the Cross. The countess, who had entered the Order of Poor Clares, had such a great devotion to Eucharistic adoration that she was called the "Spouse of the Blessed Sacrament." Once, when asked what she did during all those hours before the Sacrament, she responded,

> What do I do in his Presence? What does a poor man do in the presence of a rich man? What does a sick person do in the presence of his doctor? What does a thirsty man do at the well? What does a starving person do before a table laden with food? He is rich; he is the physician; he is the fountain; he is the bread from heaven. And his love for us is so great that he died that he might dwell among us. Why? That he might enrich us, heal us, refresh and nourish us.

May 22
Burn Brightly

You are my lamp, O LORD; the LORD turns my darkness into light.
(2 Samuel 22:29)

One evening a man took a small candle from a box and began to climb a long winding stairway. "Where are we going?" asked the candle. "We're going up higher than a house to show the ships the way to the harbor." "But no ship in the harbor could ever see my light," the candle said. "It's too small."

"If your light is small," the man said, "just keep on burning brightly and leave the rest to me." When they reached the top of the long stairs, they came to a large lamp. Then he took the little candle and lit the lamp. Soon the large polished mirrors behind the lamp sent beams of light out across the miles of sea.

We are God's candle, called to keep on shining. The success of our work is in his hands. The small flame of our good example and kindness can actually change the lives of others without our knowing it. Our calling is simply to shine.

May 23
Let Me Bless the Almighty God

How many are your works, O LORD! In wisdom you made them all; the earth is full of your creatures. There is the sea, vast and spacious, teeming with creatures beyond number—living things both large and small. There the ships go to and fro, and the leviathan, which you formed to frolic there.
(Psalm 104:24–26)

The following is an ancient prayer from the Elegy for St. Columba by Dallan Forgaill, written in about AD 597. It is from the Celtic tradition and is believed to have been passed down by word of mouth until finally recorded by scribes in the thirteenth century. It speaks to us even today of the majesty and beauty of God.

Columba's Rock

Delightful it is to stand on the peak of a rock,
in the bosom of the isle, gazing on the face
of the sea.

I hear the heaving waves chanting a tune to
God in heaven, I see their glittering surf.

I see the golden beaches, their sands sparkling,
I hear the joyous shrieks of the swooping gulls.

I hear the waves breaking, crashing on rocks,
like thunder in heaven. I see the mighty whales.

I watch the ebb and flow of the ocean tide,
it holds my secret, my mournful flight from Eire.

Contrition fills my heart as I hear the sea;
it chants my sins, sins too numerous to confess.

Let me bless almighty God, whose power extends
over sea and land, whose angels watch over all.

Let me study sacred books to calm my soul;
I pray for peace, kneeling at heaven's gates.

Let me do my daily work, gathering seaweed,
catching fish, giving food to the poor.

Let me say my daily prayers, sometimes chanting,
sometimes quiet, always thanking God.

Delightful it is to live on a peaceful isle, in a
quiet cell, serving the King of Kings.

May 24
The Hanoi Hilton

Then he opened their minds so they could understand the Scriptures. (Luke 24:45)

The most notorious prisoner-of-war camp in North Vietnam was Hoa Loa, which the American prisoners called the Hanoi Hilton. On Christmas Eve of 1971, the camp commander passed out several Bibles to the prisoners as a token Christmas present of sorts, but with the stipulation that they would be collected again later that night. The Americans decided to use the time to the best advantage. They made pens out of wire and ink out of brick dust and water, while toilet tissue served as writing paper. They then copied key passages from the Scriptures to use in their prayer and worship services.

Among the passages they copied was the parable of the lost sheep, which many of them identified with, in which Christ compares his Father to a shepherd who seeks out the lost and injured. They also copied Psalm 23: "The LORD is my Shepherd; I shall not be in want. . . Even though I walk through the valley of the shadow of death, I will fear no evil, for you are with me."

For many, their survival and their sanity were based in the conviction that the Shepherd would one day lead them out of the darkness and suffering that surrounded them.

May 25

"Ah, Let's See What We Can Do Together..."

Guide me in your truth and teach me, for you are God my Savior, and my hope is in you all day long. (Psalm 25:5)

There is an interesting story about the famous Polish pianist Paderewski. A mother had a small son who was learning to play the piano. In order to encourage him she took him to a concert by Paderewski. They arrived early at the concert hall and soon the mother was in conversation with one of her friends. Meanwhile, her son wandered off.

When it was eight o'clock, the spotlights came on and the stage curtain opened. And there was her son seated at the piano innocently playing, "Twinkle, Twinkle, Little Star." Then Paderewski came on stage and approached the piano. "Ah, let's see what we can do together," he announced. To the little boy he whispered, "Don't stop. Just keep on playing." Then he leaned over him and put his hands on the keyboard next to the boy's hands. The child kept repeating and repeating the simple refrain, and beside him the pianist was weaving beautiful and intricate variations around it, with what must have been musical genius. The audience of course was delighted by the spontaneous concert, and the incident later became part of Paderewski lore.

As we play our small melody in our daily life, Christ whispers to us, "Don't stop, keep on playing. . . ." And he makes a masterpiece out of our simple music.

May 26
Feast of St. Philip Neri

But he brought his people out like a flock;
he led them like sheep through the desert.
He guided them safely, so they were unafraid;
but the sea engulfed their enemies.
Thus he brought them to the border of his holy land,
to the hill country his right hand had taken.
(Psalm 78:52–54)

Since his early youth, St. Philip Neri (d. 1595) allowed Christ to guide him with a free hand. Love of others, simplicity of life, and a playful humor accurately describes his life and spirit. A priest and friend of the young Philip also had a great love for the sick and the poor, sharing their lot in order to be close to them in the streets of Rome.

His street ministry also included the unemployed, the homeless, the shopkeepers, and especially wayward young people. He worked to help them improve themselves materially and to appreciate the spiritual as well. After a busy day on the streets, he very often spent the night in prayer. His spirit of joyful service inspired the priests who joined him in the Congregation of the Oratory, which he founded in 1564. His eye was always on Christ, who he said guided each step of his life. Known as the *amabile santo*, or lovable saint, he once wrote: "Cheerfulness strengthens the heart, and so in dealing with our neighbor we must assume as much pleasantness of manner as we can, and by this affability win him to the ways of virtue."

May 27

The Virgin of Girkalnis

Therefore confess your sins to each other and pray for each other so that you may be healed. The prayer of a righteous man is powerful and effective. (*James 5:16*)

The following prayer is an invocation to the Virgin of Girkalnis, a village in Lithuania. It was written by a young Lithuanian woman who was deported to Siberia during the persecutions by Stalin.

O Mother, We Are Lost

We are lost,
we are tired and frozen. . . .
But you have not abandoned us,
O Mother of Mercy,
in the days of sorrow and misfortune.

O Mother,
to whom shall we have recourse,
upon whom shall we call,
in this hour of great tragedy?

Look upon us, O Mother,
upon our hearts racked
with anguish and memories;
see our lips discolored
by cold and hunger.

Make us return to the land
that heaven itself has given us,
the land of crosses and churches,
the land that you have loved for centuries.

Enable us to see once more
the images that are famous for their graces,
your sanctuaries.

Grant us
to be able to sing together once again
hymns of gratitude and love
to the merciful Jesus and to you,
O Mother of Mercy,
who have promised to obtain
the pardon of all faults.
Amen.

May 28

Christ in Vietnam

And just as we have borne the likeness of the earthly man, so shall we bear the likeness of the man from heaven. (1 Corinthians 15:49)

During the Vietnam War, a company of American marines was marching down a narrow, dust-covered street in a small village. They believed it was a safe, friendly village of children and the elderly. Suddenly a young soldier dashed from the door of one of the huts just ahead of them. From the same hut came the crack of rifles, and the fleeing soldier was killed in moments.

He was a young American lieutenant who had been in command of the very marine company that walked into the village that day. Three days earlier he had been captured, taken to this village, and held as a hostage in a hut where the Vietcong were lying in ambush, ready to slaughter the approaching group of marines. The lieutenant needed to warn his men, and he waited and watched. When his marines were near enough, he broke for the door and rushed into the street, instantly drawing the fire of his captors. He died immediately. But he had warned his men of the danger, saving many of their lives.

When the fight was over, the men he saved carried his body in reverence and in silence to a field hospital in the rear, where it could be transported back to the United States and to his family. At some point all of the men must have thought of the lieutenant's action as identical to that of Christ, the willing self-sacrifice that is the essence of divine Love.

May 29

The Word of God

All Scripture is God-breathed and is useful for teaching, rebuking, correcting and training in righteousness, so that the man of God may be thoroughly equipped for every good work. (*2 Timothy* 3:16–17)

A record price of two million dollars was paid recently for a copy of the Latin Gospels, dated 997. The book, originally printed in Germany, is nine by six by two inches and consists of 168 parchment pages illustrated with colorful scenes from Scripture.

Those who place such value on works of art might gain a far richer treasure if they were to become as motivated to study the Scriptures as were the monks who adorned them so beautifully. The original artists devoted painstaking effort to the long and arduous task of copying the Gospels by hand and embellishing the margins. They were sparked by the ardent desire to glorify God and to remind their fellow men and women of the lasting beauty of his inspired word.

May 30
White Crosses

When the perishable has been clothed with the imperishable, and the mortal with immortality, then the saying that is written will come true: "Death has been swallowed up in victory." (1 Corinthians 15:54)

In his book *Straws from the Crib*, Fr. Joseph Manton speaks of visiting the graves of American soldiers killed during the Second World War:

> I think the greatest general reaction has occurred whenever we passed an American military cemetery, as we did at Anzio and Florence, and today at Belleau Wood. There is something about those endless rows of white crosses standing at eternal attention that makes people think, and starts them wondering why this tragedy of war must happen over and over again.
>
> At Anzio we got off the bus and wandered up and down amid graves, and read the names on each gleaming marble cross. To be sure we covered only a few rows, because there were more than seven thousand American boys there, but we found several names from Massachusetts. At the end we said some brief, sad prayers. One consolation: the cemetery is in excellent care, and the man who showed us around seemed to be as moved as we were when we came upon those smaller, simpler crosses pathetically marked "Unknown."

Prayer

Lord, keep us ever mindful
    of the fighting men who sleep
In Arlington and foreign lands,
    so we may ever keep
The Light of Freedom burning
    in their honor through the years,
And hear their cry for peace on earth
    resounding in our ears.
Amen.

May 31

In Memoriam

But your dead will live;
their bodies will rise.
You who dwell in the dust,
wake up and shout for joy.
Your dew is like the dew of the morning;
the earth will give birth to her dead.
(Isaiah 26:19)

The small town of Columbus, Mississippi, was in the very path of some of the bloodiest struggles of our Civil War, and hundreds of men from the area had lost their lives. Their bodies were buried in a little cemetery, along with some forty men who had fought for the North.

It was a spring day in 1869 when three young ladies of Columbus filled their arms with flowers and trudged out to this cemetery. Tenderly they laid their wreaths on the graves of friends and relatives. One day they invited the widow of one of the soldiers to come with them.

As usual they stooped to place their bouquets on the graves, but the widow noticed the graves that had no flowers. She said to her companions, "Why don't we take our bouquets apart and put a flower on every grave?" For a moment the trio faltered. Then generously they untied their bouquets and began to place blossoms on every mound. Soon they were joined by a number of other Columbus women, so that for the first time each grave in the cemetery was wearing some mark of tribute.

They decided to do this yearly, and the custom spread far and wide, eventually giving birth to Memorial Day.

June

June 1

Big Men in Shining Garments

Then no harm will befall you,
no disaster will come near your tent.
For he will command his angels concerning you
to guard you in all your ways;
they will lift you up in their hands,
so that you will not strike your foot against a stone.
(Psalm 91:10–12)

While Maryknoll priest John Meridan and four missionary brothers were in the New Hebrides Islands, several hundred hostile natives surrounded their mission headquarters one night, intent on burning the mission and killing them. The friars spent the night in prayer and at dawn they were amazed to see the attackers just turn and leave.

A year later the chief of that very tribe was converted to the faith. Fr. Meridan then asked what had kept him and his men from burning down the mission and killing them that night. The chief asked him a question in return: "Who were all those men you had with you there?" The priest told him there had been no one except the brothers and himself, but the chief insisted that they had seen hundreds of men standing guard—big men in shining garments with drawn swords.

As Psalm 91 reassures us, God intends to "guard us in all our ways" through the angels he has created. They are often portrayed as little winged cherubs, but nothing could be farther from the truth. We know they are pure spirit, without form, and that they wield divine power. They are another expression of God's love for us.

June 2

Because She Was So Loved

And we, who with unveiled faces all reflect the Lord's glory, are being transformed into his likeness with ever-increasing glory, which comes from the Lord, who is the Spirit. (2 Corinthians 3:18)

During my first parish assignment, I used to take Communion to a World War I veteran and his wife, who shared the same room in a nursing home. They always radiated a deep happiness. The wife especially, who was almost unable to move because of old age and illness and in whose kind old face the joys and sufferings of many years had etched a hundred lines, was filled with such a gratitude for life that I was always inspired in just talking with her. Involuntarily, I asked myself what could possibly be the source of this kindly person's radiance. In every other respect they were common people, and their room indicated only the most simple lifestyle. But suddenly I knew where it all came from, for I saw those two speaking to each other, and their eyes hanging upon each other. All at once it became clear to me that this woman was dearly loved.

It was not because she was a cheerful and pleasant person that she was loved by her husband all those years. It was the other way around. Because she was so loved she became the person I saw before me.

June 3
"You Speak to Me, O Lord"

Let the name of the LORD be praised,
both now and forevermore.
From the rising of the sun to the place where it sets,
the name of the LORD is to be praised.
The LORD is exalted over all the nations,
his glory above the heavens.
(Psalm 113:2–4)

Love and gratitude for the beauty of creation is something God has put in every heart that listens to his Spirit. This has been true from the most ancient peoples to the present day, as we see in these verses from a Native American:

Creation

The beauty of the trees, the softness of the air,
the fragrance of the grass, You speak to me, O Lord.

The summit of the mountain, the thunder of the sky
the rhythm of the sea,
You speak to me, O Lord.

The faintness of the stars, the freshness of the morning,
the dewdrop in the flower,
You speak to me, O Lord.

The strength of the fire,
the taste of the salmon,
the trail of the sun,
and the life that never goes away,
they speak to me, O Lord.

And my heart soars.

June 4

Letter to the Red Cross

When the congregation was dismissed, many of the Jews and devout converts to Judaism followed Paul and Barnabas, who talked with them and urged them to continue in the grace of God. (Acts 13:43)

St. Paul's conversion on the road to Damascus is repeated countless times as individuals experience God's love and find their lives forever changed. One story speaks of this in a beautiful way.

The American Red Cross was gathering supplies, medicine, clothing, food, and the like for the suffering people of Rwanda. Inside one of the boxes that showed up at the collecting depot one day was a letter. It read, "I've recently experienced a conversion to Christ and because of this I'd like to try to help. I won't ever need these again. Can you use them for something?" Inside the box were several Ku Klux Klan garments. The Red Cross workers proceeded to cut them into strips, and they were eventually used to bandage the wounds of suffering people in Africa.

It could hardly be more dramatic—from symbols of hatred to bandages of love—the fruit of one opened heart.

June 5
The Weed Patch

Teach them the decrees and laws, and show them the way to live and the duties they are to perform. (Exodus 18:20)

There is a story of the poet Samuel Coleridge, who one day listened to a visitor's vehement argument against the religious education of the young. His acquaintance had concluded with a statement of his determination not to prejudice his children toward any faith or religion, but to let them make up their own minds when they reached maturity.

Coleridge made no immediate comment, but shortly afterward asked his visitor if he would like to see his garden, and then led him to a strip of lawn that was overgrown with weeds.

"Why, this is no garden. It's nothing but a weed patch," said his guest.

"Oh," replied Coleridge, "that's because it hasn't come to its maturity yet. The weeds, you see, have taken the opportunity to grow, and I thought it would be unfair of me to prejudice the soil toward roses and strawberries."

Clearly one of the responsibilities of faith is to pass it on to the next generation. If we believe our faith to be the most precious of gifts, then we will be anxious to share it with others, especially those closest to us.

June 6

The Image of Christ

Greater love has no one than this, that he lay down his life for his friends. (John 15:13)

During the hijacking of a TWA flight on June 14, 1985, Robert Stethem, one of six navy divers on board, was beaten, tortured, and then shot to death. Subsequently the hijackers were put on trial, including Mohammed Ali Hamadi, who was convicted of air piracy and murder.

During the trial a sixteen-year-old girl named Ruth Henderson was called to the witness stand. She had been sitting with Mr. Stethem on the plane after he had been beaten and shortly before he was killed. "His injuries included a bleeding head and back," she told the court. "His wrists had been tied very tightly and he had no feeling in his hands. His knees and ribs caused terrible pain."

She continued, "We talked about unimportant things, about his diving, about Greece. By talking about normal things, he seemed to relax and forget the pain. It helped keep both our minds off the ordeal. He said it might be better for us if he died. He believed that someone would die on the plane, one of the navy men, and he said that he might be the one. He spoke with a clear mind. He didn't believe that all of us could get out alive. He felt it was all right that he die so that the rest of us could live."

In 1995, the U.S. Navy commissioned the USS Stethem, the first U.S. Navy warship named to honor the life of a serviceman, Robert Dean Stethem. Beneath its coat of arms it bore this motto: "Steadfast and Courageous."

Prayer

Lord Jesus, we thank you for providing the grace and power to handle even the most desperate situations. Help us to remember that we are never alone when darkness enters our lives. Amen.

June 7

The Doge of Venice

We have not received the spirit of the world but the Spirit who is from God, that we may understand what God has freely given us. (*1 Corinthians* 2:12)

In today's secular society, it's encouraging now and again to hear the story of someone who had everything the world could offer but left it to find something greater still.

Such a man was Peter Orseolo (d. 987), a Venetian nobleman who at the remarkable age of twenty became the commander of the Venetian navy, conducting successful campaigns against the pirates who preyed on ships in the Adriatic. In 976 he was chosen Doge (chief magistrate) of Venice, and showed himself a remarkable statesman, one of the greatest to rule the ancient province. He rebuilt the city, nearly destroyed by fire, and from his own wealth restored the cathedral of St. Mark. He promoted peace in the region, built hospitals, and created social programs to help widows, orphans, and pilgrims.

With these tasks completed, Peter suddenly disappeared from the city one night. He walked 500 miles westward to enter a Benedictine monastery located at the foot of the eastern Pyrenees, in another country. As he neared the abbey, he took off his shoes and walked the remaining steps of the journey barefoot.

As a monk, he was known for his love, humility, and devotion to prayer. Later, at the suggestion of St. Romuald, he retired into even greater solitude.

His break with the world was the sensation of the age and was the talk of Venice for decades. He died in 987, and his tomb soon became a place of pilgrimage.

Prayer

Father, help us to remember that it is never too late to change the direction of our lives, and that you may have been preparing us for this change for a long time, though we were unaware of it. Grant us a trusting spirit as we venture into new territory. Amen.

June 8

Amazing Grace

As he neared Damascus on his journey, suddenly a light from heaven flashed around him. He fell to the ground and heard a voice say to him, "Saul, Saul, why do you persecute me?"

"Who are you, Lord?" Saul asked.

"I am Jesus, whom you are persecuting," he replied. "Now get up and go into the city, and you will be told what you must do."

(Acts 9:3–6)

John Newton had fallen into such a corrupt and sordid state that his own devout Christian mother would never have recognized him. But some remarkable things began to happen in his life.

On one voyage at sea one of Newton's shipmates, for some unknown reason, had brought a copy of St. Thomas à Kempis's *The Imitation of Christ* on board. With time on his hands, John began to read it. And something began to stir within his soul. The spiritual seeds that his mother had planted long years before began to sprout.

Then the ship ran into a storm of such force that even the most seasoned sailors thought it would surely go down. In this confrontation with death, Newton realized somehow that he was not meant to die. As a result of these and other experiences, he turned his life completely around.

At age thirty-nine, he became an ordained clergyman in the Church of England. He was assigned to a parish, where the people came to love him not only because of his compassion and preaching, but because he was such a great singer! It was then that he began to write hymns. His first collection included the greatest interfaith hymn of all time, "Amazing Grace."

June 9

The Little Prince

May the Lord show mercy to the household of Onesiphorus, because he often refreshed me and was not ashamed of my chains. On the contrary, when he was in Rome, he searched hard for me until he found me. May the Lord grant that he will find mercy from the Lord on that day! (2 *Timothy* 1:16–18a)

The Little Prince is one of those rare literary gems, simple enough for children, yet profound enough to keep adults thinking all their lives. The Little Prince comes to earth from another planet, and he needs a lot of help adjusting to our ways. One of the earthly beings that befriends him is the fox. As the fox begins to teach him, a deep friendship develops. At one point in the story they are trying to agree on a time for their next meeting. They finally agree to meet at four o'clock. But the Little Prince cannot understand why the fox must know the exact time. "Oh," says the fox, "if you will come at four o'clock, then I will begin to be happy at three."

From the lyrics of a song by Charlie Daniels (Written en route to the funeral of his friend Ronnie Van Zant):

> A brief candle; both ends burning
> An endless mile; a bus wheel turning
> A friend to share the lonesome times
> A handshake and a sip of wine
> So say it loud and let it ring
> We are all a part of everything
> The future, present and the past
> Fly on proud bird
> You're free at last.

As we see in the life of Christ, who had twelve special friends to support and encourage him, friendship can be one of the great joys of life. A friend, as Daniels writes, can "share the lonesome times / A handshake and a sip of wine." And we have the promise that friendship extends into eternity.

June 10

The Character of a Man

When pride comes, then comes disgrace, but with humility comes wisdom. (Proverbs 11:2)

Some years ago in Florida, the *St. Petersburg Times* carried a story about Don Shula, the former coach of the Miami Dolphins, winners of both Super Bowl VII and VIII. He was vacationing with his family in a small town in northern Maine. One afternoon it was raining, so Shula, his wife, and his five children decided to attend a matinee movie in the town's only theater. When they arrived, the houselights were still on. There were only six other people present. When Shula and his family walked in, all six people stood up and applauded. He waved and smiled. As he sat down, he turned to his wife and said, "We're a thousand miles from Miami and they're giving me a standing ovation. They must get the Dolphins on television all the way up here."

Then a man came up to shake his hand. Shula beamed and said, "How did you recognize me?" The man replied, "Mister, I don't know who you are. All I know is that just before you and your family walked in, the theater manager told us that unless four more people showed up we wouldn't have a movie today."

Humility is one of the great measures of a man. It's revealing that this was one of Don Shula's favorite stories to tell to friends—and newspapers.

June 11

Hope of the Hopeless

Be strong and take heart, all you who hope in the L*ORD. (Psalm 31:24)*

The closing scene of Sholem Asch's great novel *The Apostle* takes place in a dungeon in Rome. Hundreds of Christians have been lowered into the dungeon through a small trapdoor, and they know that they will never come out except to die in the arena. In fact many die in the dungeon itself.

The scene as described by Asch is one of darkness and horror. Suddenly the trapdoor opens and there is a shaft of light for a brief moment and a man is lowered. And as the man is lowered into this place of indescribable darkness and death and despair, he is singing psalms of praise to God.

The word spreads like wildfire among the people in the dungeon: "It's Paul! It's Paul! Paul has come!" And Paul's joy is so contagious that before long he has all the people in the dungeon singing songs of praise and thanksgiving. A whole new spirit has taken hold of them. In this, Asch has given us an accurate description of the New Testament spirit. Even in the darkest dungeons of life God gives his people hope and, through his people, he gives joy to the world.

■

June 12

The Trinity Within

Jesus said to her, "I am the resurrection and the life. He who believes in me will live, even though he dies." (John 11:25)

Christ's resurrection was God's greatest act of love for mankind and ultimately leads the believer to intensely seek intimacy with the Trinity. This was the essence of a Franciscan friar's meditation, to help John Paul II prepare for Holy Week in 1991.

The Holy Father joined members of the Roman Curia to hear the final Lenten preaching of Capuchin Father Raniero Cantalamessa, the papal household's preacher.

"With Christ's resurrection, the Father breaks the silence and expresses his judgment on Christ's action and, of course, on those who crucified him. It is a source of hope and joy for us because the Scriptures assure us that what God did for Jesus, he will do for us. One day he will come close to our tomb and he will say the same thing to us as Jesus said to the dead young man: 'Son, it is I who speak: get up.' This is how we, too, will resurrect."

Yet, "we do not have to wait to meet the Trinity after our death. We have to find it in this world, and not outside ourselves, but in our interior."

June 13

The High Noble One

The virgin's name was Mary. (Luke 1:27b)

For centuries Our Lady's name has been venerated by the Church, culminating in 1513 with a feast day in honor of the Holy Name of Mary.

The Virgin's name was originally Miryam in Hebrew and Maryam in Aramaic, the common language spoken in Palestine during her lifetime. Modern philology, the study of languages and their development, has been able to decipher three possible meanings of her name. The first connects the name with the Egyptian *mara*, meaning *satiated*, or *corpulent*, characteristics of a lovely woman in the ancient Middle East; hence *Mary* could be translated as *beautiful*. The second connects Mary with another Egyptian word, *mari*, which means *beloved*.

The third meaning, and perhaps the most probable, is derived from Ugaritic, a language of ancient Palestine that is akin to Hebrew. The use of the name *Myrm* was relatively common and was derived from the verb *rwm*, which literally means *high* or *lofty*, hence *exalted* or *august*. In this case Mary would mean the exalted one, the high noble one, or the sublime one, appropriate indeed for the Mother of God.

June 14

"Thus I Am Not Afraid"

For this reason I kneel before the Father, from whom his whole family in heaven and on earth derives its name. (*Ephesians* 3:14–15)

The following prayer is by an anonymous writer in Ghana, West Africa. It speaks to all people of all times:

The sun has disappeared,
I have switched off the light,
and my wife and children are asleep.
The animals in the forest are full of fear,
and so are the people on their mats.
They prefer the day with your sun
to the night.
But I still know that your moon is
there,
and your eyes and also your hands.
Thus I am not afraid.
This day again
you led us wonderfully.
Everybody went to his mat
satisfied and full.
Renew us during our sleep,
that in the morning
we may come afresh to our daily jobs.
Amen.

June 15

Abandonment to God

But I trust in you, O LORD; I say, "You are my God." (Psalm 31:14)

Surrender to God means trusting him enough to carry our problems, worries, relationships, and joys. It means falling backward into his arms, the game a child might play with his parents. This trust usually comes by degrees rather than all at once, but still requires risk—another word for faith.

The following prayer was composed by Blessed Charles Eugène de Foucauld (d. 1916), who led a life of solitude, study, and prayer in the Algerian Sahara and sought to be a "universal brother" to the people of the region. His life was based on the words of this prayer:

Father, I abandon myself into your hands;
do with me what you will.
Whatever you may do, I thank you;
I am ready for all, I accept all.
Let only your will be done in me
and in all your creatures.
I wish no more than this, O Lord.
Into your hands I commend my soul;
I offer it to you with all the love of my heart,
for I love you, Lord,
and so need to give myself,
to surrender myself into your hands,
without reserve, and with boundless confidence,
for you are my Father.

June 16
Daniel O'Connell

Turn from evil and do good; seek peace and pursue it. (*Psalm 34:14*)

Daniel O'Connell (d. 1847), known as the Liberator, was Ireland's predominant political leader in the first half of the nineteenth century, the time of severe political and economic oppression. He campaigned for Catholic emancipation—the right of Catholics to sit in the British Parliament, denied for over 100 years—and the repeal of the forced union with Great Britain that had nearly turned Ireland into a slave state.

He is remembered as the founder of a nonviolent form of Irish nationalism, and with the help of the clergy, he mobilized the Catholic community into a political force. If you saw Daniel praying the Rosary in church you might look twice, since the beads dangled from a pure white glove. When he was a young man, he had accepted the challenge of a duel, killed his opponent, and thereafter, to show his remorse and repentance, never approached the altar except when his hand was gloved in immaculate white.

But O'Connell prayed the Rosary in other places besides church. One day in the corridor of the House of Commons, he was pacing up and down, head bowed and hands clasped behind his back, apparently deep in thought. Suddenly a fellow Irishman came bolting out of the chamber, saw O'Connell, and stopped dead. "Glory be to God, O'Connell, what are you doing out here? Don't you know that your country's fate is at stake in there?" And O'Connell looked at him and said quietly, "Maybe I'm doing more for Ireland out here than the pack of you in there. Listen." And he jingled his beads behind his back. "Do you hear them? Ah, they only tinkle, but in a few minutes O'Connell will go in there and thunder, and it will be the Mother of God herself who will put the words in his mouth."

June 17

Medjugorje

In the last days, God says, I will pour out my Spirit on all people. Your sons and daughters will prophesy, your young men will see visions, your old men will dream dreams. (Acts 2:17)

On June 24, 1981, two teenage girls went for a walk in the rocky hills above their village of Medjugorje in Bosnia, a former state of Yugoslavia. Suddenly, one of them saw in the distance the luminous silhouette of a young woman. "Mirjana, look! It's Our Lady!" Ivanka said. But her companion, without bothering to look, replied, "Now, why would Our Lady appear to us!?"

Returning to the village, they spoke of their experience and were later joined at the hill by four friends, who also saw the apparition. But that night at their homes no one believed their story.

The next day four members of the original group, along with two friends who had not been with them the previous day, went to the hill (Mt. Podbrdo) at the same time, about 6:30 PM. These six constituted the group of visionaries from that time on and included Ivanka Ivankovic, fifteen years old; Mirjana Dragicevic, sixteen; Vicka Ivankovic, sixteen; Ivan Dragicevic, sixteen; Marija Pavlovic, fifteen; and Jacov Colo, ten years old.

On the second day they saw the apparition close up for the first time. The woman appeared young, nineteen or twenty, and was "beautiful beyond anything in this world," they later said. She wore a silver-gray gown and a white veil, with a circle of twelve stars around her head. Her hair was dark and her eyes light blue. She looked at them with extraordinary affection. She spoke for the first time, identifying herself as the Blessed Virgin Mary. (*Continued*)

June 18
Medjugorje II

I spoke to the prophets, gave them many visions and told parables through them. (*Hosea* 12:10)

Medjugorje has seen the longest series of Marian apparitions in church history, from 1981 until the present day. The six visionaries began to experience daily appearances of the Virgin, who said she had come to bring peace and reconciliation to a world that was intent on destroying itself. This was the time of the nuclear arms race, Communist expansionism, the Iron Curtain, and the Berlin Wall. Yugoslavia itself was under the heel of a Communist dictatorship. Even in the West, the moral fabric of society continued to unravel: "Darkness reigns over the entire earth," the Virgin said. "Faith is being extinguished."

In the course of her messages, the Blessed Mother gave the specific means to achieve her plan. These are the core messages of Medjugorje: prayer, conversion, penance, peace, and fasting. They were given essentially within the first days of the apparitions, and the following years have served to underline their importance. According to the visionaries, tied in to the urgent tone of the messages are ten secrets regarding the destiny of the world that will be revealed as events unfold.

The appearances of the Mother of God in Medjugorje have been accompanied by a number of miracles, including physical healings, reports of the sun dancing or spinning in the sky, rosary links and medals that apparently change from silver to gold, and other phenomena. But the most frequently reported miracles are those of the spirit-deep conversions, the grace of inner peace, the indwelling of a new hope and a deeper love. "This is a time of grace the world has not known since ancient times," the Madonna said. (*Continued*)

June 19

Medjugorje III

To these four young men God gave knowledge and understanding of all kinds of literature and learning. And Daniel could understand visions and dreams of all kinds. (Daniel 1:17)

Just as Christ worked miracles during his earthly life to authenticate his teaching and ministry, so Our Lady of Medjugorje seems to be using miracles to validate her presence and messages, which, as always, direct us to her Son. "I do nothing on my own," she once said, "but only the will of God." This is an essential aspect of the apparitions—that they are the initiative of God and that Mary is the intermediary he has chosen to use.

The Catholic Church has withheld judgment of the Medjugorje events until the official investigating commission reports its findings, probably not before the apparitions end. Pope John Paul II watched the unfolding of events with great interest, and privately affirmed the spiritual fruits of Medjugorje. In answer to a question by a delegation of Italian bishops in 1986, the Pontiff said, "Let the people go to Medjugorje if they pray, fast, do penance, confess, and convert" (the Virgin's five core messages).

From all accounts, Medjugorje has had a profound effect on the lives of countless Catholics. It is the fountainhead of a number of apparition sites around the world, including San Nicolas, Argentina; Damascus, Syria; Escorial, Spain; Kibeho, Rwanda (Africa); Cairo, Egypt; and Oliveto Citra, Italy. It is a time of grace that the world has rarely seen.

The most comprehensive website on the apparitions is www.Medjugorje.org, which includes all of Our Lady's messages. You may also wish to consult the author's previous book Medjugorje Day by Day.

June 20

"A Peace Gathers in My Heart..."

In this important verse, St. Paul gives the ultimate meaning behind Christian sacrifice:

Now I rejoice in what was suffered for you, and I fill up in my flesh what is still lacking in regard to Christ's afflictions, for the sake of his body, which is the church. (Colossians 1:24).

Dr. Tom Dooley was a young doctor who organized hospitals, raised money, and poured out his life in the service of the afflicted peoples of Southeast Asia. He was a man whose deep relationship with God motivated him to a great sacrifice indeed, abandoning a promising medical career in the United States for a desperately difficult ministry overseas. In the end, that relationship enabled him to die in great peace at the age of thirty-four. The following is the letter he wrote to the president of Notre Dame, his alma mater:

Dear Father Hesburgh:

They've got me down. Flat on the back, with plaster, sand bags, and hot water bottles. I've contrived a way of pumping the bed up a bit so that, with a long reach, I can get to my typewriter. . . . Two things prompt this note to you. The first is that whenever my cancer acts up a bit, and it is certainly "acting up" now, I turn inward. Less do I think of my hospitals around the world, or of 94 doctors, fund-raisers, and the like. More do I think of one Divine Doctor and my personal fund of grace. It has become pretty definite that the cancer has spread to the lumbar vertebra, accounting for all the back problems over the last two months.

I have monstrous phantoms; all men do. And inside and outside the wind blows. But then the time comes, like now, when the storm around me does not matter. The winds within me do not matter. Nothing human or earthly can touch me. A peace gathers in my heart. What seems unpossessable, I can possess. What seems unfathomable, I can fathom. What is unutterable, I can utter. Because I can pray. I can communicate. How do people endure anything on earth if they cannot have God?

Dr. Tom Dooley
December 1, 1960

June 21
Beloved of God

Surely goodness and love will follow me all the days of my life, and I will dwell in the house of the LORD forever. (Psalm 23:6)

Fr. Henri Nouwen, psychologist, teacher, and spiritual writer, addresses one of the crucial aspects of the spiritual life: our self-concept. He writes:

> The greatest gift my friendship can give to you is the gift of your Belovedness. I can give that gift only insofar as I have claimed it for myself. Isn't that what friendship is all about: giving to each other the gift of our Belovedness?
>
> Yes, there is that voice, the voice that speaks from above and from within and that whispers softly or declares loudly: "You are my Beloved, on you my favor rests." It certainly is not easy to hear that voice in a world filled with voices that shout: "You are no good, you are ugly; you are worthless. . . ."
>
> These negative voices are so loud and so persistent that it is easy to believe them. That's the great trap. It is the trap of self-rejection.

June 22
The Key to Vocations

Then he said to his disciples, "The harvest is plentiful but the workers are few. Ask the Lord of the harvest, therefore, to send out workers into his harvest field." (Matthew 9:37–38)

In a locution to Matthew Kelly, our Lord was reported to say, "The greatest dignity that I can bestow on a man is to be a priest. If I call a man to be a priest, that man was chosen from the beginning of time for that task."

There are two conditions on which vocations to the priesthood and religious life hinge. The first, as we see in the Scripture passage above, is prayer. Through prayer an individual discerns the call of God, and through prayer God's people help to plant the seeds of vocations.

Second, the environment and support of a Christian family nourishes these budding vocations. I have a friend from a farming family who was working in a field one day with his father. In the course of their conversation on Ken's future, his father said, "Have you ever thought of the priesthood?" That's all it took. Those seven words contained approval and encouragement for such a career, which is what boy needed to think seriously about it. Today he is one of the most esteemed pastors in his diocese.

Is there a young man or woman in your family or among your friends that might consider a religious vocation? Have you ever mentioned it to them, or encouraged them?

June 23

Brother Joseph Dutton

Do not seek revenge or bear a grudge against one of your people, but love your neighbor as yourself. I am the LORD. *(Leviticus 19:18)*

Ira Dutton was born on a farm in Vermont, was a teenage dropout from school, and an enlistee in the Northern army when the Civil War broke out. Eventually promoted to officer's rank, he was twenty-two when the war ended.

From there he began the tragic downward spiral of alcoholism. For years he led a kind of double life, sober in the daytime, but drunk and carousing at night, until that time when the disease entered its final, terminal stage. At this juncture he experienced, through the intercession of the Blessed Virgin, a life-changing conversion and a miraculous healing of his alcoholism.

At the age of forty, he was received into the Catholic Church and changed his first name to Joseph. Two years later he read about Fr. Damien and determined to go and help him with the lepers. When he met Damien on the beach of Molokai in 1886, he told him he wanted no special treatment: "I wish only to serve my fellow man." Fr. Damien already had leprosy, and in another few months he was dead. Brother Joseph lived for another forty years on Molokai, devoting himself to the care of the lepers until his own death in 1926.

Whatever our past, it is never too late to begin a dedicated, purposeful life. We need only be open to the promptings of the Holy Spirit, who will guide us in the right direction and the right decisions.

June 24

You Are as Young as Your Faith

Be happy, young man, while you are young,
and let your heart give you joy in the days of your youth.
Follow the ways of your heart
and whatever your eyes see,
but know that for all these things
God will bring you to judgment.
(Ecclesiastes 11:9)

It's interesting that nearly all the apparitions of Our Lady have been to children, perhaps because children are open, innocent, and full of wonder. Yet we are all called to these qualities, as the following words by an anonymous author relate:

Youth is not a time of life . . . it is a state of mind. Nobody grows old by merely living a number of years; people grow old only by deserting their ideals. Years wrinkle the skin, but to give up enthusiasm wrinkles the soul. Worry, doubt, self-distrust, fear, and despair . . . these are the long, long years that bow the head and turn the growing spirit back to dust.

Whether seventy or sixteen, there is in every being's heart the love of wonder, the sweet amazement of the stars and the star-like things and thoughts, the undaunted challenge of events, the unfailing childlike appetite for what is next, and the joy of the game of life.

You are as young as your faith, as old as your doubt; as young as your self-discipline, as old as your fear; as young as your hope, as old as your despair.

June 25

All Homes, O God, Embrace

So then, just as you received Christ Jesus as Lord, continue to live in him, rooted and built up in him, strengthened in the faith as you were taught, and overflowing with thankfulness. (Colossians 2:6–7)

The following is a seventh-century prayer from Ireland, by an anonymous author, and is part of the Church's great Irish heritage:

God's Joy

I should like a great lake of finest ale
For the King of kings.
I should like a table of the choicest food
For the family of heaven. Let the ale be made from the fruits
of faith,
And the food be forgiving love.

I should welcome the poor to my feast,
For they are God's children.
I should welcome the sick to my feast,

For they are God's joy.
Let the poor sit with Jesus at the highest
  place,
And the sick dance with the angels.

God bless the poor,
God bless the sick,
And bless our human race.
God bless our food,
God bless our drink,
All homes, O God, embrace.

June 26

Beyond Words

Here am I, and the children the LORD has given me. We are signs and symbols in Israel from the LORD Almighty, who dwells on Mount Zion. (*Isaiah* 8:18)

Around 2300 BC the holy man Kakua was the first Japanese to study Zen at its birthplace in China. He did not travel at all. He just meditated continuously. Whenever people sought him out and asked him to preach, he would say a few words and then escape to another part of the forest where he would not be disturbed.

On his return to Japan from China, the emperor heard of him and commanded him to preach at court and explain all that he had learned about Zen. Kakua stood silent and helpless. Then he pulled out a flute from the folds of his robe and played a simple, peaceful melody. At the end, Kakua bowed deeply to the emperor and disappeared.

Some realities cannot be conveyed in words, but can be reflected by symbol, which touches a deeper part of us, like Kakua's melody—or a hymn or chant. Within the Church, we use fire, water, altar, cross, and other symbols to convey the reality of a God who is beyond words. The greatest of all are the sacraments, outward *signs* of inward grace, with the Eucharist as the greatest of all. But here the bread and wine not only symbolize Christ, but *are* him, in flesh and blood, soul and divinity.

■

June 27

Highway to Heaven

Not only so, but we also rejoice in our sufferings, because we know that suffering produces perseverance; perseverance, character; and character, hope. And hope does not disappoint us, because God has poured out his love into our hearts by the Holy Spirit, whom he has given us. (Romans 5:3–5)

One of the shows in the television series *Highway to Heaven* dealt with children with cancer. The late Michael Landon, who himself died of cancer, got the idea to have real-life victims play the parts.

One victim was a boy named Josh Wood. His case was especially tragic because he had already lost a leg to cancer. But what bothered little Josh even more was the fact that he had a speech defect that caused him to stammer badly. People avoided talking to him, and the more they did this the more he stammered.

Michael Landon surprised everybody by asking Josh to audition for one of the parts, saying to the boy: "The important thing about acting is to be a good actor. If you stammer, that's all right. You're just a good actor who stammers." To everyone's amazement, when the boy read for the part, his stammer disappeared completely. Josh's cancer is in remission—and his stammer has never come back.

Josh Wood is a living example of the tremendous power that loving kindness has, of the great power that is contained in a little assurance, a little affirmation. He is a living example of kindness working a miracle.

■

June 28

The Sacred and Profane

For whoever wants to save his life will lose it, but whoever loses his life for me will find it. (*Matthew* 16:25)

We are given an insight into the cultural split of our time from college president William Banowski, who interviewed Hugh Hefner a few years ago. He wrote of the encounter:

> I was made keenly aware of the universal appeal of Jesus Christ during one of my conversations with Hugh Hefner in Chicago. As we talked, Mr. Hefner surprised me by saying, "If Christ was here today and had to choose between being on the staff of one of the joy-killing, pleasure-denying churches, he would, of course, immediately join us." What most offended Jesus' contemporaries, and what modern men find even harder to accept, is his insistence that to find life we must first lose it. Hugh Hefner writes: "We reject any philosophy which holds that a man must deny himself for others." The playboy cult holds that every man ought to love himself preeminently and pursue his own pleasure constantly.
>
> Nowhere is the clash between popular playboyism and the ethical realism of Jesus any sharper than over how the good life is to be achieved. Hugh Hefner tells us to get all we can. Jesus tells us to give all we can. Because the clash is total, there is no way to gloss over it. Our culture today teaches that to get life you must grab it; Jesus taught that to win we must surrender. The conflict is absolute and irrevocable.

June 29

The Testimony

For if you forgive men when they sin against you, your heavenly Father will also forgive you. (*Matthew* 6:14)

There is a story of a quiet act of forgiveness that began a chain of events that still survives. Deep in one of Siberia's prison camps a Jewish doctor by the name of Dr. Boris Kornfeld was imprisoned. As a physician he worked in surgery and otherwise helped both the staff and the prisoners. He met a Catholic, whose name is unknown, whose quiet faith and frequent praying of the Rosary moved the doctor.

One day, while repairing a guard's artery that had been cut in a knifing, he seriously considered suturing it in such a way that he would bleed to death a little while later. Then, appalled by the hatred and violence he saw in his own heart, he found himself repeating the words of the nameless prisoner: "Forgive us our sins as we forgive those who sin against us."

Shortly after that prayer the physician began to refuse to go along with some of the standard practices of the prison camp, including one day turning in an orderly who had stolen food from a dying patient. After that he knew his life was in danger, so he began to spend as much time as possible in the relative safety of the hospital.

One afternoon he examined a patient who had just been operated on for cancer of the intestines, a man whose eyes and face reflected a depth of spiritual misery and emptiness that moved Kornfeld. So the doctor began to talk to the patient, telling him the entire story, an incredible confession of secret faith.

That night someone broke in and smashed Dr. Kornfeld's head while he was asleep; he died a few hours later.

The physician's testimony did not die. The patient who had been moved by his confession became a believer himself. And he survived the prison camp and went on to tell the world what he had learned there. The patient was Aleksandr Solzhenitsyn.

June 30

Our Lady as Mediatrix

For the L*ORD God is a sun and shield;*
the L*ORD bestows favor and honor;*
no good thing does he withhold
from those whose walk is blameless.
(Psalm 84:11)

There has been much discussion since Vatican II about the role of Mary in the church. Perhaps the best way to understand her position is to actually study what the Council said. The following is from the Council's document *Lumen Gentium* #61–62:

> . . . in suffering with Him as He died on the cross, she cooperated in the work of the Savior, in an altogether unique way, by obedience, faith, hope, and burning love, to restore supernatural life to souls. As a result she is our Mother in the order of grace. This motherhood of Mary in the economy of grace lasts without interruption, from the consent which she gave in faith at the annunciation, and which she unhesitatingly bore with under the cross, even to the perpetual consummation of all the elect. For after being assumed into heaven, she has not put aside this saving function, but by her manifold intercession, she continues to win the gifts of eternal salvation for us. By her motherly love, she takes care of the brothers of her Son who are still in pilgrimage and in dangers and difficulties, until they be led through to the happy fatherland. For this reason, the Blessed Virgin is invoked in the Church under the titles of Advocate, Auxiliatrix, Adiutrix, and Mediatrix. This however is to be so understood that it takes nothing away, or adds nothing to the dignity and efficacy of Christ the one Mediator. For no creature can ever be put on the same level with the Incarnate Word and Redeemer. . . .

In short, Mary looks after us, helps us, and prays for us as a true mother, sharing in the work of her Son at his behest. The question we might ask is, "How do I respond to her love?"

July

Miracles

When the Sabbath came, he began to teach in the synagogue, and many who heard him were amazed. "Where did this man get these things?" they asked. "What's this wisdom that has been given him, that he even does miracles!" (Mark 6:2–3)

During my first parish assignment, I met a remarkable lady by the name of Rita. When just out of college, she was diagnosed with breast cancer and almost immediately a double mastectomy was scheduled. However, she decided first to make a pilgrimage to the Shrine of Our Lady of Lourdes. While there, she was immersed in the water of Lourdes three times and spent several more days in prayer.

When she returned, her surgeon decided to take a final set of X-rays before surgery, and to his amazement there was no longer any sign of the cancer. Needless to say, Rita was overwhelmed with gratitude. To this day, she spends two weeks every summer at Lourdes helping at the Shrine's hospital.

A *Newsweek* poll found that four out of five Americans believe that God performs miracles—and over half believe they have experienced or witnessed one. Yet we're constantly confronted by a secular media that not only ignores the spiritual and religious, but denigrates it.

What this tells us is that, first, the media is indeed out of touch with the spirituality of Americans; second, the public doesn't buy into the media's secular values to the extent we feared; and third, the grace of God transcends even the most constant and powerful efforts to obviate the gospel.

July 2

Autumn Beauty

Praise the LORD from the earth, you great sea creatures and all ocean depths, lightning and hail, snow and clouds, stormy winds that do his bidding, you mountains and all hills, fruit trees and all cedars. (Psalm 148:7–9)

It was the autumn of the year, mid-October, and the trees along the Blue Ridge Parkway were ablaze in shades of red, yellow, and orange. At a scenic overlook, I stood near a woman who was showing the view to her elderly mother. "Isn't it wonderful of God to take something just before it dies and make it so beautiful?" the daughter commented as she gazed at some falling leaves. "Wouldn't it be nice if he did that with people?" the mother mused. The younger woman looked at the stooped, white-haired figure beside her. "Sometimes he does," she answered so softly that she thought no one heard.

May the Lord of heaven and earth make us more beautiful with the passing of the years. May he enable us to thank him for all the gifts we have discovered in the course of our lifetimes.

July 3
The Pianist

Everyone who believes that Jesus is the Christ is born of God, and everyone who loves the father loves his child as well. (1 John 5:1)

Members of American Atheists, the Freedom from Religion Foundation, and other such groups suffer from a blindness, it seems to me, that robs them of most of the beauty, love, and meaning of life. In this sense, I feel a genuine sympathy for them and admit to praying daily that they will one day experience the love of God.

There is a story that comes to mind. It has to do with a family of mice who lived all their lives, of all places, in a grand piano. Into their piano-world came beautiful music, filling all the dark spaces with sound and harmony. At first the mice were impressed by it. They drew comfort and wonder from the thought that there was Someone who made the music—though invisible to them—yet apparently close. They loved to think of the Great Player whom they could not see.

Then one day a daring mouse climbed up part of the piano and returned, very thoughtful. He had found out how the music was made. Wires were the secret; tightly stretched wires of graduated lengths that trembled and vibrated. They must revise all their old beliefs; none but the most conservative could any longer believe in the Unseen Player.

Later, another explorer carried the explanation further. Hammers were now the secret, numbers of hammers dancing and leaping on the wires. This was a more complicated theory, but it all went to demonstrate that they lived in a purely mechanical and mathematical world. The Unseen Player came to be thought of as a myth.

But the Pianist continued to play, and the music was as beautiful as ever.

July 4

Corrie ten Boom

If someone strikes you on the right cheek, turn to him the other also. And if someone wants to sue you and take your tunic, let him have your cloak as well. If someone forces you to go one mile, go with him two miles.
(Matthew 5:39b–41)

Corrie ten Boom, author of *The Hiding Place*, was a prisoner in the Nazi concentration camp at Ravensbruck. After the war she traveled about Europe, giving talks and urging citizens of rival nations to forgive one another.

One night a man approached her and held out his hand. When Corrie saw who it was, she was shocked, for it was one of the most hated guards of the camp. She froze. Try as she might, she couldn't reach out and take his hand. As she stood there, she began to pray, saying, "Oh, Jesus. I can't forgive this man. Help me to forgive him." At that moment, she said later, some mysterious power helped her reach out and grasp the guard's hand.

That experience taught Corrie an important truth. The same Christ who gave us the command to love our enemies gives us the grace to obey the command.

■

July 5

The Tree of Life

Consequently, you are no longer foreigners and aliens, but fellow citizens with God's people and members of God's household, built on the foundation of the apostles and prophets, with Christ Jesus himself as the chief cornerstone. In him the whole building is joined together and rises to become a holy temple in the Lord.
(Ephesians 2:19–21)

St. Paul's favorite image of the church was that of the Body of Christ. A similar image is that of the Tree of Life. The trunk and roots of the tree are Christ himself. The branches are his people. The green, flowing branches at the top are the souls in heaven. Midway down are the branches of the souls in purification. The lower branches are those still living on earth. These lower branches can be healthy and strong, those in love with Christ and seeking to do his will, or they can be withered and dying branches, those who have fallen into serious sin and poison the rest of the lower third of the tree. Hence we can find sin and corruption, as well as beauty and virtue, within the church in any given age.

But the dead and diseased limbs finally fall away and new ones sprout. The one constant is the root and trunk of the tree, which is the divine Christ himself. In this sense, the Tree of Life, the Body of Christ, is forever holy. Branches may fall away, but the essence of the tree is divine.

■

July 6
Into the Love of God

And now these three remain: faith, hope and love. But the greatest of these is love. (1 Corinthians 13:13)

The following is one of the prayers composed by Thomas à Kempis (1380–1471), the author of one of the great classics of Catholic spirituality, *The Imitation of Christ*:

O Lord, let Your love dissolve my hard heart.
Let Your love raise me above myself.
Let Your love reveal to me joy beyond imagination.
Let my soul exhaust itself by singing the praises of Your love.
Let me love You more than I love myself,
and let me love myself only for Your sake.
And let me see Your love shining in the hearts of all people,
that I may love them as I love You.

July 7

In the Ruins of Pompeii

The men of Nineveh will stand up at the judgment with this generation and condemn it; for they repented at the preaching of Jonah, and now one greater than Jonah is here. (Matthew 12:41)

In the ancient ruins of Pompeii, there was found a petrified woman who, instead of trying to flee from the city, had spent her time in gathering up her jewels. In another house was found the skeleton of a man who, for the sake of a few coins, a small plate, and a saucepan of silver, had stayed in his house until the street was half-filled with volcanic ash, then tried to escape through the window.

Because life (and death) is built around priorities, Jesus presses us to put God and spiritual things first in our lives. This boils down to the various decisions we make every day. Thus deciding for God, or conversion, is an ongoing process.

July 8

Where Is God Now?

Jesus said to his disciples: "Things that cause people to sin are bound to come, but woe to that person through whom they come." (Luke 17:1)

From the writings of Jewish author Elie Wiesel:

> The SS hanged two Jewish men and a youth in front of the whole camp. The men died quickly, but the throes of the youth lasted for half an hour. "Where is God? Where is He?" someone asked behind me. As the young man still hung in torment in the noose after a long time, I heard the man call again, "Where is God now?" And I heard a voice in myself answer: "Where is He? He is here. He is hanging there on the gallows."

It's no surprise to any of us that great evil is caused by man himself, but we all suffer the consequences in that we are one body in Christ. It was precisely this unbearable evil that forced our Lord to intervene, offering his own torture and death as the price of his people's salvation. But nonetheless our wills remain free, capable of the greatest evil or the greatest good. And the consequences are felt all through the body of Christ. We never sin alone or suffer sin's consequences alone.

July 9

Follow Me

My sheep listen to my voice; I know them, and they follow me. I give them eternal life, and they shall never perish; no one can snatch them out of my hand. (John 10:27–28)

An American traveling in the Middle East came upon several shepherds whose flocks had intermingled while drinking water from the same brook. After an exchange of greetings, one of the shepherds turned toward the sheep and called out, "Manah . . . manah . . . manah," which means "follow me" in Arabic. His sheep then came forward, separating themselves from the rest. Then one of the two remaining shepherds did the same thing, and again his sheep left the common flock to follow him. The traveler then said to the third shepherd, "I'd like to try that. Let me put on your cloak and turban and see if I can get the rest of the sheep to follow me." He simply smiled as the traveler wrapped himself in his cloak and put his turban on his head. The imposter then called out, "Manah . . . manah." But the sheep didn't respond to the stranger's voice. Not one of them moved toward him. "Will that flock ever follow someone other than you?" the traveler asked. "Oh yes," the shepherd replied. "Sometimes a sheep gets sick, and then it will follow anyone."

Note that the sheep don't need to be herded like cattle or geese. They follow the shepherd, who walks ahead of them. Are we aware of whom we follow, or what we follow? There are so many possibilities today, that sometimes we need to consciously say to ourselves, "I follow you, Lord Jesus. You are my shepherd."

July 10
Miracle at Pitcairn Island

Blessed are the peacemakers, for they will be called sons of God. (Matthew 5:9)

One of the great stories of the effects of Christianity comes to us from the story of the mutiny on the *Bounty*. The mutineers were put ashore on Pitcairn Island. There were nine mutineers, six native men, ten native women, and a fifteen-year-old girl. One of them succeeded in making crude alcohol. A terrible situation ensued. They all died except Alexander Smith, a man of great faith who also had a Bible in his possession. He tried to apply its teachings to the society of natives that lived on the island.

It was twenty years before an American sloop landed at the island. They found a completely Christian community. There was no jail because there was no crime, and there was no illiteracy. And nowhere in the world was human life respected so profoundly.

Peace begins within the heart of each individual, who then brings this peace to others, as did Alexander Smith. This is the mission of all Christians. The question is then, "How can I be a peacemaker today?"

July 11
Awe and Wonder

Sing to him, sing praise to him; tell of all his wonderful acts. (Psalm 105:2)

Awe or wonder are great for the soul. They put us in touch with the unimaginable power and creativity of God, our own Father, who wishes to share everything with us.

For instance, as Stephen Hawking writes of the dawn of creation, "If the rate of expansion one second after the Big Bang had been smaller by one part in a hundred thousand million, it would all have re-collapsed" and there would be nothing. On the other hand, if it had been greater by one part in a million, the universe would have expanded too rapidly for planets to form. That incredible equilibrium is, even today, still balanced on the same razor's edge.

In the first seconds that followed the great explosion, for every one billion antiprotons in the universe, there were one billion and *one* protons. The billion pairs annihilated each other to produce radiation, but one proton was left over. A greater or smaller number of survivors (or no surviving protons at all if they had been evenly matched) and again, there would not be a universe. Adding to the anomaly, normally there is a perfect symmetrical balance between particles (a billion protons for a billion antiprotons). Why the billion and *one*? It seems that even in the realm of deep physics, God is trying to tell us something.

July 12

Awe and Wonder II

Let them give thanks to the LORD for his unfailing love and his wonderful deeds for men. (Psalm 107:15)

Yesterday we spoke of how awe and wonder are good for the soul. It puts us in touch with the magnificent and powerful God who chooses to share all of his incredible works with his children. Now, the universe.

It began about 15 billion years ago with an explosion (the big bang), emanating from something that was tinier than a single atom. If the nuclear force caused by the explosion had been even slightly weaker, the universe would be composed solely of hydrogen. If it had been even slightly stronger, all the hydrogen would have been converted to helium.

The explosion was just strong enough so that carbon could form, but if it had been any stronger all the carbon would have been converted to oxygen. Again, had there been a variation within a *millionth of a part*, there would have been no earth and no life.

The sheer complexity that evolved out this big bang is beyond comprehension. One example: there are a hundred *trillion* synapses (points at which a nerve impulse passes from one neuron to another) in a human brain, and the number of possible ways of connecting them is greater than the *number of atoms in the universe.*

The origins of the universe, the earth, and human life can only be described as a miracle, something beyond the human imagination. And it was created out of love, for the children of God.

July 13
Wedding Ring

Moses agreed to stay with the man, who gave his daughter Zipporah to Moses in marriage. (Exodus 2:21)

A few years ago divers located a four-hundred-year-old sunken ship off the coast of northern Ireland. Among the treasures they found on the ship was a man's wedding ring. When they cleaned it up, they noticed that it had an inscription on it. Etched on the wide band was a hand holding a heart. Under the etching were these words: "I have nothing more to give you." Of all the treasures found on the sunken ship, none moved the divers more than the ring and its beautiful inscription.

Tertullian (d. 235), one of the early church fathers, has well expressed the greatness of married life and its beauty: "How can I ever express the happiness of the marriage that is joined together by the Church, strengthened by an offering, sealed by a blessing, and announced by angels and ratified by the Father? . . . How wonderful the bond between two believers with a single hope, a single desire, a single observance, a single service! They are both brethren and both fellow-servants; there is no separation between them in spirit or flesh; in fact they are truly two in one flesh and where the flesh is one, one is the spirit."

Marriage is beyond itself, so to speak. The self-giving love between husband and wife is a witness to all the circles they move in, and like that of the early Christians, will hopefully evoke the response, "See how they love one another"—in good times and in bad, in sickness and in health, for richer or poorer. Sacramental marriage "signs" to us the unconditional love of God for his people and inclines us to love in the same way.

July 14

Chaplain Al Schmitt, USN

Therefore, I urge you, brothers, in view of God's mercy, to offer your bodies as living sacrifices, holy and pleasing to God—this is your spiritual act of worship. (Romans 12:1)

The attack on Pearl Harbor produced acts of extraordinary courage and sacrifice that would be repeated again and again as the war progressed. One example is found in a letter written by Chaplain Thomas Maguire to the sister of Fr. Al Schmitt, a Catholic chaplain serving with the navy:

December, 1941.

. . . It is consoling to tell you that Al was one of the true heroes of the raid on Pearl Harbor. The circumstances of his death are well-known by eye-witnesses. I have been able to authenticate the following account:

Before his ship sank, Father Al succeeded in passing at least three men through a narrow air duct to the surface of the ship. But despite the efforts of the same men, assisted by a fourth, they were unable to pull Fr. Al upward to safety. He is quoted as having said: "Push me back. . . . There's other men who need to get out. You guys get clear of the ship." He returned to the interior of the ship and continued to help other sailors until the end came.

Prayer

Lord Jesus, we thank you for the courageous men and women who have lived their faith with such heroism. May their example inspire us to be faithful and bold in our own faith and the loving demands it makes upon us. Amen.

July 15

General Foch

For day after day they seek me out; they seem eager to know my ways, as if they were a nation that does what is right and has not forsaken the commands of its God. They ask me for just decisions and seem eager for God to come near them. (Isaiah 58:2)

In the first part of 1918, when the final German offensive seemed to be overwhelming the Allies, General Ferdinand Foch was appointed supreme commander of the Western front. The great counterattack by the Allies was to occur on July 18th. The entire war depended on the success of this counterattack. At the Allied headquarters the evening before, all preparations were completed, except the precise time for the start of the massive offensive. General Foch left headquarters, asking his staff officers to leave him undisturbed for an hour.

A few minutes later a messenger suddenly rushed into headquarters with a telegram from several Allied leaders, requesting that the time for the attack be set immediately. Thinking he was catching some sleep, his staff officers went to his billet, but he wasn't there. Then his orderly, who knew the general's habits, led them to the village church. There was Foch, kneeling motionless before the altar. He read the telegram and gave his answer. As the officers left the church, they saw him already on his knees again, with his eyes on the Blessed Sacrament.

"Always when I leave his temple," wrote General Foch later, "I feel stronger, and above all more certain. It is there that I have taken the greatest decisions of the war."

July 16
Our Lady of Mount Carmel

It will burst into bloom;
it will rejoice greatly and shout for joy.
The glory of Lebanon will be given to it,
the splendor of Carmel and Sharon;
they will see the glory of the LORD,
the splendor of our God.
(Isaiah 35:2)

Mount Carmel is twenty miles from Nazareth. Because of its luxurious vegetation, as we see in the verse above, it was a symbol of grace, blessing, and beauty in ancient Israel. But for the Israelites it was above all the mount of the renewal of the Covenant and of God's interventions through Elijah the Prophet (1 Kings 18:20–40).

Around 1150 Mount Carmel became a place of veneration of Our Lady. A group of Latin hermits built a small church there in her honor and became known as the Brothers of the Blessed Virgin of Mount Carmel. They were the forerunners of the Carmelite Order, whose spirituality is distinctively Marian and contemplative in nature. It was to a Carmelite, St. Simon Stock, that Our Lady appeared and presented the Brown Scapular, one of the most widespread of Marian devotions.

July 17

Deliver Me from Fear

And anyone who does not take his cross and follow me is not worthy of me. Whoever finds his life will lose it, and whoever loses his life for my sake will find it. (*Matthew* 10:38–39)

Dietrich Bonhoeffer (d. 1945), was one of the great opponents of Nazism as well as a man of great spirituality. The following verses were smuggled out of the concentration camp where he was executed on April 9, 1945:

Waking in a Nazi Prison

O God, early in the morning I cry to You.
Help me to pray, and to think only of You.
I cannot pray alone.

In me there is darkness,
But with You there is light.
I am lonely, but You never leave me.

I am feeble in heart, but You are always strong.
I am restless, but in You there is peace.
In me there is bitterness, but with You patience.
Your ways are beyond my understanding,
but You know the way for me.

Lord Jesus Christ,
You were poor and wretched,
You were a captive as I am,
Cut off from your friends as I am.
You know all human distress.

You abide in me, in my isolation.
You do not forget me, but seek me out.
You desire that I should know and love You.
Lord, I hear your call and follow You.

Holy Spirit,
Grant me the faith that will protect me from despair.
Pour into me such love for You and for all people,
that any hatred and bitterness will be blotted out.
Grant me the faith that will deliver me from fear.

July 18

Dancing with God

Praise him with tambourine and dancing, praise him with the strings and flute. (Psalm 150:4)

The great spiritual writers of the church teach us that the Holy Spirit normally expresses his will for us through gentle urgings of the heart, which is why periods of prayerful silence can be so important in the spiritual life. These subtle promptings have been likened to a dance with the Divine. Needless to say, if both parties in a slow dance try to lead, it becomes awkward and frustrating. The movement doesn't flow with the music and the dance becomes uncomfortable and jerky. But when one partner allows the other to take the lead, both bodies begin to flow rhythmically with the music. The one who leads gives gentle cues, perhaps with a nudge to the back or by pressing lightly in one direction or another. It's as if two become one body, moving gracefully together.

The dance requires acquiescence, willingness, and attentiveness from one partner and gentle guidance and skill from the other. It's when we allow the Spirit to take the lead that our lives become infused with the peace and purpose that God longs to give us, and that we all long to receive.

July 19

The Prince's Rose

I am a rose of Sharon,
a lily of the valleys.
Like a lily among thorns
is my darling among the maidens.
Like an apple tree among the trees of the forest
is my lover among the young men.
I delight to sit in his shade,
and his fruit is sweet to my taste.
(Song of Solomon 2:1–3)

The Little Prince had one possession he considered unique in all the universe. His rose was the most beautiful creature he could ever imagine, and he had raised her and joyfully cared for her. By day he would gently water her and tend the soil around her delicate stem, and at night he would cover her with a glass glove to protect her from any harm. Her soft laughter filled him with the most amazing feelings of fulfillment, and her singular beauty made his small planet complete.

When the prince came to visit earth, one of the first sights he happened upon was a whole garden filled with roses, all laughing and chatting and filling the air with their familiar perfume. He stared at them, overcome with the realization that his rose was only one of numberless others that flourished in the universe. He lay down on the ground and wept.

But slowly, as he listened to the joyful sounds flowing out of the garden, a deeper thought came to him, and a familiar feeling of contentment began to stir. He began to realize that his rose was unique. In all of creation there was not a rose so lovely as she, nor one who was cared for with so much love and attention. His rose was unique because she belonged to him, and because he loved her.

We belong to God in all of our uniqueness and individuality, and as we grow and flourish among all the roses in the garden, we will forever be unique in all the universe, and lovely in his eyes.

July 20

Standing Watch

He will not let your foot slip—
he who watches over you will not slumber;
indeed, he who watches over Israel
will neither slumber nor sleep.
(Psalm 121:3–4)

God's invisible protection of each of us, even when we are completely unaware of his presence, is the subject of a Native American parable.

It seems there was an Native American boy who, on his thirteenth birthday, was led out into the deep forest. It was a test of his courage before he would be accepted as an adult in the tribe. He was going to be left on his own all night to test his bravery. But every leaf that fell, every branch that swayed, every sound from the undergrowth, terrified him. He knew he couldn't run away—where could he run to in the dark forest? Of course he was unable to sleep.

He never, ever thought a night could be so long, and he felt the morning would never come. He hung on and eventually morning did come. As his eyes became accustomed to the dawning light, he looked around and was amazed to see, standing behind a tree, right near him—his father. His father had been on duty all night with a spear, on guard. And the boy's first words were, "Father, if I'd known that you were there, I could have slept all night long!"

How unaware most of us are that God stands watch over each of us, sparing us the fear and anxiety that we conjure up as if we were alone.

July 21

The Good Hunter

"I am the good shepherd. The good shepherd lays down his life for the sheep." (John 10:11)

Mother Teresa of Calcutta once said that if we are to imitate Christ, we must love until it hurts—and the greatest love of all entails the greatest sacrifice of all.

During hard times in deep winter in an Alaskan Eskimo village, a young man of great courage might go out into the bitter cold in search of food for his people. Armed only with a pointed stick and his compassion for his starving village, he would wander, anticipating the attack of a polar bear. Having no natural fear of humans, a polar bear will stalk and eat a man. In the attack the Eskimo hunter would wave his hands and spear to anger the bear and make him rise up on his hind legs to over ten feet in height; and then, with the spear braced to his foot, the hunter would aim for the heart as the weight of the bear came down upon his spear. With heart pierced, the bear might live long enough to maim or kill this noble hunter. Loving family and friends would then follow his tracks out of the village and find food for their survival and evidence of profound courage—and profound love.

Early missionaries to these Native Americans drew upon these stories and spoke of Christ as the Good Hunter who sacrificed his life for the family of mankind.

July 22
The Gift of God

For you created my inmost being; you knit me together in my mother's womb. (Psalm 139:13)

Referring to the family and the unborn, Mother Teresa of Calcutta once wrote:

> If we have today so many unhappy and broken families, and if we have in the world so much unhappiness and so much suffering, I think it is because the mother is not in the home! It is very painful to accept what is happening in Western countries: a child is destroyed by the fear of having too many children and having to feed it or to educate it. I think these parents are the poorest people in the world, who do an act like that. A child is a gift of God. I feel that the poorest country is the country that has to kill the unborn child to be able to have extra pleasures. They are afraid to have to feed one more child!

Taking up this theme, John Paul II wrote in 2002, "The church affirms the right to life to every innocent human being at the moment of its existence. . . . There is a grave danger posed by the false interpretation of human rights in that it does not take into account the reality of human nature, and which can drive democratic regimes to transform themselves into totalitarian regimes. . . . Every human being, from his conception to his natural death, has the inviolable right to life and deserves all the respect due to the human person."

July 23
Filming in Calcutta

And he has given us this command: Whoever loves God must also love his brother. (1 John 4:21)

Some years ago the BBC sent its star journalist, Malcolm Muggeridge, to India to do a documentary on Mother Teresa. The BBC wanted to televise her and her sisters picking up the dying in the slums of Calcutta and caring for them at a shelter they ran. Here the dying are washed up and cared for, as Mother Teresa puts it, "within the sight of a loving face."

The shelter is dimly lit by tiny windows high up in the walls. The television crew had not anticipated the poor lighting inside the building, and had not brought any portable lights with them. They concluded that it was useless to try to film the sisters working with the dying inside the building. But someone suggested they do it anyway. Perhaps some of the footage would be usable. To everyone's surprise the footage turned out to be absolutely spectacular. The whole interior was bathed in a mysterious warm light. Technically speaking, the camera crew said, the results were impossible to explain.

Mr. Muggeridge has his own theory about the mysterious light: "Mother Teresa's home for the dying is overflowing with love. . . This love is luminous, like the haloes artists have seen and made visible round the heads of the saints. I find it not at all surprising that the luminosity should register on photographic film."

July 24
Silent Violins

"But you will receive power when the Holy Spirit comes on you; and you will be my witnesses in Jerusalem, and in all Judea and Samaria, and to the ends of the earth." (Acts 1:8)

Luigi Tarisio was found dead one morning with hardly a comfort in his home, but with 246 exquisite violins, which he had been collecting all his life. They were crammed into an attic, the best in the bottom drawer of an old rickety bureau. In his very devotion to the violin, he had robbed the world of all the music those violins could have produced during the time he treasured them. Others had done the same before him, so that when the greatest of his collection, a Stradivarius, was first played, it had been silent for 147 years.

Yet, how many of Christ's people are like old Tarisio? In our very love for Christ and his church, we sometimes fail to spread his word outside it; in our zeal for the truth, we forget to publish it. Through our confirmation we were commissioned to bear witness to our faith, and God invariably presents us with opportunities throughout our lives. We should not be fainting violets in this regard, but allow our voices and books and music to be heard whenever we discern the time is right.

July 25

Cardinal O'Connor on Life

"See, I set before you today life and prosperity, death and destruction. . . . This day I call heaven and earth as witnesses against you that I have set before you life and death, blessings and curses. Now choose life."
(Deuteronomy 30:15, 19a)

Referring to the passage above, John Cardinal O'Connor gave the following message on Respect Life Sunday on October 7, 1990:

> Moses put it very simply. At the time he was close to death. Moses knew something about choice. At the time of his birth it was the law of the land that all male Hebrew babies be immediately put to death at birth. The midwives had a direct order from the king to throw every male Hebrew baby into the Nile River. The midwives had to

make a choice between their own possible deaths for disobeying the law, and the lives of Hebrew babies. The Scripture tells us: "But the midwives were God-fearing and so did not obey the king; instead, they let the boys live." One such male Hebrew baby that they chose to save was Moses. Moses grew up to lead the Israelites out of slavery under the Egyptians toward the Promised Land.

No wonder Moses told his people: choose life.

July 26

Daring and Adventurous Spirits

I write to you, dear children,
because you have known the Father.
I write to you, fathers,
because you have known him who is from the beginning.
I write to you, young men,
because you are strong,
and the word of God lives in you,
and you have overcome the evil one.
(1 John 2:13b–14)

Two fifteen-year-old boys alarmed onlookers in Norfolk, Virginia, who watched them drift down the forty-foot-deep Elizabeth River on a makeshift raft. It was a three-by-six-foot mortar box used by brick masons. The Coast Guard finally rescued them as they were floating toward the open ocean in their unseaworthy craft.

Young people are blessed with a daring and adventurous spirit. But it is important that their enthusiasm and resourcefulness be wisely directed. At the same time, great care must be taken not to suppress their spirit and potential.

The Lord himself encouraged his apostles to "launch out into the deep" as fishers of men. But at the same time he made sure they were rooted in divine truth and love. Through prayer and example, we can help young people to be daring in faith.

July 27

The Sacrament of Matrimony

"Haven't you read," he replied, "that at the beginning the Creator 'made them male and female,' and said, 'For this reason a man will leave his father and mother and be united to his wife, and the two will become one flesh'? So they are no longer two, but one. Therefore what God has joined together, let man not separate." (Matthew 19:4–6)

Success in marriage," wrote B.R. Brickner, "is more than finding the right person: it is a matter of being the right person."

The Sacrament of Matrimony received special treatment from the fathers of Vatican II; some of the thoughts expressed were quite beautiful, including the following:

> Authentic married love is caught up into divine love, and is governed and enriched by Christ's redeeming love. . . . Such love, merging the human with the divine, leads the spouses to a free and mutual gift of themselves, a gift proving itself by gentle affection and by deed. Such love pervades the whole of their lives. Indeed, by its generous activity, it grows better and grows greater. . . .
>
> Sealed by mutual faithfulness and hallowed above all by Christ's Sacrament, this love remains steadfastly true in body and in mind, in bright days or dark. . . .

July 28

You Have Not Forgotten Anyone

He has brought down rulers from their thrones but has lifted up the humble. (Luke 1:52)

Søren Kierkegaard (d.1855) was a prolific nineteenth-century Danish philospher and theologian. The following is one of his most profound prayers:

God in Heaven! Great is your presence in all the world. You bear the weight of the stars and govern the forces of the world through immense spaces. Numberless as the sands are those who have life and being through you. And yet, you hear the cry of all the creatures, and the cry of the man and woman whom you have especially formed.

You hear the cry of all men and women without confusing our mixed voices and without distinguishing one from another as though you played favorites. You hear not only the voice of one who is responsible for others and prays to you in their name. You hear not only the voice of one who prays for loved ones . . . . You hear also the most anguished man and woman, the most abandoned, the most solitary one alone in the desert, alone in the multitude.

Even if the forgotten one is separated from all others, and in the crowd has become unknown—having ceased to be a person except on a list—you know that person. You have not forgotten anyone. You remember our names. You know us where we are, retired, hidden in the desert, unseen in the crowd, alone in the multitude. And if in the thick shadows of dread, in the prey of terrible thoughts, we are abandoned, you hear that anguish, too.

July 29

The Inspiration of Genius

"Send me, therefore, a man skilled to work in gold and silver, bronze and iron, and in purple, crimson and blue yarn, and experienced in the art of engraving, to work in Judah and Jerusalem with my skilled craftsmen, whom my father David provided." (2 Chronicles 2:7)

In the Sistine Chapel at the Vatican is Michelangelo's great wall-to-wall painting of the Last Judgment. It's breathtaking to behold, and if you look closely enough, you will discover a detail that is often missed. As a sinner is plunging into the flaming abyss of hell, the Madonna bends over him from the heights of heaven, flinging out her rosary to him like a lifeline, and the sinner's hands are desperately clutching the strong, powerful beads.

It's a colorful, swirling scene, the projection of a powerful imagination. Michelangelo himself—who perhaps could make canvas glow and marble breathe like no other artist in history—prayed the Rosary each evening after his grueling work. Perhaps this is why he considered his art a ministry. He lived in austere quarters and slept in a room with the rest of his workmen and assistants. He shunned the trappings of fortune and fame and rarely created a work of art that was not religious in nature. And over and over again, he created resplendent images of the Blessed Virgin, the great love of his life.

Throughout the ages men and women have seen the Virgin Mary as the great inspiration of their lives and have devoted themselves to her in a special way, as we see in the life of John Paul II. Her response is to forever love, protect, and intercede for her faithful people.

■

July 30

Tabernacle Door

When he was at the table with them, he took bread, gave thanks, broke it and began to give it to them. Then their eyes were opened and they recognized him, and he disappeared from their sight. (Luke 24:30–31)

An artist designed a beautiful tabernacle door for the cathedral in Bonn, Germany, dividing it into four panels. Each panel was decorated with a set of symbols that was related to the Eucharist. The first was decorated with six water jars; the second with loaves and two fish; the third with thirteen people seated around a table; and the fourth, with three people seated at a table.

The three people seated at a table symbolized the Emmaus supper on Easter Sunday night, when the risen Jesus broke bread and revealed himself to two disciples. The artist interpreted the Emmaus supper as being the first celebration of the Eucharist, which Christ instituted at the Last Supper. And so the tabernacle door served as a summary of the Eucharist, tracing it from Cana, where it was previewed, to Capernaum, where it was promised, to Jerusalem, where it was instituted, and to Emmaus, where it was first celebrated.

With roots that extend far back into the Old Testament, the Eucharist has been pre-figured time and again, all leading up to the moment Christ gave his body and blood as food for all the faithful for all ages. Are we aware of the tremendous gift we have been given?

■

July 31
Feast of Ignatius of Loyola

Then I will teach transgressors your ways, and sinners will turn back to you. (Psalm 51:13)

Ignatius Loyola, a worldly and ambitious Spanish nobleman, was directing the defense of Pamplona against the French in 1521. A cannon ball passed between his legs, breaking his leg right below the knee. The garrison lost heart and surrendered, but the French treated the brave officer well and carried him to his own castle of Loyola, where his leg was broken again, to be re-set clumsily, necessitating further painful surgery and a very tedious convalescence.

Ignatius asked for some of his favorite romances to read; they brought him the only books in the castle, a life of Christ and a volume of the lives of the saints. For lack of anything better, he read these, and they took him into a new world of heroes serving a King far more worthy than any king on earth. In that great company, he felt his ambition take a radical new direction. Like St. Augustine, he said: "If these men and women could do such remarkable things, I believe I can, too." Sometimes his mind reverted to the old daydreams of worldly love and riches, but now there seemed nothing in them compared with his new goals. By the time his leg had mended, his soul was healed as well, and he was fully determined to pursue the new goal of his life.

■

August

August 1

"The Voice in My Silence"

Then Jesus answered, "Woman, you have great faith! Your request is granted." (Matthew 15:28)

Helen Keller (d. 1968) was an author, lecturer, and activist as well as the first deaf and blind person to graduate from college. The following is an excerpt from one of her writings called "I Believe":

> I believe that we can live on earth according to the teachings of Jesus, and that the greatest happiness will come to the world when man obeys His commandment "Love one another."
>
> I believe that we can live on earth according to the fulfillment of God's will, and that when the will of God is done on earth as it is done in heaven, every man will love his fellowmen, and act toward them as he desires they should act toward him. I believe that the welfare of each is bound up in the welfare of all.
>
> I believe that life is given us so we may grow in love, and I believe that God is in me as the sun is in the color and fragrance of a flower—the Light in my darkness, the Voice in my silence.

I believe that only in broken gleams has the Sun of Truth yet shone upon men. I believe that love will finally establish the kingdom of God on earth, and that the cornerstones of that kingdom will be liberty, truth, brotherhood, and service. . . .

August 2

Our Lady of Good Counsel

I will instruct you and teach you in the way you should go; I will counsel you and watch over you. (Psalm 32:8)

The title "Our Lady of Good Counsel" is reminiscent of Mary, Seat of Wisdom, for good counsel or advice is always generated from a store of knowledge or wisdom. We can imagine the countless times that Christ, as a young boy and adolescent, relied upon the counsel of his Mother, even up to the wedding feast at Cana. As spiritual Mother of all the faithful, she continues to guide and counsel all who seek her assistance.

Our Lady of Good Counsel also refers to a miraculous image of Our Lady that mysteriously appeared in a church at Genazzano, Italy, near Rome, in 1467. As the people prayed before the picture, extraordinary graces and miracles began to be reported, even to the present day. Pope Urban VII and Pius IX went on pilgrimage to this shrine, and Benedict XIV approved the Union of Our Lady of Good Council and became its first member. Another pope, Leo XIII, added the title to the Litany of Loreto, and in 1986 John Paul II approved a new Marian Mass entitled, "The Blessed Virgin Mary, Mother of Good Counsel."

Prayer

Our Lady of Good Counsel, help me to exercise good judgment in every situation and to become wiser with the years. May you always help me in solving the problems I face each day. In your Son's name, I pray. Amen.

August 3

Achieving the Impossible

He mocks proud mockers but gives grace to the humble. (Proverbs 3:34)

A wealthy businessman hosted a spectacular party in which he had filled his swimming pool with sharks, barracuda, and other assorted dangerous fish. He announced to his guests that he would like to challenge any of them to try swimming across the pool, and he would offer a first prize of either a new home in the mountains, or a trip around the world for two, or a share of his business. No sooner had he made the announcement than there was a splash and a man swam rapidly across the infested waters and bounded out on the other side. The millionaire said to the dripping man, "That was a stunning performance. What prize do you want?" The man answered tersely, "Right now I really don't care about the prize. I just want to get the name of the turkey that pushed me in."

It's true, given the right circumstances, we can do what we think is impossible. But when we think back, we realize it was the amazing grace of God that did for us what we could not.

August 4

To Serve Love

If anyone acknowledges that Jesus is the Son of God, God lives in him and he in God. And so we know and rely on the love God has for us. (1 John 4:15–16)

Ultimately love is the motivation of our faith, our hope, and our service to others. St. John even capsulated the divine nature in saying simply: "God is love."

It was the startling experience of this love, during a dark period of my life, that drew me to the priesthood. My whole understanding of God, of faith, of life itself, was changed profoundly. I saw love as the center of everything, and it was then that I decided on the goal of my life: to serve love. This was my conversion, the opening to a new life.

Having been reared a Catholic, I found that the priesthood seemed a natural way to live out this goal. Then came seminary, books, theology, and training. But the first thing was the experience of God's love. In the words of Angelus Silesius (d. 1677), the German mystic and poet:

> The longest way to God, the indirect,
> lies through the intellect.
> The shortest way lies through the heart.
> Here is my journey's end, and here its start.

August 5

Care for the Earth

God blessed them and said to them, "Be fruitful and increase in number; fill the earth and subdue it. Rule over the fish of the sea and the birds of the air and over every living creature that moves on the ground." (Genesis 1:28)

It was the tradition of the Navajos to remove every trace of their temporary encampments. They buried the embers of the cooking fires and the remnants of the food, spread out any stones they had piled together, and filled up the holes they had scooped in the sand. Just as it was the white man's way to assert himself in any landscape, to change it, and make it over at least a bit, it was the Native American's way to pass through a country without disturbing anything; to pass and leave no trace, like fish through the water, or birds through the air.

In an address on November 11, 2000, Pope John Paul II echoed this respectful attitude:

> Without doubt, the most important value at stake when we look at the earth and at those who work is the principle that brings the earth

back to her Creator: the earth belongs to God! It must therefore be treated according to his law.

If, with regard to natural resources, especially under the pressure of industrialization, an irresponsible culture of "dominion" has been reinforced with devastating ecological consequences, this certainly does not correspond to God's plan. "Fill the earth and subdue it; and have dominion over the fish of the sea and over the birds of the air" (Genesis 1:28). These famous words of Genesis entrust the earth to man's use, not abuse. They do not make man the absolute arbiter of the earth's governance, but the Creator's "co-worker": a stupendous mission, but one which is also marked by precise boundaries that can never be transgressed with impunity.

August 6

God in Music

Hear this, you kings! Listen, you rulers!
I will sing to the LORD, I will sing;
I will make music to the LORD, the God of Israel.
(Judges 5:3)

"Come, Love! Sing On! Let me hear you sing this song—sing for joy and laugh, for I the Creator am truly subject to all creatures," sings the mystic Mechtild of Magdeburg. Truly life without joy and song and playfulness is incomplete. The beauty of music uplifts our spirits and shows us the face of our Creator.

For many, music is also a means of meditation and contact with God. When we experience the creativity of a musical piece, as it speaks to us, we take a step beyond the practical world, into the profound level of creation.

Some might say, "How can you celebrate when there is so much suffering, so much to grieve about?" Yet we have all grieved; we continue to grieve alongside our joy. But we need not pour all our energies into the painful and sad. Life is also wonderful. Music and dance and the joy of love enrich our lives and strengthen us to go on.

August 7

Safe Harbor

When the perishable has been clothed with the imperishable, and the mortal with immortality, then the saying that is written will come true: "Death has been swallowed up in victory."

"Where, O death, is your victory?
Where, O death, is your sting?"

(1 Corinthians 15:54–55)

Colonel David Marcus was killed in battle during the Israeli War in June 1948. Later a note was found in his wallet that spoke of his thoughts on death. He wrote:

> I am standing upon the seashore. A ship at my side spreads her white sails to the morning breeze and starts for the ocean. She is an object of beauty and strength. And I stand and watch her, until at length she is only a ribbon of white cloud just where the sea and sky come to mingle with each other.
>
> Then someone at my side says, "There! She's gone!" But gone where? Gone from my sight—that is all. She is just as large in mast and hull and spar as she was when she left my side, and just as able to bear her load of living freight to the place of destination. Her diminished size is in me, not in her. And just at the moment when someone at my side says, "There! She's gone!" there are other voices ready to take up the glad shout, "There! She comes!" And that is dying.

August 8

Between Myself and the Powers of Darkness

My God is my rock, in whom I take refuge,
my shield and the horn of my salvation.
He is my stronghold, my refuge and my savior—
from violent men you save me.
(2 *Samuel* 22:3)

St. Patrick (390–461), the great missionary to Ireland, wrote several prayers that have come down to us. The following is one of the most profound:

God's Protection

At Tara today in this fateful hour
I place all heaven within its power
And the sun with its brightness
And the snow with its whiteness
And the fire with all the strength it hath,
And lightning with its rapid wrath,
And the winds with their swiftness along their path,
And the sea with its deepness,
And the earth with its starkness:
All these I place,
By God's almighty grace,
Between myself and the powers of darkness.

May we always be mindful that the major decisions we make in our lives are ultimately tied to life or death, blessing or curse, and by God's grace, seek always to place the universe "between myself and the powers of darkness."

August 9

Feast of St. Therese Benedicta of the Cross

You know, brothers, that our visit to you was not a failure. We had previously suffered and been insulted in Philippi, as you know, but with the help of our God we dared to tell you his gospel in spite of strong opposition.
(1 Thessalonians 2:1–2)

Edith Stein was born of a Jewish family in 1891 and raised and educated in Germany. A brilliant student, she received her doctorate in philosophy cum laude from the University of Freiburg, where she later became assistant to Professor Edmund Husserl, the eminent philosopher. In 1922 she entered the Catholic Church and thereafter devoted her time to teaching, lecturing, and writing. In 1932, she was offered a professorship at the University of Muenster.

A year later, as the Nazis came to power, her varied activities were curtailed. She was, however, permitted to enter the cloistered Carmelite convent in Cologne, taking the name Therese Benedicta of the Cross. She prayed that God would accept her life and her death in expiation for the sins of unbelievers, the salvation of Germany, and for peace in the world. Her Calvary was Auschwitz. She died there in the gas chambers on August 9, 1942. On May 1, 1987, she was beatified by Pope John Paul II at Cologne, Germany, where he said, "The Church honors 'a daughter of Israel' who, as a Catholic during Nazi persecution, remained faithful to the crucified Lord Jesus Christ and, as a Jew, to her people in loving faithfulness."

August 10

"Thank You, My God"

You turned my wailing into dancing; you removed my sackcloth and clothed me with joy, that my heart may sing to you and not be silent. O LORD my God, I will give you thanks forever. (Psalm 30:11–12)

During World War II, many Hollywood stars donated their time and talent to entertain American servicemen here and abroad. Elsa Lancaster, the British-born actress, frequently gave informal parties for soldiers at her home in Los Angeles. As each of her guests was about to leave, she asked him to write his name and address in her Soldier's Book, as she called it. She then said to her guests, "I promise each of you that I will pray constantly that God will protect you and bring you safely home."

As the months rolled into years, a number of these soldiers, sailors, and marines returned. Many of them made a point to stop and thank Elsa before they took trains for home. After they left, the actress would take out her Soldier's Book, find the name of the one who had returned safely, and write next to the name, "Thank you, my God."

Spiritual writers consistently tell us that gratitude to God is the key to a happy life, for our glass will always be half full or half empty. It is so important in recovery from addiction that recovery is deemed impossible without gratitude. Today we might ask ourselves the last time we paused to add up our blessings.

August 11

Feast of St. Clare

I tell you the truth, anyone who has faith in me will do what I have been doing. He will do even greater things than these, because I am going to the Father. (*John* 14:12)

Next to St. Francis of Assisi, St. Clare (1193–1253) was most responsible for the growth and spread of the Franciscan ideal that changed the face of the church in the thirteenth century.

Born in Assisi of wealthy parents, Clare heard a sermon by St. Francis when she was a teenager. It affected her to such a degree that she left home to join him and his followers, and to live the life of Gospel poverty. Francis gave her the veil when she was nineteen years old, and she was shortly joined by her two sisters and, later, her mother. While she was living at the convent at the church of San Damiano, Francis charged her under obedience to accept the office of abbess, which she then held for nearly forty years until her death.

Clare's understanding of poverty, embodied in the Rule of Poor Clare Nuns, was designed to bring the individual into intimate union with Christ and away from all earthly attachments. She founded monasteries for her nuns in Italy, France, Germany, and Hungary, and was credited with many miracles throughout her life, notably the saving of her convent and the town of Assisi from the Saracen invaders. Her story, and that of St. Francis, is told in a beautiful film by Franco Zeffirelli called *Brother Son, Sister Moon.*

August 12

"She Is the World to Me..."

Husbands, love your wives, just as Christ loved the church and gave himself up for her. (*Ephesians* 5:25)

In May 1946, a newspaper related the story of a woman who suffered from the dreaded disease of leprosy. She was to be sent to the leper asylum at Carville, Louisiana. But her husband, a major during World War II, insisted on going with her, saying simply, "I need to be with my wife, who is the world to me." Major Hornbostel had been a highly decorated officer in the army of the Pacific. There, he and his wife had been captured by the Japanese and imprisoned in a jail where disease was rampant and starvation killed half the prisoners. She had the opportunity to be released, but refused, preferring to stay in prison with her husband. It was there she contracted leprosy. Accompanying the news article was a picture of the major embracing his wife.

We can hardly imagine a more striking example of self-giving love, reminding us of the sacrificial love God has for each individual and the call he gives to imitate him, for it is the gateway to fulfillment and peace in our lives.

August 13

The Gift of Perseverance

Be faithful, even to the point of death, and I will give you the crown of life. (Revelation 2:10b)

A missionary named Noreen Towers had worked for years among the poor in Nigeria. In spite of all her efforts, she saw absolutely no progress. She says: "I became despondent. I finally reached the breaking point one night. . . . I was beaten. When I went to bed, I didn't know how I could continue."

The next morning, shortly after she awoke, something strange happened to her. It was as though Christ himself said to her, "Can you not trust my plan for you?" She writes, "Then I realized that I did not have to see the plan; I only had to trust him. I rose from my bed a different person. My encounter with the living Christ changed me from a broken, defeated person into a person with unshakable hope and faith."

Today, this woman's work among the poor is bearing remarkable fruit.

Like all the virtues, perseverance is a gift of grace, yet God never fails to bestow it on those who ask. This is the primary challenge—to rely not on our own strength and endurance, but on that of Jesus Christ.

August 14

Feast of Maximilian Kolbe

"For whoever wants to save his life will lose it, but whoever loses his life for me and for the gospel will save it." (Mark 8:35)

In one of the Nazi concentration camps of the Second World War, a Polish priest named Fr. Maximilian Kolbe was interned for publishing writings unfavorable to the Third Reich. On one occasion, several prisoners escaped from the compound, and the camp commandant, to punish the prisoners, ordered ten of them to die through starvation.

Among the condemned prisoners was a young man who was known to have a wife and children. When the prisoner's numbers were called out, Fr. Kolbe stepped forward and insisted on taking the young man's place.

Incarcerated in the death cell, he helped his companions prepare for death. Through the long days, the guards did not hear the usual sounds of pleading and anguish, but the subdued sounds of hymns and prayers. Fr. Kolbe was the last to die, and because he had taken so long, they injected him with carbolic acid.

After his death, a picture of Christ on the cross was found scratched with his nails on the wall of his death cell. His life is a reminder not only of Christian heroism, but also of Jesus' promise to sustain us no matter what happens in our lives.

August 15

Feast of the Assumption of Mary

Devote yourselves to prayer, being watchful and thankful. (Colossians 4:2)

James Ryman (d.1492), poet and Franciscan friar of the Canterbury house, is renowned for the beauty of the many carol-poems that he composed. The following is one of his finest and very fitting for today's feast:

A Carol on the Assumption

Come, my dear spouse and Lady free;
 come to thy Son in heaven's bliss.
For why? Next to me your place shall be;
 come now, to be crowned.

Come, my mild dove, to thy abode,
 with joy and bliss replete which is.
For why? It is your heritage;
 come now, to be crowned.

Your blessed body was my bower;
 wherefore my bliss you shall not miss,
and all saints shall honor you.
 Come now, to be crowned.

With your fragrance so pure and sweet
 You have led me; wherefore, then,
of heaven's bliss you shall be queen.
 Come now, to be crowned.

August 16

Trust

Whoever can be trusted with very little can also be trusted with much, and whoever is dishonest with very little will also be dishonest with much. (*Luke 16:10*)

A young lady was soaking up the sun's rays on a Florida beach when a little boy in his swimming trunks, carrying a towel, came up and asked her, "Do you believe in God?" She was surprised by the question but replied, "Well, yes, I do." Then he asked her: "Do you go to church every Sunday?" Again, her answer was "Yes!" Then he asked: "Do you pray every day?" Again she said, "Yes!" But by now her curiosity was very much aroused. At last the boy sighed and said, with obvious relief, "Will you hold my quarter while I go in swimming?"

Trust grows, of course, as a relationship deepens, and this is especially true of our relationship with Christ. "Ambush theology" is the false idea that if we really put all our trust in God, he will somehow ambush us and send us off to be missionaries in Africa or some such scenario. Nothing could be further from the truth. The God of love never betrays our trust, but rather gives us gift upon gift to assure our happiness in this life and the next. "Do not let your hearts be troubled. Trust in God; trust also in me" (John 14:1).

August 17

The Wisdom of Parenting

Jesus said, "Let the little children come to me, and do not hinder them, for the kingdom of heaven belongs to such as these." (*Matthew 19:14*)

Dr. David Elkind is a child psychologist and the author of such groundbreaking books as *The Hurried Child* and *Miseducation*. He has written of the importance of parents being present to see their children perform, whether it be an athletic competition, a puppet show, a spelling bee, or a musical recital. He illustrates his point with a story: "I remember visiting my middle son's nursery school class, at the request of his teacher, so that I could observe a 'problem child' in the class. It so happened that I was sitting and observing a group of boys, including my son, who sat in a circle nearby." He continues, "Their conversation went like this: Child A: 'My daddy is a doctor and he makes a lot of money and we have a swimming pool.' Child B: 'My daddy is a lawyer and he flies to Washington and talks to the president.' Child C: 'My daddy owns a company and we have our own airplane.' Then my son (with aplomb, of course): 'My daddy is here!' with a proud look in my direction."

Dr. Elkind concludes that children regard the presence of their parents as a visible symbol of caring "that is far more significant than any material support could ever be."

August 18

Oneness

Naked I came from my mother's womb,
and naked I will depart.
The LORD gave and the LORD has taken away;
may the name of the LORD be praised.
(Job 1:21)

Surrender to God is one of most difficult tasks of the spiritual life, for we are ingrained with a self-centeredness and egotism (original sin) that impels us to seek control not only over our own lives, but also over everyone and everything around us. Left unchecked, this sometimes unconscious attitude leads inevitably to frustration and despair.

However, turning from self to God allows us to enter a new life of God-centeredness, oneness, and joy that we were created for. Instead of moving inward, we move outward, and become free. It all begins with a conscious choice.

August 19

God's Shield to Protect Me

Rather, clothe yourselves with the Lord Jesus Christ, and do not think about how to gratify the desires of the sinful nature. (Romans 13:14)

St. Patrick, the saint who converted the people of Ireland to Christianity, composed poetry that contained not one wasted word, but rather a profundity that has weathered the ages. The following is one of his finest efforts:

God's Strength to Comfort Me

I gird myself today with the might of heaven.
The rays of the sun,
the beams of the moon,
the glory of fire,
the speed of wind,
the depth of sea,
the stability of earth,
the hardness of rock.

I gird myself today with the power of God:
God's strength to comfort me,
God's might to uphold me,
God's wisdom to guide me,
God's eye to look before me,
God's ear to hear me,
God's word to speak for me,
God's hand to lead me,
God's way to lie before me,
God's shield to protect me,
God's angels to save me
from the snares of the devil,
from temptations to sin,
from all who wish me ill,
both far and near,
alone and with others.

August 20
Our Lady of the Rosary

So your servant has found courage to offer you this prayer. (*2 Samuel* 7:27)

The prayer most associated with the Blessed Virgin is the Rosary, a form of meditation that has been strongly recommended for centuries not only by saints and popes alike, but also by Our Lady herself in her many apparitions, including those of Lourdes and Fatima. In a public audience on the feast of the Holy Name of Mary (September 12, 1961), Pope John XXIII remarked:

> "Mary" is a magical name that moves heaven and earth, as well we know. We have proof of this every time she has come back among us, with her visible appearances in places that have since become centers of devotion to her. Meanwhile we pray to her continually and call upon her name. We have the holy Rosary, a summary of the whole story of the redemption in its fifteen mysteries. That is why we ask you all to recite the Rosary, not only with the mechanical movements of your lips, or of your fingers on the beads, but really pondering each individual mystery.

■

August 21
False Prophets

Jesus answered: "Watch out that no one deceives you. For many will come in my name, claiming, 'I am the Christ,' and will deceive many."
(*Matthew* 24:4–5)

But not everyone who speaks of the spirit is a prophet, but only if he follows the conduct of the Lord." This excerpt from the apocryphal *Teaching of the Twelve Apostles* is another way of putting the old adage "actions speak louder than words," or "by their fruit you shall know them."

The gauge of a teacher, a prophet, or any Christian lies in his behavior rather than in his words. Does he live the spirit of the Scriptures? Does he help others in concrete ways? Do his words and actions promote peace or dissention? Before placing any trust in would-be prophets, preachers, or evangelists, look carefully at their lives as well as their words.

Fortunately, as Catholics, we have the safeguard of the Magisterium, or teaching arm, of the Church, which has preserved the body of faith in its essential form since the time of Christ, often against fierce opponents, cults, and false teachings. In fact, the primary responsibility of the pope and the bishops is to teach and preserve the faith, so carefully passed down through the ages. This ultimately is the work of the Holy Spirit, who remains with us always, protecting the legacy of faith until the coming of God's kingdom.

August 22

My Yoke Is Easy

Take my yoke upon you and learn from me, for I am gentle and humble in heart, and you will find rest for your souls. For my yoke is easy and my burden is light. (Matthew 11:29–30)

In today's Scripture passage, Christ speaks of his yoke as easy. The word *easy* in Greek is *chrestos*, which can mean well-fitting. In Palestine ox-yokes were made of wood; the ox was brought in and measurements were taken. The yoke was then roughed out and the ox was brought back to have the yoke tried on. It was carefully adjusted so that it would fit well, and would not gall (chaff) the neck of the patient beast. The yoke was tailor-made to fit the ox.

It is possible that as a carpenter, Jesus made ox-yokes and would have been familiar with the skill involved in making a yoke "easy" for the ox to bear. In any event, there is no doubt that the burdens we bear are made lighter when we invite God to bear them with us.

August 23

A Last Conversation

Sons are a heritage from the L*ORD, children a reward from him. (Psalm 127:3)*

Writing in Catholic Mother Magazine, *Cathy Collins recalled her last conversation with Msgr. Donald Neumann, a longtime friend and mentor who was suffering from a terminal illness.*

During the conversation, when asked for advice on raising her large family, he responded, "My father always said to try to speak to each of the children privately daily, in a casual way, as they follow you up the stairs, or as you do dishes together. Let them know that you know them and see what they do. Praise them, thank them for whatever good they have done. Try especially to give correction in private. . . . [T]he heart speaks to heart clearly. . . . I have tried to do this even with my caregivers, thanking them for their particular kindnesses to me."

He continued in a serious tone, "Also, offer sacrifices each day for them, offering things one day for each child. Keep it simple; name them in your morning offering, say one decade of the rosary for them, take only one cookie at tea time rather than two. . . . You may find that if you are having a particularly hard day, that day's child is in special need of graces. You will find out in heaven that it was necessary for his salvation."

The author concluded, "I will always treasure and ponder his last lesson to me about the value of solidarity, sacrifice and kindness. They are the acts that nurture human beings and save souls, that define the kind of mother we all want to be."

August 24

Kneeling in the Barracks

If anyone is ashamed of me and my words, the Son of Man will be ashamed of him when he comes in his glory and in the glory of the Father and of the holy angels. (Luke 9:26)

Some time ago a newspaper columnist shared with his readers an important moment in his earlier life. It happened when he was drafted into the Royal Air Force and found himself in a military barracks with thirty other men.

On the first night he had to make a big decision. He had always knelt to offer his evening prayers. Should he continue to kneel now that he was in the military service? He squirmed a little bit and then said to himself, "Why should I change just because people might be watching? Am I going to begin my life away from home by letting other people dictate what I should and should not do?" He decided to kneel. By the time he finished, he was aware that everyone else was aware of him. And when he made the Sign of the Cross, he was aware that everyone else knew that he was a Catholic. As it turned out, he was the only Catholic in the barracks. Yet, night after night, he knelt. He said that those ten minutes on his knees often led to discussions that lasted for hours.

Prayer

Lord Jesus Christ, help us never to be ashamed of bearing witness to you, that we may gently draw others to the faith that is the meaning of our lives. Amen.

August 25
A Special Obligation

Do not seek revenge or bear a grudge against one of your people, but love your neighbor as yourself. I am the LORD. (Leviticus 19:18)

The love of neighbor," George MacDonald wrote, "is the only door out of the dungeon of self." Christ emphasizes the love of neighbor as the highest Christian calling other than the love of God himself. Indeed, one is not possible without the other. "He alone loves the creator perfectly," wrote St. Bede, "who manifests a pure love for his neighbor." The Second Vatican Council speaks of this love:

> In our times a special obligation binds us to make ourselves the neighbor of absolutely every person, and of actively helping him when he comes across our path, whether he be an old person abandoned by all, or a foreign laborer unjustly looked down upon, a refugee, a child born of an unlawful union and wrongly suffering for a sin he did not commit, or a hungry person who disturbs our conscience.

August 26
Room for Peace

God has called us to live in peace. (1 Corinthians 7:15)

Personal peace is often grounded in quiet reflection, as exemplified in Mary's own life, for she was a contemplative. When things happened that were strange or puzzling, she "thought," she "pondered," she "kept . . . in her heart." The unusual, the irritating, the puzzling, did not hurry her into action. She didn't make snap judgments or speak on impulse. At the Annunciation "she was deeply troubled by these words"—and she thought.

The story the shepherds told of angelic choirs amazed her mother's heart—and she pondered, Luke tells us. When Jesus was lost in the temple she was certainly anxious, and didn't understand his mysterious reply; yet she was not piqued at being left in ignorance—she just "kept all these things in her heart."

Mary's life serves as a lesson in peace. Sometimes we are so quick, unreflective, impulsive. But Our Lady's example encourages us to slow down, to reflect, to think—to make room for peace in our lives.

■

August 27

A Child Will Lead Them

The wolf will live with the lamb, the leopard will lie down with the goat, the calf and the lion and the yearling together; and a little child will lead them. (Isaiah 11:6)

Some time ago a little boy named Johnny was told by his doctor that he could save his sister's life by giving her some blood. The six-year-old girl was near death, the victim of a disease from which the boy himself had made a full recovery two years earlier. His sister's only chance for recovery was a blood transfusion from someone who had previously conquered the illness. Since the two children had the same rare blood type, the boy was the ideal donor.

"Johnny, would you like to give your blood for Mary?" the doctor asked.

The boy hesitated. His lower lip started to tremble. Then he smiled, and said, "Sure, Doc. I'll give my blood for my sister."

Soon the two children were wheeled into the operating room—Mary, pale and thin; Johnny, robust and the picture of health. Neither spoke, but when their eyes met, Johnny grinned.

As his blood siphoned into Mary's veins, one could almost see new life come into her tired body. The ordeal was almost over when Johnny's brave little voice broke the silence, "Say Doc, when do I die?"

It was only then that the doctor realized what the moment of hesitation, the trembling of the lip, had meant earlier. Little Johnny actually thought that in giving his blood to his sister he was giving up his life! And in that brief moment, he had made his great decision.

"And a little child will lead them," we read in Isaiah. The example of their simple trust and love speaks of the nature of Jesus Christ, who once said we must become like them if we are to inherit the kingdom.

August 28

Feast of St. Augustine

In reading this, then, you will be able to understand my insight into the mystery of Christ. (Ephesians 3:4)

St. Augustine of Hippo (d. 430), after his conversion at the age of thirty-three, became a bishop, a saint, a writer, and one of the greatest figures in the church's history. His final conversion (for which his mother Monica had prayed incessantly) came through his reading about St. Anthony of Egypt and the thousands of monks who gave up the world's pleasure for the love of God. Could he not do the same? In agony of mind he lay in his garden; from the next house came by chance the sound of a boy's voice repeating the words *Tole, lege*—take up and read.

Augustine took this as a sign from God, for there happened to be a book lying near him. He opened it (like St. Anthony with the Gospels) at random and then saw the words: "Put on the Lord Jesus Christ, and make no provision for the flesh." From that moment he made the decision to put the love of God before everything else, and soon he and his friends were baptized.

August 29

To Be Light

Put your trust in the light while you have it, so that you may become sons of light. (*John 12:36*)

There is a famous cave, some sixty miles from Auckland in New Zealand. It is known as the cave of the glowworms. You reach it in a boat that is pulled by a cable for silence. As you glide down the stream, you suddenly come across a soft light gleaming in the distance; then you enter a magic world. From the top of the cave, thousands of threads hang down from the glowing insects. So great is the light that it is possible to read a book there. But if there is the slightest noise, the bright light dies out, just as if a switch had been turned off.

The light of one enthusiastic Catholic can illuminate not only that Catholic's family, but also the parish and community in which that Catholic lives. But the light is dependent on its source, which is prayer, and deep personal prayer in turn requires silence, the delicate atmosphere in which God infuses the soul with the manifold gifts of the Holy Spirit and empowers us to become beacons of his love.

August 30

Lord of My Heart, Give Me Trust

For I tell you that unless your righteousness surpasses that of the Pharisees and the teachers of the law, you will certainly not enter the kingdom of heaven. (Matthew 5:20)

The following is an ancient prayer from the Celtic oral tradition. It speaks to us of love, discernment, courage, and trust in God, just as it did to the sons of St. Patrick fifteen hundred years ago.

Lord of My Heart

Lord of My Heart, give me vision to inspire me, that, working or resting, I may always think of you.
Lord of My Heart, give me light to guide me, that at home or abroad, I may always walk in Your way.
Lord of my heart, give me wisdom to direct me, that, thinking or acting, I may always discern right from wrong.
Lord of my heart, give me courage to strengthen me, that amongst friends or enemies, I may always proclaim Your justice.
Lord of my heart, give me trust to console me, that, hungry or well-fed, I may always rely on Your mercy.
Lord of my heart, save me from empty praise, that I may always boast of You.
Lord of my heart, save me from worldly wealth, that I may always look to the riches of heaven.
Lord of my heart, save me from military prowess, that I may always seek Your protection.
Lord of my heart, save me from vain knowledge, that I may always study Your word.
Lord of my heart, save me from unhealthy pleasures, that I may always find joy in Your beautiful creation.
Lord of my heart, whatever may befall me, rule over my thoughts and feelings, my words and actions.

August 31

One People

I have other sheep that are not of this sheep pen. I must bring them also. They too will listen to my voice, and there shall be one flock and one shepherd. (*John 10:16*)

When Fr. Egerton Young first preached the gospel to the Native peoples in Saskatchewan, the idea of the fatherhood of God fascinated people who had hitherto seen God only in the thunder and the lightning and storms. An old chief said to Fr. Young, "Did I hear you say to God, 'Our Father'? "

"I did," he said.

"God is your Father?" asked the chief.

"Yes," Young answered.

"And he is also my Father?"

"He certainly is."

Suddenly the chief's face lit up with a new radiance. His hand went out. "Then," he said like a man making a dazzling discovery, "you and I are brothers."

Within Catholicism, our brotherhood is most obvious in the Eucharist, when we eat of the one Bread, Jesus Christ, whose life infuses each of his members so that they are mystically transformed into one body, all interrelated and divinized in the Spirit of God.

September

September 1

Faith on the Wire

I tell you the truth, if you have faith as small as a mustard seed, you can say to this mountain, "Move from here to there" and it will move. Nothing will be impossible for you. (Matthew 17:20)

Imagine a steel cable stretched from city hall across Main Street to the bank building. A lone individual stands atop city hall and announces that he intends to walk across the cable to the bank. Along his route a large crowd gathers to witness the extraordinary event.

The tightrope walker asks if they believe he can make it across. They all encourage him and shout, "Yes!" Carefully, slowly, he teeters his way across, with a couple of close calls. Finally he reaches the other side safely and is greeted with applause and shouts of praise.

At this point he shows the crowd a wheelbarrow and says, "I have a great finale for you. Do you think I can go one further and push this across ahead of me?" Some again shout, "Yes!"—but others tell him it's too dangerous.

The tightrope walker then singles out a man and yells down to him, "Sir, do you think I can make it?" He shouts up, "Yes!"—whereupon the daredevil says, "OK, then! Climb in the wheelbarrow!"

Christ also calls to each one of us personally and persistently, promising that he will safely guide us over life with its insecurities, dangers, and joys. It takes trust and courage to say "Yes!" and give ourselves completely into his hands.

Talking of faith and trust is easy, but will we really ride in the wheelbarrow?

September 2

Love and Surrender

Submit to God and be at peace with him; in this way prosperity will come to you. (Job 22:21)

Why do we often resist surrendering ourselves to Christ? Perhaps it's because we don't really trust God to handle our lives. There was once a young woman who was talking to a priest about consecration to the Sacred Heart—of giving oneself wholly to God. She said, "I don't dare give myself totally to the Lord, for fear he might have suffering in mind, or something bad." The priest answered, "If some cold, snowy morning a little bird should come, half-frozen, pecking at your window, would you take it in and feed it, thereby putting itself entirely in your power. What would you do? Would you grip it in your hand and crush it? Or would you give it shelter, warmth, food, and care?" She paused a moment and then said, "It's really about love then, isn't it?"

September 3

The Challenge of Confirmation

You know that the household of Stephanas were the first converts in Achaia, and they have devoted themselves to the service of the saints. I urge you, brothers, to submit to such as these and to everyone who joins in the work, and labors at it. (*1 Corinthians 16:15–16*)

At our confirmation we were commissioned to assume an active role in the Church as adult Christians. In today's Scripture quotation, St. Paul reminds us of that role. There is an interesting story that comes to mind:

In the 1930s a young traveler was exploring the French Alps when he came upon a vast stretch of barren, desolate land. In the middle of this vast wasteland was a stooped old man with a sack of acorns on his back and a four-foot-long iron pipe in his hand. The man was using the iron pipe to punch holes in the ground. Then from the sack he would take an acorn and put it in the hole. The old man told the traveler, "I've planted over 100,000 acorns. Maybe only a tenth of them will grow." The old man's wife and son had died, and this was how he spent his final years.

Twenty-five years later the traveler happened to return to the same desolate spot. What he saw amazed him—the land was covered with a beautiful forest two miles wide and five miles long. Birds were singing, animals were playing, and wildflowers perfumed the air—all because someone cared.

We are called to action as well, to do our part in spreading God's kingdom on earth. We may not be able to change the whole world, but we can change part of it, just as the old man did. We received our sack of acorns and our iron pipe when we were confirmed. Now it's up to us to put them to use.

September 4

A Legacy of Love

You are my hiding place; you will protect me from trouble and surround me with songs of deliverance. (Psalm 32:7)

There's a moving story in the autobiography of Jimmy Cagney, the late Hollywood actor. It takes place in Cagney's youth when his mother was on her deathbed. Around the bed were the four Cagney boys and Jeannie, the only sister. Because of a stroke, Mrs. Cagney could no longer speak. After she had hugged each of her five children, she lifted her right arm, the only one that was still functioning. Jimmy describes what happened next:

"Mom indicated Harry with the index finger of her useless hand, she indicated me with her second finger, she indicated Eddie with her third finger, and with her fourth finger indicated Bill. Then she took the thumb, moved it to the middle of her palm, and clasped the thumb tightly under the other four fingers. Then she patted this fist with her good hand." Cagney said the gesture was beautiful. Everyone knew what it meant. The four brothers were to protect Jeannie after their mother was gone. It was a gesture that no words could have duplicated in beauty and meaning.

Do we see the protection and nourishment of others as part of the mission God has given us in life? Is there someone in our family or among our friends who needs our help and encouragement right now?

September 5
A Conscious Choice

Give thanks to the LORD, for he is good. His love endures forever. (*Psalm* 136:1)

Norskov Olsen, former president of Loma Linda University, once wrote,

"Thankfulness leaves no room for discouragement. I once read a legend of a man who found the barn where Satan kept his seeds ready to be sown in the human heart, and on finding the seeds of discouragement more numerous than others, he learned that those seeds could be made to grow almost anywhere. When Satan was questioned, he reluctantly admitted that there was one place in which he could never get them to thrive. 'And where is that?' asked the man. Satan replied sadly, 'In the heart of a grateful man.' "

Both abundance and lack exist simultaneously in our lives, as parallel realities. It is always our conscious choice which secret garden we will tend. When we choose not to focus on what is missing from our lives but are grateful for the abundance that is present—love, health, family, friends, work, the joys of nature, and personal pursuits that bring us pleasure—the wasteland of illusion falls away and we experience a part of heaven on earth.

■

September 6
The Seven Sorrows

I tell you the truth, you will weep and mourn while the world rejoices. You will grieve, but your grief will turn to joy. (*John* 16:20)

The devotion of the Seven Sorrows of Mary appeared toward the beginning of the fourteenth century, originating in the Dominican Order and advocated by Blessed Henry Suso (d. 1366) and other Rhenish mystics. It spread throughout the church and reached its present form in 1482. The Seven Sorrows of Mary are these:

1. The prophecy of Simeon
2. The flight into Egypt
3. The loss of the boy Jesus
4. The way of the cross
5. The crucifixion and death of Christ
6. Jesus taken down from the cross
7. Jesus laid in the tomb

Devotion to the Seven Sorrows became so widespread that a Confraternity of Our Lady of Sorrows developed and was approved without delay by the pope.

Meditation on the Seven Sorrows is a way of sharing in Mary's life. As we pray the Our Father, the Hail Mary, and the Glory Be for each sorrow, we ponder the pain she endured along with her Son, and we become one with them, offering everything to the Father for the salvation of humanity. We also become aware of the effects of our own sins. This leads us to repentance, conversion, and ultimately freedom and new life.

■

September 7

The Fruit of Forgiveness

In him we have redemption through his blood, the forgiveness of sins, in accordance with the riches of God's grace that he lavished on us with all wisdom and understanding. (Ephesians 1:7–8)

God's forgiveness is life-giving, an expression of his immense love for us. But the same is true of the forgiveness we extend to others, especially that radical forgiveness that Christ empowers us to give. A striking example of this is an incident that occurred during the Korean War. A South Korean Catholic was arrested by the Communists and ordered to be shot. But when the young Communist leader in charge learned that his prisoner was the director of an orphanage, caring for small children, he decided to spare him and kill his son instead. So they took his nineteen-year-old son and shot him in front of his father.

Later, when the tides of war changed and the same young leader was captured by the UN forces, he himself was tried and condemned to death. But before the sentence could be carried out, the Christian whose son had been killed came and pleaded for the life of the killer. He declared that the man was young and didn't know what he was doing. He said, "Give him to me and I'll be responsible." The UN forces granted the request, and the father took the murderer of his boy into his own home and cared for him. Today the young man, formerly a Communist, is a Catholic priest.

This is the power of forgiving love that can only be described as miraculous, the kind of love the dying Stephen reflected in the book of Acts, the kind of love Jesus invoked in his words from the cross, "Father, forgive them, for they know not what they do."

September 8

What Love Is This?

The chief priests and our rulers handed him over to be sentenced to death, and they crucified him. (*Luke* 24:20)

The Jewish leaders flung one last challenge at Jesus: "Come down from the cross and we will believe in you." This was precisely the wrong challenge, for it's because Jesus didn't come down from the cross that he demonstrated the limitless, fathomless, impossible love of God. Did he have to endure a torturous death to redeem us? Of course not. The Incarnation itself was enough to deify human beings and all creation as well. Why then his excruciating death? Solely to prove his love, that there was nothing in heaven or earth that he would not endure for our sakes, that he was prepared to suffer anything, cross any line, to make us his own.

What love is this? It is the question that has dumbfounded theologians and scholars for two millennia and continues to mystify us. It ultimately comes down to a divine, sacrificial love that in the end is incomprehensible. This is the Good News in its nakedness: from the cross, the Son of God says to us, "See how I love you. It is a love without limits, a love that will bear every suffering earth has to offer, for I love you with a fiery love that will make you mine forever."

September 9

Resisting the Sirens

His mouth is sweetness itself;
he is altogether lovely.
This is my lover, this my friend,
O daughters of Jerusalem.
(Song of Solomon 5:16)

In Greek legend two famous travelers passed the rocks where the Sirens sang. They sat on the rocks and sang with such sweetness that they lured mariners irresistibly to their doom. Ulysses sailed past these rocks. His method was to plug the sailor's ears so that they could not hear, and order them to bind him to the mast with ropes so that, however much he struggled, he wouldn't be able to answer to that seductive sweetness. He resisted by compulsion.

The other traveler was Orpheus, the sweetest musician of all. His method was to play and sing with such surpassing sweetness as his ship passed the rocks of the Sirens, that the attraction of their song was not experienced due to the attraction of the song he himself sang. His method was to answer the appeal of seduction with a still greater appeal.

Orpheus represents God's way. He seeks to make us love him so much that his voice is more sweetly insistent to us than all the voices that call us away from him.

September 10
You Are the Peace of All Things Calm

Sing joyfully to the LORD, you righteous; it is fitting for the upright to praise him. (Psalm 33:1)

The greatest form of prayer is praise. We do not ask anything for ourselves but simply praise God for who he is and all he has done for us. The following is an ancient prayer of praise from the Celtic oral tradition—passed down by word of mouth over the centuries:

You Are God

You are the peace of all things calm
You are the place to hide from harm
You are the light that shines in dark
You are the heart's eternal spark
You are the door that's open wide
You are the guest who waits inside
You are the stranger at the door
You are the calling of the poor
You are my Lord and with me still
You are my love, keep me from ill
You are the light, the truth, the way
You are my Savior this very day.

■

September 11
New Slavery

For we know that our old self was crucified with him so that the body of sin might be done away with, that we should no longer be slaves to sin. (Romans 6:6)

In 1838, after a strong emancipation movement among blacks, slavery was abolished in Jamaica. This emancipation was to take effect on August 1st. On the evening of July 31st, a large company of former slaves gathered on the beach for a solemn occasion. A large mahogany coffin had been constructed and placed on the sand next to a burial plot in the beach.

All evening the soon-to-be-emancipated slaves placed in the coffin, with ceremony, symbols of their enslavement. There were chains, leg-irons, whips, padlocks, and other similar symbols of slavery. A few minutes before midnight the box was lowered into the hole in the beach. Pushing sand into the hole to cover the coffin, all joined their voices with one accord and sang: "Praise God from whom all blessings flow, praise him all creatures here below, praise him above ye heavenly host, praise Father, Son, and Holy Ghost." They were free.

Today the Church warns us of the danger of falling into the slavery of materialism, and reminds us that this trap is being actively prepared by the evil one. Vigilance and prayer are necessary to protect our liberty as free sons and daughters of God.

September 12

The Idea of Penance

But if a wicked man turns away from all the sins he has committed and keeps all my decrees and does what is just and right, he will surely live; he will not die. (Ezekiel 18:21)

The concept of renunciation or penance often has a negative connotation: to give up something for Lent or Advent seems to be an imposition that no one welcomes. Yet, the actual effect of penance is to help set us spiritually free. We develop a greater desire for God and a growing freedom from material things—and so peace begins to take root in our hearts. When we begin to live this interior freedom from exterior things, we begin to grow rapidly in the spiritual life.

The late Fr. Slavko Barbaric, spiritual writer and director, has written:

Once you embrace God, you let go of other things, because there is no room for them anymore. So the core issue is not giving up luxury or wealth; you have found something *better* when you have found God. God leaves no room in your life for other things.

For instance, a candidate for the Olympic swimming team will need to "renounce" smoking if he is to realize his dream of competing for the gold medal. When we choose a penance or sacrifice, it is so that we can win in the spiritual life.

September 13
I Knew You'd Come Back

My command is this: Love each other as I have loved you. Greater love has no one than this, that he lay down his life for his friends. (John 15:12–13)

Joseph Dimino, former archbishop for the military services, wrote of an incident during the First World War in which two friends were part of a night patrol in the French countryside. When they returned to their trenches under heavy gunfire, one of the friends was missing. By that time it was daybreak, and it was certain death to be out on top. But the other friend insisted on crawling out to look for his mate—and reluctantly the officer in charge gave his permission.

They watched him slowly working his way into no-man's-land, from shell-hole to shell-hole, and at last, when it became dark again, he again crawled back from his mission and dropped into the trench, himself mortally wounded.

While the medics were attending to him, the officer said gently, "I hear you found your friend." "Yes, sir, but he only lived for a few minutes." "I'm sorry, Jack. I wish I hadn't let you go." "Oh, no," he replied. "It was worth it. When I found Tommy he said to me, 'Good old Jack . . . I knew you'd come back.' "

The love of Christ is like this. He will always come back for us, no matter what the cost.

September 14

Not Where or What, but How

But I trust in you, O LORD; I say, "You are my God." (Psalm 31:14)

Fr. Henri Nouwen brought to his writing not only a deep knowledge of traditional Catholic spirituality, but also insights from the science of psychology as well as his personal experience. In the following excerpt from his work, he speaks of our spiritual state of mind and heart:

> Today, I realized that the question of where to live and what to do is really insignificant compared to the question of how to keep the eyes of my heart focused on the Lord. I can be teaching at Yale, working in the bakery at the Genesee Abbey, or walking around with poor children in Peru and feel totally useless, miserable, and depressed in all these situations. I am sure of it, because it has happened. There is not such a thing as the right place or the right job. I can be happy and unhappy in all situations. I am sure of it, because I have been. I have felt distraught and joyful in situations of abundance as well as poverty, in situations of popularity and anonymity, in situations of success and failure. The difference was never based on the situation itself, but always on my state of mind and heart. When I knew that I was walking with the Lord, I always felt happy and at peace. When I was entangled in my own complaints and emotional needs, I always felt restless and divided.
>
> It is a simple truth that comes to me in a time when I have to decide about my future. Coming to Lima or not for five, ten, or twenty years is no great decision. Turning fully, unconditionally, and without fear to the Lord is.

September 15

"If I Should Never See the Moon Again..."

Now we see but a poor reflection as in a mirror; then we shall see face to face. Now I know in part; then I shall know fully, even as I am fully known. And now these three remain: faith, hope and love. But the greatest of these is love. (*1 Corinthians* 13:12–13)

Clearly, love is the very essence of God's nature and the motivating force of our faith. We could spend our lives attempting to fathom its depth.

For centuries, writers and poets have sought to express this love in their verse. In our age, one beautiful passage was written by Major Malcolm Boyle, who was killed in action after the landing on D-day in June 1944. He had written the following lines in his Bible:

If I should never see the moon again
rising red gold across the harvest field,
or feel the stinging of soft April rain,
as the brown earth her hidden treasures yield.
If I should never taste the salt sea spray
as the ship beats her course against the breeze,
or smell the dog-rose and the new mown hay,
or moss and primrose beneath the tree.

If I should never hear the thrushes wake
long before the sunrise in the glimmering dawn,
or watch the huge Atlantic rollers break
against the rugged cliffs in baffling scorn.
If I have said goodbye to stream and wood,
to the wide ocean and the green clad hill,
I know that he who made this world so good
has somewhere made a heaven better still.
This I bear witness with my latest breath;
knowing the love of God, I fear not death.

September 16

"Rest Your Head on My Heart..."

Hear my prayer, O God; listen to the words of my mouth. (Psalm 54:2)

In the month of January I spoke of the extraordinary love and intimacy conveyed by Christ in his messages to Gabrielle Bossis (d. 1950), compiled in the book *He and I.* What Christ says of prayer strikes to the heart of its purpose:

* Why do you talk to me as though I were so far away? I'm very near . . . in your heart.

* Sometimes you feel me more, sometimes less, but I never change. Don't let praying tire you. Why do you give yourself so much trouble? Let it be utterly simple and heart-warming, a family chat. . . .

* Don't aim at saying an exact number of wordy prayers. Just love me simply. A look of your heart. The tender smile of a friend. . . .

* Gabrielle to Christ: "Perhaps I talk to you too familiarly?"

* His response: But since we are a family nothing could give me greater pleasure. One who understands my desire opens his heart at all times. I have so much love for a soul that its faintest call finds an echo in me. Don't be afraid of expressing yourself. Put your mouth to my ear. I'm listening.

* Don't say your prayers just to get them finished, but saturate your soul with love. Otherwise it would be better to say less.

* My child, rest your head on my heart and listen . . . you don't listen enough, so how can you hear? And how can we have intimate conversations, not just mouth to mouth, but heart to heart? Without any words, with sighs, with the soul's breath. What beautiful intimacy. . . .

September 17

To Grow in His Likeness

Let the morning bring me word of your unfailing love,
for I have put my trust in you.
Show me the way I should go,
for to you I lift up my soul.
(Psalm 143:8)

As Catholics, we believe our ultimate goal in life is to become more and more like Jesus Christ, that is, Godlike, steadily growing in all the qualities that characterized his life. As a result, there is an urgency to human life, for our time is limited. A physician battling a chronic illness speaks of this in a letter to his best friend:

> I felt I hadn't given enough to the Lord—I didn't have much to show him, and I hoped with more time I could offer him more in heaven. I wanted more time to grow into his likeness; more time to detach myself from worldly goods and concerns, and thus yearn more and more to be with him. To disdain this world and eagerly rejoice in going to the next.
>
> I felt a great desire to die more and more to myself, that Jesus would be everything to me. To do only his will, to trust him completely and totally. I felt a need to slow down. To take time with the patients, unhurried. To always pray for the dying: for the dying we pray, that they will be filled with radiant hope and peace as they are reborn to eternal life, the purpose of their creation.
>
> I felt a need to fast—to make more sacrifices for Jesus and Mary. And to truly put first things first: prayer, patients, ministry of writing—of loving.
>
> O my Lord Jesus, my Blessed Mother Mary, I thank you with all my heart for letting me live on earth a while longer, so I can detach myself more from the world and begin to live entirely for you, to put first things first, not to hurry, and to have the chance to give you more, show you more, when at last I enter into your presence.
>
> Oh Jesus, help me to grow in complete trust in you, to disdain this world, and desire and seek with all my heart to be with you in heaven. Your grace is everything, and I love you, I adore you, and I thank you with every fiber of my being. My Lord, thank you.

September 18

Adoration of the Eucharist

This is the bread that came down from heaven. Your forefathers ate manna and died, but he who feeds on this bread will live forever. (John 6:58)

Immediately after the consecration, the living Christ, in the form of simple bread, is elevated by the priest for the people to adore. For some reason liturgists have abbreviated this moment, but I personally follow the example of Pope John Paul II, who solemnly elevated the host and gazed at it with awe and joy.

On this subject, there was an old Irish lay brother in a monastery in Madrid, Edwin O'Brien, who always showed extraordinary devotion at the elevation of the Sacred Host and was present at every elevation he could manage. When asked why, he would answer to this effect:

> Some years ago, one morning I came in at the back of this church when it was full of people attending Mass. It was All Saints' Day, and the bell was ringing for the elevation. And as I came in I was given an extraordinary vision. Over the altar I saw the Saints in Heaven in bright robes and glorious light, kneeling to adore the Sacred Host. There seemed thousands of them, right up into the roof of the church. I could see Our Lady and the Apostles, and St. Lawrence and St. Agnes and many more I recognized.
>
> Then I looked lower down, because all the people in church were bowing low, and I could see over their heads, and behind the altar there seemed to be a sort of great cavern opening, and the souls in purgatory had gathered in hundreds around each side of the altar, in dark colored clothes and all lifting up their arms to the elevated Host.
>
> God showed me all this in a moment or two, and left me weeping in great joy, thinking how close we are to heaven and the souls in purgatory. And always ever since I have a great desire to adore Our Lord at the elevation together with all of them.

September 19

Milagros

And the prayer offered in faith will make the sick person well; the Lord will raise him up. If he has sinned, he will be forgiven. (James 5:15)

In our sacramental Church we use symbols to represent what words alone cannot express, to point to spiritual realities beyond speech, such as the bread and wine used in the Eucharist or the water in baptism. Besides the seven primary sacraments, the Church also has a number of sacramentals.

One of these is the milagro, meaning *miracle*, which is much like a votive candle in that it represents or symbolizes a special prayer, often a petition or thanksgiving. For instance, the milagro in the shape of a heart may reflect a prayer for healing before heart surgery or perhaps a request to find a good husband. A milagro in the shape of a small leg can represent a prayer for the healing of arthritis or the request for a safe journey. Milagros are about the size of bracelet charms and are usually made of metal.

The use of milagros accompanied the Spaniards as they arrived in Central and South America. Milagros are often placed on the side altar of a church or attached to a picture or statue of Christ, the Blessed Virgin, or a particular saint, at home or in the church. They are not magical, of course, but are the visible sign of an inward prayer, and that is why they are considered holy.

■

September 20

Empathy

Be completely humble and gentle; be patient, bearing with one another in love. (*Ephesians* 4:2)

Leon Goldensohn, the psychiatrist who examined the leaders of the Third Reich during the Nurenburg trials, concluded his study by stating that they had one thing in common—a complete lack of empathy, an inability to understand or feel compassion for other human beings. This is also the height of evil: cold indifference to others, despite their suffering or needs. According to his confidantes, the highest compliment Hitler could pay a crony was to say he was ice cold.

In complete contrast, Christ taught that we are one body, mystically united and interwoven with each other so that what affects one member affects the whole. The great sign or sacrament of this oneness is the Eucharist, where we eat of the one bread and drink of the one cup, and in St. Paul's words, "become one in Christ."

September 21

You Shall Always Be My Hope

For you have been my hope, O Sovereign LORD, my confidence since my youth. (Psalm 71:5)

St. Bonaventure (d. 1274) was a medieval Scholastic theologian and philosopher, a contemporary of Thomas Aquinas, and a Doctor of the Church. The following is considered his most beautiful prayer:

> May your fragrance fill my soul! May it always thirst for you, O fountain of life, O fountain of wisdom, O fountain of knowledge, O fountain of eternal light, O torrent of desire and fertility in the mansion of God! May my soul always rove around you, and seek you and find you!
>
> Let it turn to you and come to you! May you be the object of its thought and of its word. Let it sing your praise and the glory of your beloved name with humility and reserve, with love and delight, with ease and tenderness, with patience and peace, with success and perseverance unto the very end.
>
> You alone shall be all in all to me, you shall always be my hope, my confidence, my riches, my charm, my pleasure, my delight, my repose, my tranquility, my peace, my suavity, my perfume, my sweetness, my refreshment, my nurture, my love, my thought, my support, my desire, my refuge, my succor, my patience, my treasure, my passion!
>
> My spirit and my heart shall always be fixed and locked and deeply rooted in you, and in you only! Amen.

September 22

Love Them Anyway

Thus you will walk in the ways of good men and keep to the paths of the righteous. (Proverbs 2:20)

Dr. Kent M. Keith is a speaker and writer whose mission is "to help people find personal meaning in a crazy world." His work and presentations deal with leadership and discovering personal meaning at home and in the workplace. His most famous work, *Anyway: The Paradoxical Commandments*, has spread around the world in the thirty years since it was written. These commandments are a new and refreshing echo of the gospel message:

The Paradoxical Commandments

1. People are illogical, unreasonable, and self-centered. Love them anyway.
2. If you do good, people will accuse you of selfish ulterior motives. Do good anyway.
3. If you are successful, you win false friends and true enemies. Succeed anyway.
4. The good you do today will be forgotten tomorrow. Do good anyway.
5. Honesty and frankness make you vulnerable. Be honest and frank anyway.
6. The biggest men with the biggest ideas can be shot down by the smallest men with the smallest minds. Think big anyway.
7. People favor underdogs, but follow only top dogs. Fight for the underdogs anyway.
8. What you spend years building may be destroyed overnight. Build anyway.
9. People really need help but may attack you if you do help them. Help people anyway.
10. Give the world the best you have and you'll get kicked in the teeth. Give the world the best you have anyway.

September 23
The Seven Joys

Splendor and majesty are before him; strength and joy in his dwelling place. (1 Chronicles 16:27)

Near to Christ," wrote Pope Paul VI, "Mary recapitulates all joys. A Mother filled with holy joy, she experienced the perfect joy promised to the church. With good reason do her children on earth turn to her, mother of hope and mother of grace, invoking her as cause of their joy."

The Seven Joys of Mary were first encouraged by the Franciscan Order, beginning as far back as its foundation in the twelfth century. They eventually took the following form:

1. The Annunciation
2. The Visitation
3. The Birth of Christ
4. The Adoration of the Magi
5. Finding Jesus in the Temple
6. The Resurrection
7. The Assumption

The usual form of this devotion is to meditate on each joy, as in the Rosary or the Seven Sorrows, following it with the Our Father, Hail Mary, and Glory Be. The Seven Joys can also be used as a seven-decade Rosary. It is especially appropriate in the Easter Season.

September 24

Mother Teresa and the Hindu Family

When they had finished eating, Jesus said to Simon Peter, "Simon son of John, do you truly love me more than these?" "Yes, Lord," he said, "you know that I love you." Jesus said, "Feed my lambs." (John 21:15)

One of the great encouragements Mother Teresa experienced in her work with the poor of Calcutta was their overwhelming gratitude for even the smallest gift, as well as their willingness to share this gift with others who were just as unfortunate. In this light she told the following story:

> Once a man came to our house and he told me, "There is a Hindu family with about eight children who have not eaten for a long time." So, I quickly took some rice for that evening and went to their family and I could see real hunger on the small faces of these children. Yet the mother had the courage to divide the rice into two portions and she went out. When she came back, I asked her, "Where did you go? What did you do?" And she said, "They are hungry too!" Who are they? "A Muslim family next door with as many children." She knew that they were hungry. What struck me the most was that she knew and because she knew, she gave until it hurt. This is something so beautiful! This is living love! She gave until it hurt.
>
> I did not bring more rice that night because I wanted them to enjoy the joy of giving, the joy of sharing. You should have seen the faces of those little ones! They understood what their mother did. Their faces were brightened up with smiles. When I came in, they looked hungry, they looked so miserable, but the act of their mother taught them what true love is.

September 25

The Nicene Creed

Guard the good deposit that was entrusted to you—guard it with the help of the Holy Spirit who lives in us. (2 Timothy 1:14)

The Nicene Creed, of course, contains the very core of Catholic belief and has been included in the liturgy since the fourth century. As soon as Constantine, the first Christian emperor, had bestowed peace on the church, he gathered the Council of Nicaea (325) to address the schism that had developed as a result of the Arian heresy. Arius was a priest of Alexandria, elderly, grave, ascetic; to him and his followers God seemed so high and remote that he could never have become man; the Son who became man was not really God, not co-eternal with the Father, but only the highest of his earthly children.

The great Council opened, with 318 bishops, some bearing the marks of torture or maiming from the persecutions. Constantine himself listened from his throne. The Patriarch of Alexandria brought with him a young deacon named Athanasius, who spoke powerfully on behalf of the divinity of Christ: "begotten, not made, one in being with the Father." In the end, the Council rejected the teaching of Arius and defined for all time the truths contained in the Nicene Creed, which we proclaim every Sunday.

September 26

Grumbling

Give thanks to the LORD, for he is good; his love endures forever. (*1 Chronicles 16:34*)

There was once a woman who was always grumbling. Her husband, she thought, made more work than other husbands, her children took less care of their clothes than other children. Her home seemed colder in winter and hotter in summer than anyone else's—in fact, she thought God had given her a heavier cross to bear than he had given to any of her neighbors.

One night she dreamed that her guardian angel stood by her bed. He told her to rise since he had something he wanted to show her. She got up and followed him down the street. Many of the doors were marked with large crosses. The angel beckoned, and she peeped through the windows. In one room she saw a mother and father kneeling by the bedside of a dying child. In another she saw a poor blind woman, sitting beside a cold fireplace. In another, the breadwinner lay dead. Every house seemed to have some trouble. At last they stopped before a house with a tiny cross on the door, and as she looked at it she realized it was her own.

When afterward she was inclined to grumble she thought of all those who were worse off than she was, and instead of grumbling she said gladly and thankfully, "Thy will be done, my beloved Lord."

September 27
Sowing Seeds

Still other seed fell on good soil, where it produced a crop—a hundred, sixty or thirty times what was sown. (*Matthew* 13:8)

When we sow the seeds of encouragement and example, we rarely know what effect the seed will have, but we're sure to be very surprised in heaven.

In the church where author H.L. Gee worshiped there was a lonely old man, old Thomas. He had outlived all his friends and hardly anyone knew him. When he died, his one acquaintance, the young writer, suspected that there would be no one at the funeral.

As Gee later wrote, there was indeed no one there, and it was a windy, wet day as well. When the funeral reached the cemetery, there was a soldier waiting at the gate. He was an officer, but on his raincoat there were no rank badges. He had come for the graveside service, and when it was over he stepped forward and, before the open grave, raised his hand in a salute that might have been given to a king. Gee wrote that he walked away with this soldier, and as they walked, the wind blew the soldier's raincoat open to reveal the shoulder badges of a brigadier.

The general said to him, "You're probably wondering what I'm doing here, but many years ago old Thomas taught me to be an altar boy. I was a wild kid and gave him a lot of trouble, but I listened more than he thought I did and came away with an understanding of my faith and the values I've built my life on. He never knew what he did for me, but I owe everything I am to old Thomas, and today I had to come to salute him at the end."

September 28

Creation of a Masterpiece

The watchman opens the gate for him, and the sheep listen to his voice. He calls his own sheep by name and leads them out. When he has brought out all his own, he goes on ahead of them, and his sheep follow him because they know his voice. (John 10:3–4)

When in Florence every visitor seeks out Michelangelo's statue of David, a striking image of the future king just before he does battle with Goliath. It is a masterpiece in marble, standing nine feet high and alert with all the wonderful expressiveness of artistic genius. The statue has a remarkable history.

Several sculptors before Michelangelo had attempted to mold the magnificent block of Carrara marble, with one inadvertently breaking a great piece out of the side, which put an end to his efforts.

There it lay for many years, "badly blocked out and supine," according to an inventory of the workshop, until the trained eye of Michelangelo rested on it. Immediately he caught the possibility that lay in the stone, and soon it was taking form. Under the artist's hand, energetically outlining and fashioning, carving and chiseling, a majestic figure was soon seen stepping from the marble, and even the mutilation that had rendered it useless to the original artist became part of the majesty of the new design. The three years of work produced what may be the most famous sculpture in the world.

Like marble in the hands of a sculptor, we are being formed into the very image of Christ, regardless of our former sins and flaws. Sometimes the chiseling may hurt, but a masterpiece is being created.

September 29

The Risk of Love

Surely it is you who love the people;
all the holy ones are in your hand.
At your feet they all bow down,
and from you receive instruction.
(Deuteronomy 33:3)

Trust in God, the certainty that we are in his hands, enables us to take risks in loving. A dramatic illustration comes from one of the most famous and decisive battles of World War II, the battle of the Philippine Sea, fought on June 20, 1944. As Admiral Mitscher's task force came within striking distance of the Japanese flotilla, he ordered the planes from his aircraft carrier to attack the planes and ships of the enemy.

After striking and badly damaging the Japanese fleet, the American pilots re-formed in groups and turned back toward their carrier and its entourage of destroyers.

But darkness was falling and their fuel was running low. Although the pilots needed to locate and land on the deck of their carrier, they discovered the ships were operating in a black-out and in radio silence, as protection from enemy submarines. A desperate situation developed.

To switch on the carrier's powerful searchlights would be to risk the lives of thousands of sailors. So with the planes circling in the darkness over his head, Admiral Mitscher had to make a decision—either risk all his ships and the lives of the men on board, or effectively doom a hundred pilots to death.

At that moment Mitscher made a decision that stamped him for all time as a hero of American military history. From his position on the bridge of the ship, he bellowed out, "Turn on the lights!"

The ships of the task force turned on all their lights. Five-inch guns fired "star" shells into the air, and the searchlights guided the planes to the deck of the carrier. The pilots landed safely. No enemy attack came.

In our own lives, may we realize that risks taken for the sake of love are the invitations of a loving God to imitate the greatest risk-taker of all, Jesus Christ.

September 30

To Give Back

You turned my wailing into dancing;
you removed my sackcloth and clothed me with joy,
that my heart may sing to you and not be silent.
O LORD my God, I will give you thanks forever.
(Psalm 30:11–12)

Some time ago, a seventy-year-old toymaker gave his toyshop to the children of Denmark. His "house of toys," one of the biggest in the world, was started 157 years ago by his family. It was a favorite haunt of fairytale writer Hans Christian Andersen, as well as hundreds of thousands of enchanted youngsters who romped through the five-story Toyland.

When the owner announced that the toy store would be placed in trust for needy youngsters, he said, "We earned all our money from children, so it comes quite naturally to us to give the money back to the children, especially to those who have never had the joy that toys can give."

Prayer

Father, every gift comes from you. May we be generous to a fault, in imitation of your Son, for it is in giving that we receive. Amen.

OCTOBER

October 1

Feast of St. Therese of Lisieux

Draw me: we will run after thee to the odour of thy ointments. The king hath brought me into his storerooms: we will be glad and rejoice in thee, remembering thy breasts more than wine: the righteous love thee.
(Song of Solomon 1:3–4 VULGATE)

In her autobiography, *The Story of a Soul,* St. Therese of Lisieux wrote of the advice she was given by Christ concerning prayer for others:

> Since I have two brothers and my little Sisters, the novices, I wanted to intercede for what each soul needed, and go into detail about it. But the days wouldn't be long enough and I fear I would forget something important. But during my thanksgiving, Jesus gave me a simple means of accomplishing my mission.
>
> He made me understand these words of the Song of Solomon: "Draw me, we shall run after you in the fragrance of your ointments."

O Jesus, it is not even necessary to say: "When drawing me, draw the souls whom I love!" This simple statement: "Draw me" suffices. I understand, Lord, that when a soul allows herself to be captivated by the fragrance of your ointments, she cannot run to you alone, but all the souls whom she loves follow in her train. This is done without effort, without constraint, for it is a natural consequence of her attraction for you. Just as a torrent, throwing itself with impetuosity into the ocean, drags after it everything it encounters in its passage. In the same way, O Jesus, the soul who plunges into the shoreless ocean of your Love, draws with her all those who are dear to her. For you know, Lord, that I have no other treasure than the souls it has pleased you to unite to mine.

■

October 2

Fire and Abyss of Love

One thing I ask of the LORD,
this is what I seek:
that I may dwell in the house of the LORD
all the days of my life,
to gaze upon the beauty of the LORD
and to seek him in his temple.
(Psalm 27:4)

St. Catherine of Siena (d. 380) was a mystic, a stigmatist, a spiritual writer, and a counselor to two popes. In 1970 she was given the rare title of Doctor of the Church. One of the great prayers she wrote is the following:

O Eternal Godhead

O eternal God, fire and abyss of love, . . . I have tasted and
seen your depth, eternal Trinity, and the beauty of your
creation.

. . . O abyss! O eternal Godhead! O deep sea! What more could you have given me than the gift of your very self? . . . You are a fire lifting all chill and giving light. In your light you have made me know your truth. . . .

Good above every good, joyous Good,
Good beyond measure and understanding! Beauty above all beauty. . . .
You who are the angels' good are given to humans with burning love.
You, garment who covers all shame,
pasture the starving within your sweetness, for you are sweet without trace of bitterness.

October 3

Meditating on the Mysteries

O Lord, let your ear be attentive to the prayer of this your servant and to the prayer of your servants who delight in revering your name. (Nehemiah 1:11)

Traditionally, October has been designated as the month of the Rosary and is a good time to reflect on the different ways the Rosary can be offered to engage the imagination and heart, ways that we may not have been aware of. Spiritual writers have offered the following suggestions:

- One way to reflect on the Rosary is simply to picture the scene of each mystery, noting some of the details and reflecting on Christ and Our Lady's reactions to the various events, such as Mary's joy at the Nativity or the thoughts of Christ in Gethsemane.

- Another way is to briefly visualize the events of each mystery and then meditate on the virtues Jesus and Mary portrayed in each, such as Mary's faith and humility at the Annunciation or Christ's love in bearing his cross. These thoughts lead us to pray for these virtues in our own lives.

- A third way is to briefly recall the events of each mystery, but rather than dwelling on the details or virtues involved, we meditate on the great themes represented in the mysteries, such as the meaning of the Incarnation, the Redemption, the forgiveness of sins through the passion of Christ, or the hope held out to us by the Resurrection.

- Fourth, utilizing a more contemplative approach, we simply gaze with love at Christ present within us, communing with him in a wordless way—while the various mysteries create a background for a more vivid realization of Christ's great love as manifested in the mysteries.

October 4

Maternal Love

Gather to me my consecrated ones, who made a covenant with me by sacrifice. (Psalm 50:5)

In the last century, a young mother was making her way across the hills of South Wales, carrying her tiny baby in her arms, when she was overtaken by a blinding blizzard. She never reached her destination, and when the blizzard had subsided, her body was found by searchers beneath a mound of snow. But they discovered that before her death, she had taken off all her outer clothing and wrapped it about her baby. When they unwrapped the child, to their great surprise and joy, they found he was alive and well. She had mounded her body over his and given her life for her child, proving the depths of her maternal love. Years later that child, David Lloyd George, grown to manhood, became prime minister of Great Britain, and was, without a doubt, one of England's greatest statesmen.

October 5

Damien's Confession

Therefore confess your sins to each other and pray for each other so that you may be healed. The prayer of a righteous man is powerful and effective. (*James 5:16*).

In the biography of *Damien the Leper*, author John Farrow speaks of an incident in which Father Damien's superior planned to visit him in Molokai. But because of the leprosy, the captain of the ship prevented him from going ashore.

As Damien's tiny boat came alongside, the captain warned the priest not to come aboard; there was a new law forbidding it. Although Damien pleaded that all he wanted was a few minutes alone with his superior so that he could go to confession, the captain insisted that the law be kept. "Then," cried Damien from his boat, "I'll make my confession from here."

Stillness settled over the deck as the heroic priest knelt in the small craft and made his confession aloud. The ship's crew and passengers crowded the railing in deep interest, but silent and respectful. Finally came the words of absolution, and the pastor of Molokai took his seat again and was rowed back to the leper colony.

Such a great witness to the Sacrament of Forgiveness was never forgotten by the Catholics of Molokai and the Hawaiian Islands.

■

October 6

Freedom and Self-Deception

And the LORD said to Satan, "Where have you come from?" Satan answered the LORD, "From roaming through the earth and going back and forth in it." (*Job 2:2*)

Christian psychologist M. Scott Peck speaks of a disguised evil in his book *People of the Lie*. Perhaps unconsciously, but certainly under the influence of evil, they are individuals who are utterly dedicated to preserving their self-image of perfection and maintaining the appearance of moral behavior. They worry about this a great deal. They are acutely sensitive to social norms and what others might think of them. They dress well, go to work on time, pay their taxes, and outwardly seem to live lives that are above reproach. Dr. Peck writes, "The words 'image,' 'appearance,' and 'outwardly' are crucial to understanding the morality of the evil. While they lack any motivation to be good, they intensely desire to appear good. Their 'goodness' is all on a level of pretense. It is, in effect, a lie. That is why they are the 'people of the lie.' Actually, the lie is designed not so much to deceive others as to deceive themselves. They cannot or will not tolerate the pain of self-reproach."

Sometimes the manifestation of a mental illness such as the narcissistic personality (in which the deception is involuntary) can be gently brought to light and healed through the grace of God. Daily prayer will give Christ and Our Lady the opening they need to infuse us with that liberating truth that leads us to real freedom.

October 7

Most Richly Blessed

Give ear to my words, O LORD,
consider my sighing.
Listen to my cry for help,
my King and my God,
for to you I pray.
(Psalm 5:1–2)

Our God answers all prayers, and yet he may not give us precisely what we ask for, if it would be harmful to us. A child, for instance, may wish to play with matches, but out of love his parent would give him a toy instead. This loving concern of God is expressed in these lines by an unknown author:

I asked God for strength that I might achieve;
I was made weak that I might learn humbly to obey.
I asked for help that I might do greater things;
I was given infirmity that I might do better things.
I asked for riches that I might be happy;
I was given poverty that I might be wise.
I asked for all things that I might enjoy life;
I was given life that I might enjoy all things.
I was given nothing that I asked for,
But everything that I had hoped for.
Despite myself, my prayers were answered;
I am among men most richly blessed.

October 8

Catching Faith

I long to see you so that I may impart to you some spiritual gift to make you strong—that is, that you and I may be mutually encouraged by each other's faith. (Romans 1:11–12)

It has been said that "faith is caught, not taught." Certainly the people closest to us have had a profound influence on our faith, beginning with our parents. As a child I remember, for instance, the great importance my mother placed on Sunday Mass, preparations for which began early in the morning. Somehow she got the five of us groomed, dressed, and transported to the church. How she got herself ready as well I don't know.

Once at Mass, we saw her in prayer, of course; after Communion, I remember my mother kneeling in thanksgiving, her hands covering her face so as not to be distracted (as the nuns had taught her as a girl). These things along with our parents' moral code, sacrifices, and faithfulness to us and to each other made a lifelong impression on their children. Even such seemingly minor things as grace before meals, the rosary on our mother's nightstand, and the crucifix on the living room wall were etched in our memory. We could not help catching the faith, for its evidence was all around us.

How can we, without words, pass on the faith to our family? Is there more we could do?

October 9

Monte Cassino

Jesus answered them, "Destroy this temple, and I will raise it again in three days." (John 2:19)

At Monte Cassino in Italy there still exists a monastery established by St. Benedict more than 1,500 years ago. Because it was perched on the side of a hill overlooking British and American forces attempting to advance northward during World War II, General Harold Alexander believed that it was occupied by the German army, despite reports by troops on the front line that no fire had come from the monastery. Consequently, on February 15, 1944, he ordered the worst saturation bombing in all of history to level it. But when the smoke cleared, no soldiers were found inside, only civilians who had fled there for refuge, and whom the bombing had killed. The Germans then proceeded to use the ruins for artillery emplacements.

After the war ended, with American help, the monastery was rebuilt on its hillside perch where it remains to this day, looking more glorious and more beautiful than ever. Actually, through its 1500-year history, the monastery was destroyed many times, by fire and earthquake and war. Always it was rebuilt to appear more beautiful than before. This history is symbolized in the monastery's coat of arms, which depicts an oak tree that has been cut down, lying next to its stump. Growing out of the stump are new branches, bearing new green leaves. Underneath this visual image are the words, "Cut down, it comes to new life." The monastery itself is a symbol of human life, which, nearly destroyed, can rise to new life through the grace of God.

October 10

The Miraculous Medal

How great are his signs,
how mighty his wonders!
His kingdom is an eternal kingdom;
his dominion endures from generation to generation.
(Daniel 4:3)

In November 1830, the Blessed Virgin appeared to Catherine Labouré, who had just entered a convent that year. The Madonna was standing on a terrestrial globe, her arms extended downward. From her open hands streamed bright rays of light, and an oval framed her, showing these words in letters of gold: "O Mary, conceived without sin, pray for us who have recourse to thee." After a while the vision began to recede, and she then saw the letter *M* mounted on a cross, beneath which were the hearts of Jesus and Mary. The whole image was encircled with twelve stars. Catherine then heard the Virgin say, "Have a medal struck after this model. Those who wear it will receive great graces. They should wear it around the neck. Abundant graces will be given to those who wear it with confidence."

The medal had originally been called the "Medal of the Immaculate Conception," but so many remarkable graces and favors were granted through it, that it quickly became known as the Miraculous Medal. The devotion has since spread throughout the world.

October 11

Forming Christ

Your hands made me and formed me; give me understanding to learn your commands. (*Psalm 119:73*)

A certain wealthy man, a patron of artists, possessed a breathtaking statue of Christ. He put an ad in the newspaper stating that he would like to present an exact duplicate to the local church, and would give a large reward to anyone who could reproduce it. Two men presented themselves. One said he was a sculptor and the other said he would use a "secret process." The patron set a limit of four weeks for each to complete his model. The sculptor labored with a chisel, chipping here and there, and finished one day before the deadline.

On the day appointed both men presented their replicas. The patron said that the sculptor had done a good job, but the work of the other man was perfect—a perfect replica, and this one he would purchase.

Curious about the "secret process," he asked about the technique that was used. With a twinkle in his eye, the man said he himself had crafted the original statue and still had the mold. All he had to do was to pour liquid bronze into it to produce the perfect replica.

We are all called to be other Christs. There are two ways of accomplishing this: we can chip away at a fault here and a sin there; or the easy, "secret" way. We can allow the Blessed Virgin to form us. Christ was formed in her. She was the mold, and given the chance, she will fashion us into a unique image of her Son. We need only ask her.

October 12

¡Viva Cristo Rey!

Be strong and courageous. Do not be afraid or discouraged because of the king of Assyria and the vast army with him, for there is a greater power with us than with him. (*2 Chronicles 32:7*)

American Catholics, indeed all Catholics in the West, have enjoyed religious freedom for so long that it's hard to conceive of the persecutions that have plagued the Church continually during its long history. Today deadly persecutions are occurring in China, Pakistan, North Korea, Somalia, Ethiopia, and Iran.

One account is found in Graham Greene's *The Power and the Glory*, which was deeply influenced by the underground work and death of Fr. Miguel Pro. During the religious persecution in Mexico in the 1920s, when Catholicism was basically outlawed, the thirty-five-year old Jesuit priest continued to secretly minister to hundreds of Mexicans day in and day out. A master of disguise, he escaped the police again and again.

Finally, however, he was arrested with his two brothers. There was no trial and no evidence was produced against the brothers, but all three were condemned to death. On the day he faced the firing squad, Fr. Miguel threw open his arms in the form of a cross and as the soldiers took aim, cried, "¡Viva Cristo Rey!" (Long live Christ the King), the rallying cry of the Catholic resistance. His example of faith and courage became a light of hope in this darkest hour of Mexican history.

We as Catholics all share in the sacred Body and Blood of Christ, making us blood brothers and sisters. Now may be an opportune time to add the plight of persecuted Catholics to our daily prayers.

October 13

I Believe; Help My Unbelief

This righteousness from God comes through faith in Jesus Christ to all who believe. (Romans 3:22)

The following is a contemporary prayer by British author Fr. Michael John Bernard (1928–2007) of the Society of St. Francis. It speaks of the vacillating faith many of us have experienced from time to time and the comfort of knowing that we are not alone in our perplexity:

I Want to Love You

Lord, I want to love you, yet I'm not sure.
I want to trust you, yet I'm afraid of being taken in.
I know I need you, yet I'm ashamed of the need.
I want to pray, yet I'm afraid of being a hypocrite.
I need my independence, yet I fear to be alone.
I want to belong, yet I must be myself.
Take me, Lord, yet leave me alone.

Lord, I believe; help thou my unbelief.
O Lord, if you are there, you do understand, don't you?
Give me what I need but leave me free to choose.
Help me work it out my own way, but don't let me go.
Let me understand myself, but don't let me despair.
Come unto me, O Lord—I want you there.
Lighten my darkness—but don't dazzle me.
Help me to see what I need to do and give me strength to do it.
O Lord, I believe; help thou my unbelief.

October 14
The Rosary

[T]hen hear from heaven their prayer and their plea, and uphold their cause. (1 Kings 8:45)

The greatest and most popular devotion to Our Lady is the Rosary. Although not always perceived as such, the Rosary is essentially a form of meditation. It has been consistently recommended and encouraged by saints and popes alike, not to mention Mary herself in the context of her many apparitions.

The Rosary transforms us: in reflecting on its mysteries—the major events in the lives of Christ and Our Lady—we are gradually changed into their likeness. We begin to see and act and feel as they did. Just as a child often takes on the personality traits of a parent, so we too acquire the mind and heart of the Christ and his Mother.

But this movement of grace can be stifled if we focus on the wrong element. It is important to avoid concentrating on the repetitive Hail Marys of the Rosary. These serve as a type of mantra in that the quiet rhythm of the prayers keeps us centered on the particular mystery on which we are meditating. "The Hail Marys of the Rosary," writes Fr. Albert Shamon, "are like background music while you are watching Our Lord's life. Background music helps us when reading and working. We don't pay much attention to the music, but it helps us." *(Continued)*

October 15
The Rosary II

Yet give attention to your servant's prayer and his plea for mercy, O Lord my God. Hear the cry and the prayer that your servant is praying in your presence. (2 Chronicles 6:19)

Many people find that the scriptural Rosary helps them to keep tuned in to the mystery. Before each Hail Mary a short Scripture verse is read, one that relates directly to the mystery that is being contemplated. After a while the verses become memorized and thus become a valuable aid in this meditative prayer. It calls to mind the analogy of Pope Paul VI that the Rosary is a "compendium of the entire gospel," a prayer "centered on the redemptive incarnation, in which the litany-like succession of Hail Marys becomes an unceasing praise of Christ." It might also be added here that the last twelve popes have all warmly recommended the Rosary and have set aside October as the special month of this prayer.

The fathers of the Second Vatican Council again recommended the Rosary to the faithful, along with the suggestion that additional events in the lives of Jesus and Mary, other than the traditional fifteen mysteries, also be meditated upon. For instance, a Rosary could be comprised of the miracles of Christ, or the beatitudes, or Jesus' discourse at the Last Supper. *(Continued)*

October 16

The Rosary III

O Lord, let your ear be attentive to the prayer of this your servant and to the prayer of your servants who delight in revering your name. (Nehemiah 1:11a)

Pope John Paul II expressed his love for the Rosary many times, even leading the Catholic world in its recitation by satellite some years ago. He also arranged for it to be recorded on cassette and compact disc for individual use. His usual gift to diplomats and VIPs visiting the Vatican is a Rosary. One of his discourses on this prayer included the following remarks:

> The Rosary is marvelous in its simplicity and in its depth. . . . Against the background of the words "Hail Mary" there passes before the eyes of the soul the main episodes in the life of Jesus Christ. They are composed altogether of the joyful, sorrowful, and glorious mysteries—and put us into living communion with Jesus through his Mother's heart.

At the same time our heart can enclose in these decades of the Rosary all the facts that make up the life of the individual, the family, the nation, the church, and all humankind. They include personal matters and those of our neighbor, particularly persons who are closest to us. Thus in the simple prayer of the Rosary beats the rhythm of human life.

October 17
The Shadow on the Wall

I will listen to what God the LORD will say;
he promises peace to his people, his saints—
but let them not return to folly.
(Psalm 85:8)

In his book *The Power and the Glory*, novelist Graham Greene describes a priest who ministered to his people in an era of religious persecution in Mexico. The danger of being caught by the police as well as the exhausting work of serving his people finally took their toll. The priest turned to drink and became an alcoholic. Eventually he was caught, sentenced to die, and put into prison to await execution.

When he awoke on the morning of his death, he had an empty brandy flask in his hand. He tried to recite an act of contrition, but he was too confused to remember the words. Suddenly he caught sight of his own shadow on the wall of the prison cell. He sat there, staring at it. Tears began to form in his eyes. He did not weep because he was afraid to die, but because he had to go to God so empty-handed. It seemed to him at that moment that it would have been easy to have been a saint. He would only have needed a little self-restraint and a little courage. He felt like someone who had missed happiness by seconds at an appointed place. He knew now that in the end there was only one thing that counted—to be a saint.

October 18

Communion at Dachau

And he took bread, gave thanks and broke it, and gave it to them, saying, "This is my body given for you." (Luke 22:19a)

The former bishop of Munich, Johannes Neuhausler, who had been a prisoner at the Dachau concentration camp, tells this story of the priests imprisoned in the compound and their amazing love for the Eucharist:

> The Polish priests . . . were not permitted to practice their religion in the block as others were, so they had to devise means to deceive the guards. Many worked in the plantation greenhouses. While one of them kept guard and the other comrades pretended to be working, the Polish priest who had spent the longest time in the camp knelt on the ground, with his face turned toward the greenhouse so as to give the impression that he was weeding. Indeed, the SS sentries might be spying from their watchtower.
>
> The kneeling priest had pressed a small portable altar into the ground and there he celebrated Mass. Many comrades hurried by, holding grass or plants in their hands as if they had some work to do there. Then they knelt down and received Holy Communion clandestinely.

Prayer

Lord Jesus Christ, throughout the ages you have freely given us your very body and blood, communicating to us your life and spirit. Help us never to lose our sense of awe when you come to us in Communion. Amen.

October 19

Fr. Michael Heller

You will increase my honor and comfort me once again. (Psalm 71:21)

The Templeton Prize was given on March 13, 2008, to Fr. Michael Heller, 72, a cosmologist and philosopher who has spent his life asking, and perhaps more impressively answering, key questions relating to science and religion.

The John Templeton Foundation, which awards grants to encourage scientific discovery on the "big questions" in science and philosophy, commended Polish-born Professor Heller for his extensive writings that have "evoked new and important consideration of some of humankind's most profound concepts."

Much of Fr. Heller's career has been dedicated to reconciling the known scientific world with the unknowable dimensions of God. Explaining his affinity for the two fields, he has said, "I always wanted to do the most important things, and what can be more important than science and religion? Science gives us knowledge, and religion gives us meaning."

Fr. Heller was born in 1936 in Tarnow, Poland, one of five children in a deeply religious family devoted to intellectual interests. His mother, a schoolteacher, and his father, a mechanical and electrical engineer, fled to Russia in 1939 before the Nazi occupation.

On returning years later to Poland, where Communist authorities sought to oppress priests and intellectuals, Professor Heller found shelter for his work in the Catholic Church.

Prayer

Father, help us see your presence in our Church that has given shelter and protection to the persecuted throughout history. Grant us the wisdom to see, with Fr. Heller, that science and God are not two separate realities, but inherently linked together. When we look at the wonders science has given us, may we also see your creative hand.

October 20

Heaven and Hell

Then I saw a new heaven and a new earth, for the first heaven and the first earth had passed away, and there was no longer any sea. (Revelation 21:1)

Pope John Paul II used to teach about heaven and hell through the story of a Korean general. He died, was judged, and assigned to paradise. But when he came before St. Peter he thought of something he would like to do. He wanted to peer into hell for just a moment, just to have an idea of it. "No problem there," said St. Peter.

So the general peered in at the door of hell and saw an enormous banquet hall. There were a number of long tables with bowls of rice and delicacies on them, well flavored, smelling delicious, inviting. The guests were sitting there hungrily, opposite one another, each with a plate of food.

What was happening? The guests all had chopsticks—which they had to use—but these were so long that, however hard they tried, not a grain of rice could they get into their mouths. And this was their torment, this was hell. "I've seen it, that's more than enough for me," said the general and went back to the gates of heaven, where he went in.

Inside, he saw the same banquet hall, the same tables, the same food, and the same long chopsticks. But the guests were cheerful, all of them smiling and laughing. Each one, having put the food onto his chopsticks, held it out to the mouth of his companion opposite, and so they managed to eat to their fill.

"Thinking of others instead of oneself," the pope said, "had solved the problem and transformed hell into heaven."

October 21
Bearing the Cross

Take my yoke upon you and learn from me, for I am gentle and humble of heart, and you will find rest for your souls. For my yoke is easy and my burden is light. (Matthew 11:29–30)

A certain nun had many afflictions and began to sink into discouragement, feeling that God had deserted her. One night he sent her a dream, appearing to her wounded, crowned with thorns, and bearing a huge cross. As he came nearer she saw that he had a second cross too, but a smaller and lighter one. He held it out for her. "Take up your cross, my daughter, and follow me."

She followed him up a steep hill, often forcing her way through thorns and briars. Her feet were soon bleeding, and the cross seemed heavier and heavier; in desperation she called to the Lord for help. He did not come back to her, but turned around and said, "The right way to carry your cross is to clasp it firmly, and place your feet in my footsteps." She clasped her cross firmly and at once it grew lighter. She carefully observed wherever the Lord's feet trod, and saw that in those places the thorns disappeared and flowers sprang up immediately in their place. The rest of the journey to the top of the hill seemed easy, and as Jesus turned to thank her she awoke with a start, but found her heart full of new insight and courage.

October 22
The Spiritual Link

Turn, O Lord, and deliver me; save me because of your unfailing love. (Psalm 6:4)

Writing in the September 1989 issue of *Columbia* magazine, author Dale Francis tells the story of a laicized priest who, after many years away, returned to the priesthood under some revealing circumstances.

He stated that he left the priesthood because the Church wasn't changing rapidly enough. Initially he had intended only to leave the priesthood, but as he found new interests and a new profession, the spiritual dimension of his life began to erode to the point that he even stopped attending Mass.

During this time, one spiritual link remained—he continued to pray the Rosary. He credited this not only with preserving his fading spark of faith, but also as the means by which he was slowly drawn back to the Church and to the priesthood.

In *The Secret of the Rosary*, St. Louis Marie de Montfort writes, "It is not just a conglomeration of Our Fathers and Hail Marys, but on the contrary it is a divine summary of the mysteries of the life, passion, death and glory of Jesus and Mary." It is, as John Paul II said, a compendium of the Gospels, and leads to an intimate relationship with Christ and his Mother.

October 23

Know That You Are Welcome

"Indeed, the very hairs of your head are all numbered. Don't be afraid; you are worth more than many sparrows." (Luke 12:7)

"Not being welcome," writes Fr. Henri Nouwen, "is your greatest fear. It connects with your birth fear, your fear of not being welcome in this life, and your death fear, your fear of not being welcome in the life after this. It is the deep-seated fear that it would have been better if you had not lived."

He continues, "Here you are facing the core of the spiritual battle. Are you going to give in to the forces of darkness that say you are not welcome in this life, or can you trust the voice of the One who came not to condemn you but to set you free from fear? You have to choose for life. At every moment you have to decide to trust the voice that says 'I love you. I knit you together in your mother's womb' " (Psalm 139:13).

Fr. Nouwen concludes, "Everything Jesus is saying to you can be summarized in the words 'Know that you are welcome.' Jesus offers you his own most intimate life with the Father."

■

October 24

The Flowing Light of the Godhead

"Before I finished praying in my heart, Rebekah came out, with her jar on her shoulder. She went down to the spring and drew water, and I said to her, 'Please give me a drink.' " (Genesis 24:45)

Mechthild of Magdeburg (d. 1285) was a medieval mystic and Cistercian nun whose book *The Flowing Light of the Godhead* describes her visions of God. In this prayer she gives us an insight into prayer of the heart:

> That prayer has the greatest power
> Which you make with all your heart.
> It makes a bitter heart grow sweet,
> A sad heart merry,
> A poor heart rich,
> A foolish heart wise,
> A timid heart brave,
> A sick heart well,
> A blind heart full of sight,
> A cold heart fervent.
> It draws the great God down to the little heart,
> It drives the thirsty soul up to the fullness of God.
> It brings together two lovers,
> God and the soul,
> In a wondrous place where they speak much of love.

■

October 25

Francis Spinelli and the Blessed Sacrament

I am the living bread that came down from heaven. If anyone eats of this bread, he will live forever. This bread is my flesh, which I will give for the life of the world. (John 6:51)

Blessed Francis Spinelli (d. 1913), was born in Milan, Italy, and seemed to have a special love for the Blessed Sacrament since his boyhood, when his mother would bring him along when she visited the church, as well as when she helped the poor of the city. Ordained to the priesthood at twenty-two, Father Spinelli began his pastoral vocation by assisting his uncle, Father Peter Cagliaroli, and the Blessed Luigi Palazzolo. In December 1875, during a visit to Rome's Church of Saint Mary Major, Father Spinelli was inspired to found a new religious congregation of women dedicated to Eucharistic adoration that would atone for the indifference of many toward the Real Presence of Christ in the Blessed Sacrament. In establishing the Sisters of Perpetual Adoration of the Blessed Sacrament, with Blessed Gertrude Comensoli, Father Spinelli assigned to the sisters an active apostolate in the service of orphans and other needy children that would flow from their prayer life.

Is there a time during the week when we could pray before the Blessed Sacrament, perhaps before or after Sunday Mass? It would be a time to bring all our problems and concerns to the Lord in a very personal and special way.

> Wherever the Sacred Host is, there is the living God, there is your Savior as truly as when he lived and spoke in Judea, and Galilee, and as truly as he is now in Paradise.
>
> —Charles de Foucauld

October 26

Accepting Forgiveness

This is my blood of the covenant, which is poured out for many for the forgiveness of sins. (Matthew 26:28)

In 1830 a man named George Wilson killed a government employee who caught him in the act of robbing the mails. Thereafter he was tried and later sentenced to be hanged. But through the efforts of family members and friends, he was extended a pardon by the president of the United States, Andrew Jackson. But unaccountably Wilson did a strange thing. He refused to accept the pardon, and no one knew what to do. Thus the case made its way to the Supreme Court.

Chief Justice John Marshall, credited as one of our greatest justices, wrote the court's opinion. He said, "A pardon is a slip of paper, the value of which is determined wholly by the *acceptance* of the person to be pardoned. If it is refused, it is no pardon."

Accepting the gratuitous forgiveness of God can be difficult for some of us, given the weight of guilt that has burdened us in the past. Sometimes pride gets in the way, or that self-hatred that has Satan as its source. But our Lord delights in forgiving his people and endured his passion and death precisely for this. And if we let him, he will replace our guilt and shame with a joyous gratitude.

October 27

Salve Regina

He alone stretches out the heavens and treads on the waves of the sea. (Job 9:8)

In the western seas the last rays of a great red sun spread a final layer of fire over the ocean, and on the scarlet sea, with sails swollen and prows pointed full at the heart of the sunset, sweep three galleons of old Spain. Suddenly on the center ship a small cannon booms. As the ships rise and fall on the breathing ocean, there rises and falls the old hymn of sailors on the sea, "Salve Regina! Hail, Holy Queen!"

This may sound like poetry, but actually it is history. Every sunset, after Columbus put out from Spain, whenever the weather was serene, the admiral reminded his little fleet that it was the hour to honor Our Lady. He was, in fact, sailing these unknown waters under her patronage. The ships bore her colors, pennants of blue and white snapping at the mastheads. Her name was emblazoned on the flagship, but not merely *Santa Maria* as school books have it, but *Santa María de la Imaculada Concepción*—"Saint Mary of the Immaculate Conception." Indeed, the Immaculate Conception came to America with Columbus.

October 28

Time and Eternity

However, as it is written: "No eye has seen, no ear has heard, no mind has conceived what God has prepared for those who love him." (1 Corinthians 2:9)

Needless to say, there has always been tremendous interest in life after death. What will it be like? Will I see my family and friends again? Will I have a body? We know few things for certain, except that we will be sharing God's life in a paradise that is beautiful beyond our imagining. But we also know that at the time of our passing we will also leave the realm of time, into what philosophers call the "eternal now." Since there will be no before or after, we may not recognize any delay between the instant of death and the instant of resurrection in a glorified body, and maybe immediately encounter all our family members and friends who were alive at the time of our death, since we're outside of time. Indeed, they may enter eternity after us in time, but in eternity there is no before or after.

Still, even the great Doctor of the Church, St. Augustine, had a difficult time describing life outside of time. "Those who consider this matter are baffled because of the tough resistance the senses and habit offer," he said. "Who can comprehend this even in a thought, so as to express it in a word? Who can explain this?" In the end, Christ's word is all we need, for where he is, there is love.

October 29

Catholicism and William F. Buckley

For wisdom will enter your heart, and knowledge will be pleasant to your soul. (Proverbs 2:10)

In the avalanche of commentary that marked William F. Buckley's death at the age of eighty-two, perhaps the most striking was the judgment of papal biographer George Weigel: "Bill Buckley may have been the most publicly influential U.S. Catholic of the twentieth century; he would certainly be on any serious list of the top five."

Almost all of what could be considered media for Catholic conservative thought—*First Things*, *InsideCatholic.com*, *Human Life Review*, *Ethics & Public Policy Center*, *The Acton Institute*, *Faith & Reason Institute*, EWTN, and a variety of others—are flourishing in ground first plowed by Buckley.

Another of his major, but often overlooked, Catholic contributions was in making mainstream American conservatism pro-life. In an article for the *National Catholic Register*, Fr. Raymond J. de Souza writes that "In the late 1960s and early 1970s, abortion politics were in transition. The Democratic Party with its heavily Irish Catholic leadership was generally on the side of life—but moving rapidly toward embracing the abortion license. The elite Republican Party of Eisenhower and Rockefeller was generally in favor of abortion liberalization (Reagan himself signed such a law as governor of California). It is generally conceded that without the steadfastness of the Catholic Church in the 1970s there would be no pro-life movement. It is likely that if William Buckley had not been staunchly pro-life himself, the ascendant Republican majority may well have equivocated on the question of abortion."

But beyond his powerful intellect and moral sense, "Bill Buckley was a man of almost inexhaustible curiosity, courtesy, generosity, and delight in the oddness of the human circumstance," said Fr. Richard John Neuhaus, editor of *First Things* and a longtime friend. "He exulted in displaying his many talents, which was not pride so much as an invitation to others to share his amazement at the possibilities in being fully alive."

October 30

Funeral for a Parish

He replied, "Because you have so little faith. I tell you the truth, if you have faith as small as a mustard seed, you can say to this mountain, 'Move from here to there' and it will move. Nothing will be impossible for you."
(Matthew 17:20)

There is a story of a priest who, because he was discouraged by the lack of response and overall indifference within his parish, announced that the church was dead and that the next Sunday, if they wouldn't mind, they would have a funeral. So, of course, the word got around and everyone was very puzzled by it.

The next Sunday, as the parishioners entered the church, they saw an open coffin in the sanctuary. With a straight, solemn face, the pastor invited the people to come up one by one to view the remains. And as they came up to look into the coffin to view the remains of the church that was dead, what they saw in the coffin was a full-length mirror. He certainly got his point across.

Needless to say, the life of a parish is dependent on the people within it, on their good will, cooperation, enthusiasm, and faith. And faith is dead if it is not expressed by good works. This is the example Christ gave us in his earthly life—healing, teaching, nourishing—and the way he has chosen for all his followers.

October 31

The Power of Example

"Now that I, your Lord and Teacher, have washed your feet, you also should wash one another's feet. I have set you an example that you should do as I have done for you." (John 13:14–15)

Loving service to others was a major theme of Christ's ministry on earth, and his example has drawn countless numbers to the faith over the ages.

One such case is Sir Henry Stanley, who in 1871 journeyed to Africa, where he encountered the missionary Dr. David Livingstone (d. 1873) and subsequently spent a few months in his company. Livingstone never spoke to Stanley about spiritual things, but throughout those months Stanley observed the old man.

Livingstone's habits were beyond his comprehension, and so was his patience. He could not understand Livingstone's love for the African people. For the sake of Christ and his gospel, the missionary doctor was patient, untiring, and eager. Stanley wrote, "When I saw that unwearied patience, that unflagging zeal, those enlightened sons of Africa, I became a Christian at his side, though he never spoke to me about it."

■

Feast of All Saints

After this I looked and there before me was a great multitude that no one could count, from every nation, tribe, people and language, standing before the throne and in front of the Lamb. They were wearing white robes and were holding palm branches in their hands. (Revelation 7:9)

Today is a great feast in honor of God's saints, but it is also a reminder of Christ's promise to us, the living, that one day we shall join them in glory. In one sense, we are united with them already in the communion of saints (which we refer to whenever we recite the Apostle's Creed). This is the union of the living, the saints in heaven, and the souls in purgatory, all joined together in a mystical oneness with the Holy Trinity.

Most of the saints are unknown to us, but probably included in that number are some of our relatives and friends who are praying that we will join them in heaven one day. In fact, just as we might ask a friend on earth to pray for us, so we can ask the saints in heaven. In honor of their feast day, it would be appropriate to offer a special prayer of thanksgiving to our patron saint, or to one whom we especially admire.

November 2

All Souls Day

Another book was opened, which is the book of life. The dead were judged according to what they had done as recorded in the books. (Revelation 20:12b)

Especially on All Souls Day, the Church calls us to remember and pray for the souls in purgatory, including our loved ones who have gone before us.

The Church's doctrine of purgatory is too often misunderstood. It is not a place where the residue of sin is remitted through suffering; it is rather a process in which we are perfected until we can unite in harmony with the fullness of love and life, which is God. Just as oil and water cannot mix, so too we must resemble the Spirit of God, free from sin, before entering into his life—the state of existence called heaven.

This process is veiled in mystery, but it is without doubt a benevolent concept, a gift from God who allows us time even after death to gain paradise. It also allows us, the living, to help those who have already died through prayer and the Mass. Those whom we have helped to achieve heaven will in turn help us when the time comes, and this is part of the beauty of the communion of saints, the bond of union with the saints in heaven, the souls in purgatory, and all the living.

November 3

Because God Loves It

Then I said: "O LORD, God of heaven, the great and awesome God, who keeps his covenant of love with those who love him and obey his commands. . . ." (Nehemiah 1:5)

Julian of Norwich (d. 1416) is considered one of the great English mystics. She was a master of the prayer of awe and praise, and the insights of her visions are startling. The following is an example:

God showed me in my palm
a little thing round as a ball
about the size of a hazelnut.

I looked at it with the eye of understanding
and asked myself:
"What is this thing?"
And I was answered: "It is everything that is created."

I wondered how it could survive since it seemed so little
it could suddenly disintegrate into nothing.

The answer came: "It endures and ever will endure,
because God loves it."

And so everything has being
because of God's love.

November 4

The Culture War

See, I am setting before you today a blessing and a curse—the blessing if you obey the commands of the LORD your God that I am giving you today; the curse if you disobey the commands of the LORD your God and turn from the way that I command you today by following other gods, which you have not known. (Deuteronomy 11:26–28).

The dissolution of American culture ranges from politicized education to corporate fraud to abortion on demand. Cheating is almost institutionalized: accounting and brokerage firms swindle their clients; pharmaceutical companies promise unsubstantiated results from their drugs; prized athletes at great universities are kept eligible for competition through bogus credits and forged transcripts of academic records. Children soon acquire the cynical assumption that lying is the normal tack for television advertisers. In the words of a *Time* magazine essay, ours is "a huckstering, show-bizzy world, jangling with hype, hullabaloo, and hooey, bull, baloney, and bamboozlement." After a while, people tend to expect not to hear the truth anymore; a Gallup poll in 2000 found that only 21 percent of Americans felt journalists were honest and ethical.

This is part of what is called the Culture War, a war of values versus secular nihilism. In winning it we must first plan our defense by consciously defining our personal values and, second, advocating those values in our homes, communities, and nation. An essential starting point is to become familiar with Catholic social action, which has many entries on the Internet, including the comprehensive document *Forming Consciences for Faithful Citizenship: A Call to Political Responsibility from the Catholic Bishops of the United States*. We might well keep in mind the famous line of Edmund Burke (d. 1797), who strongly influenced the founders of America: "All that is necessary for the triumph of evil is that good men do nothing."

November 5

The Test of Love

The crucible for silver and the furnace for gold, but the L*ORD tests the heart.* *(Proverbs 17:3)*

In the Northeast of the United States, codfish are a big commercial business. There is a large market for eastern cod, especially in sections farthest removed from the northeast coastline. But the public demand posed a problem to the shippers. At first they froze the cod, then shipped them out, but the freeze took away much of the flavor. So they experimented with shipping them alive, in tanks of seawater, but that proved even worse.

Finally, someone solved the problem in a strange way. The fish were placed in the tank of water along with their natural enemy—the catfish, which chased the cod all over the tank. Consequently, when the cod arrived at the market, they were as fresh as when they were first caught.

Each of us is in a tank of unique and inescapable circumstances. This can be distressing at times, especially when we encounter those God-appointed catfish. But they bring a sufficient tension that keeps us alive, alert, fresh, and growing. It's all part of God's project to shape our character so we will be more like his Son. Although we don't always understand why the catfish are in our tank, we do know that they are part of God's method of producing compassion, character, and trust in our lives.

November 6

Rabbi Leo Beck

Blessed is he
whose transgressions are forgiven,
whose sins are covered.
Blessed is the man
whose sin the LORD does not count against him
and in whose spirit is no deceit.
(Psalm 32:1–2)

Psalm 32 celebrates forgiveness, the love of God that heals and renews our souls. We too are called to forgive one another in imitation of Christ, and this too, takes great love.

Rabbi Leo Beck, a German scholar who took the leadership of German Jews in Hitler's time, testified by his own life to this love. He was five times arrested, and finally sent to a concentration camp, where he served on the convicts' committee of management. According to the English educator F. H. Drinkwater, on the very day he was to have been shot, the Russian troops arrived. Beck could have escaped at once, but stayed behind to argue with the Russians, to persuade them to spare the lives of the German camp guards. And when the Russians decided the guards should be handed over to the inmates, Beck then argued with them and managed to persuade them not to take the vengeance that they were thirsting for.

From St. Augustine (d. 371), one of the church fathers: "There are many kinds of alms, the giving of which helps us to obtain pardon for our sins; but none is greater than that by which we forgive from our heart a sin that someone has committed against us."

November 7
Chaplain Emil Kapaun

Have I not commanded you? Be strong and courageous. Do not be terrified; do not be discouraged, for the LORD your God will be with you wherever you go." (Joshua 1:9)

In 1950 Chaplain Emil Kapaun, a Catholic priest from Kansas, was captured by the Chinese during the Korean War. He was thrown into a prison camp along with some eighty other officers. There he found not only starvation, cruelty, and death, but an atmosphere of despair.

Fr. Kapaun changed the picture. As he worked and prayed, he persuaded the other prisoners to follow his example, no matter what their faith or lack of it. He shared his own meager food and even stole food for the starving. They dubbed him "The Good Thief." He bandaged their wounds, washed the clothing of the weak, and cared for the sick. He held dying men in his arms and later buried them. He refuted the brainwashing tactics of the Communists, bearing their threats and punishments with patience and love.

Starvation and disease led to his death in May 1951. When his fellow prisoners were released some months later, all they could talk about was this heroic priest. "He was the bravest and kindest man I ever knew," a fellow prisoner said. A number of them testified that if Chaplain Kapaun could live and die with such love, it must in great measure be due to his great faith. Fifteen of the chaplain's fellow prisoners were later baptized into the Catholic faith.

The archdiocese for military affairs is seriously considering taking up the cause of his beatification.

■

November 8

Never Too Late

"Do not be afraid," Samuel replied. "You have done all this evil; yet do not turn away from the LORD, but serve the LORD with all your heart."
(1 Samuel 12:20)

Over and over again, the saints and theologians of the church have reminded us that it is never too late to turn to Christ in full faith and commitment. The English poet Alfred, Lord Tennyson wrote of the new horizons that await even those who have been "made weak by time and fate":

I am a part of all that I have met;
yet all experience is an arch wherethrough
gleams that untraveled world whose margin fades
for ever and for ever when I move.
How dull it is to pause, to make an end,
to rust unburnished, not to shine in use!
As though to breathe were life. Life piled on life
were all too little. . . .
Come, my friends,
'tis not too late to seek a newer world.
Push off, and sitting well in order smite
the sounding furrows; for my purpose holds
to sail beyond the sunset, and the baths
of all the western stars, until I die.

It may be the gulfs will wash us down;
it may be we shall touch the Happy Isles,
and see the great Achilles, whom we knew.

Though much is taken, much bides; and though
we are not now that strength which in old days
moved earth and heaven, that which we are, we are;
one equal temper of heroic hearts,
made weak by time and fate, but strong in will
to strive, to seek, to find, and not to yield.

November 9

Greatest of Gifts

The Blessed Sacrament was pre-figured in the Old Testament:
A tabernacle was set up. In the first room were the lampstand, the table and the consecrated bread; this was called the Holy Place. (Hebrews 9:2)

Archbishop Joseph Dimino tells the poignant story of Fr. Anthony Conway, who bore witness to the Blessed Sacrament in a profound and terrible way.

In July 1944 Fr. Conway was with a large contingent of marines on a ship off the coast of Japanese-held Guam. They would land at dawn the next day as the invasion began. After Mass that afternoon, he placed as many hosts as possible in a gold pyx (a small container for the Eucharist). Several years earlier he had mentioned to a group of other Catholic chaplains that he did not believe it irreverent, as someone suggested, to take the Blessed Sacrament with him on upcoming island assaults. He said simply, "If I have to go into combat with my marines, I want Our Lord right there with us."

The next morning Fr. Conway placed the cord holding the pyx around his neck, under his uniform. With his marines he was transferred to a landing craft, and as it approached the beach there was heavy shellfire all around. When it hit the beach, he and his men quickly waded ashore. But as he first stepped on dry sand, an enemy shell exploded almost precisely where he stood.

Another priest in the contingent rushed to the spot to see if he could help, but discovered that the priest had disintegrated in the explosion. All that was found was his right hand, severed at the wrist. When his fingers were opened, in his hand was found the golden pyx containing the holy Eucharist.

He had held on to what had been most precious to him, and in the miracle of the surviving Sacrament we too are called to hold closely to our hearts this greatest of gifts.

November 10

Love on File

But I trust in your unfailing love; my heart rejoices in your salvation. (Psalm 13:5)

After several years in parish ministry, Fr. Mulligan went to his file cabinet to pull out the "Love" file. He discovered he didn't have one. Impossible! It must be misfiled. He searched among Faith and Fasting, between Healing and Heaven. Perhaps it was sandwiched between Christology and Christian Ed. After all, these have to do with Love, don't they? But it wasn't there, nor was it found after Money or ahead of Missions.

When he stopped to reflect, the Holy Spirit solved the mystery. The Love file was scattered, yet not misfiled. Parts of it were found under Patience, Kindness, Humility, Trust, Hope, Loyalty, and Perseverance. But the pastor found the greatest part of the Love file, squarely centered and deeply seated, in Forgiveness.

In the words of French Cardinal François De La Rochefoucauld (d. 1645), "We pardon in the degree that we love."

■

November 11

Feast of St. Martin of Tours

There will always be poor people in the land. Therefore I command you to be openhanded toward your brothers and toward the poor and needy in your land. (Deuteronomy 15:11)

In the winter of AD 334 Martin of Tours was riding with his regiment through the snow and slush into the city of Amiens, in the Roman district of Gaul. Crowds had gathered to watch the soldiers coming in, worn and weary, with sodden equipment, ragged cloaks and uniforms. As they passed through the city gate, a young Roman officer dismounted. He'd seen a poor man among the crowd, nearly naked, blue with cold, holding out a trembling hand for alms. The officer flung off his cloak, and drawing his sword, cut it in two. Gently he wrapped one half of it around the shivering shoulders of the beggar.

That night, as he lay asleep in his billet, he saw a vision—the one-half of a military cloak. And he heard a voice that asked him to look at it carefully, and whether he had seen it before. As he looked, he expected to see beneath the cloak the features of the shivering beggar at the city gate, but was startled to see Jesus himself.

This was the sign that changed Martin's life from that of a warrior to one of the great teachers of the church, rivaling St. Paul in his enthusiasm and travels throughout the Roman world. He was later elected bishop of Tours and was the most venerated saint during the Middle Ages.

November 12
The Church as Family and Refuge

I am the vine; you are the branches. If a man remains in me and I in him, he will bear much fruit; apart from me you can do nothing. (John 15:5)

The great Russian novelist Leo Tolstoy told the story of a man who stopped to give alms to a beggar. To his dismay, he found that he had left his money at home. Stammering his explanation, he said, "I'm sorry, brother, but I don't have anything." "Never mind, brother," was the beggar's answer, "that too was a gift." It seems that the word "brother" meant even more to him than the money.

One of the finest things about our Church is the care and concern we have for one another. In a real sense, we are all brothers and sisters. We have a stake in each other's salvation, and we have learned from the gospel to value and strengthen each other. Our Church becomes our family, our fortress, and our refuge.

There is a wedding prayer that says, "Now our joys are doubled, because the happiness of one is also the happiness of the other. Now our burdens are cut in half, since when we share them we divide the load." As members of the universal as well as the local church, we double our joys and cut our burdens in half. We become a family, the body of Christ, instead of isolated individuals.

November 13

You Have Made Us for Yourself

David and all the Israelites were celebrating with all their might before God, with songs and with harps, lyres, tambourines, cymbals and trumpets.
(1 Chronicles 13:8)

St. Augustine (d. 430) was a philosopher, a theologian, and the bishop of the North African city of Hippo during the last third of his life. He is one of the most important figures in the development of Western Christianity and is honored as a church father. He framed the concepts of original sin and the just war theory, and is a preeminent Doctor of the Church and the patron of the Augustinian religious order. The following is one of his most famous prayers:

> How great you are, O Lord, and how greatly to be praised!
> How incomparable is your power and how infinite your understanding.
> We may be but a speck in your vast creation,
> but we want to praise you.
> We may carry around with us our mortality and our sin as mute testimony to the truth that
> "God resists the proud," but even so we want to praise your name.
> You have thrilled us by giving us delight in your praise.
> You have made us for yourself, O Lord,
> and our hearts are restless until they rest in you.

November 14
The Virgin's Crown

"[F]or the Mighty One has done great things for me—holy is his name." (Luke 1:49)

After Pizarro's conquest of Peru in 1532, his followers founded the town of Popayán, which became immensely wealthy. Fifty years later a plague struck the city, killing hundreds of Spaniards and natives. The people made a novena to the Blessed Virgin, and to their amazement the city was saved. To express their gratitude they resolved to make the Virgin the finest crown in the world. They gathered over 100 pounds of gold and 453 emeralds, weighing 1,532 carats. The goldsmiths were given but one order: "The crown must exceed in beauty, in grandeur and in value the crown of any reigning monarch on earth, for it is destined as a gift to the Queen of heaven." On the eve of the Immaculate Conception, December 8, 1599, the richest crown in the world—15 inches high and 12 inches in diameter—was placed upon the head of the Virgin Mother. Every year on the anniversary, the people of Popayán placed the crown anew upon the head of their protectress. Often they had to fight off bandits and pirates who wanted to steal the priceless treasure. It was fittingly called "The Crown of the Immaculate Conception."

November 15
The Role of Adversity

Although the Lord gives you the bread of adversity and the water of affliction, your teachers will be hidden no more; with your own eyes you will see them. Whether you turn to the right or to the left, your ears will hear a voice behind you, saying, "This is the way; walk in it." (*Isaiah* 30:20–21)

Carlo Carretto's *Letters from the Desert* share the thoughts of a person who went into the desert to learn to pray. In one chapter, Carretto says that he often lost his way in the desert during the day "because the sun was too high in the sky." But at night he found his way again, "guided by the stars."

The same is true of our journey to God. We can sometimes lose our way during the day, when we walk in the sunlight of prosperity. But we rediscover our own way again at night, when we walk in the starlight of adversity. It was adversity that brought the centurion to Christ. A deeply Christian question for us is whether we look upon adversity as a stepping-stone or a stumbling block to God.

November 16
37 Pennies

No one can serve two masters. Either he will hate the one and love the other, or he will be devoted to the one and despise the other. You cannot serve both God and Money. (*Matthew* 6:24)

There is a story about a young man who found a silver dollar. From that time on he never raised his eyes from the ground when he walked. In the next thirty years, he accumulated $3.50 in silver, 37 pennies, 18,478 buttons, 14,369 pins, a hunched back, a miserly character, and a rotten disposition. He lost the beauty and glory of the sunshine, the smiles of friends, the glorious colors and beauty of flowers and trees, blue skies, and all there is that makes life worthwhile.

So keep your head up, your eyes towards the stars. You may miss finding a few pennies, but you will find all the beautiful things that make life a wonderful adventure. In the end, we can serve only one master, as Christ reminds us today. In our consumer society, it is easy to become obsessed by money and the things it will buy. This is the danger, the materialistic trap, that we are warned of today. As Paul says in his letter to Timothy, "For the love of money is a root of all kinds of evil. Some people, eager for money, have wandered from the faith and pierced themselves with many griefs" (1 Timothy 6:10).

■

November 17

Miracle Flight

So God created the great creatures of the sea and every living and moving thing with which the water teems, according to their kinds, and every winged bird according to its kind. And God saw that it was good. (Genesis 1:21)

The Manx Shearwater, a seagull-like bird, makes its home in tiny holes in a cliff on an island off the coast of Wales. One day a researcher caught one of these birds, put a band on its leg, and had it flown 3,000 miles to Boston. There it was released by another researcher. Twelve and a half days later, it showed up again at the exact tiny hole from which it was taken.

Scientists still can't figure out how these birds have acquired such a remarkable power of navigation. The most logical answer is the one given in today's reading: they are creations of God, who simply gave them this remarkable power.

■

November 18

Brother Gerard

How great are his signs,
how mighty his wonders!
His kingdom is an eternal kingdom;
his dominion endures from generation to generation.
(Daniel 4:3)

For over thirty years I have taken retreats at New Melleray Trappist Monastery in the countryside near Dubuque, Iowa. One of the monks I came to know well was Brother Gerard McDonough, a great grizzly bear of a man with the heart of a little boy. At one time he was the beekeeper, producing the honey that was sold to help support the abbey.

Now and then we took walks in the woods and hills surrounding the monastery, always stopping at the beehives where Brother Gerard would elaborate on the art of beekeeping. Sadly, Gerard had several minor heart attacks, but he said even these were blessings, since he had a "life-after-life" experience of floating out of his body and watching the doctors work to resuscitate him. "During that time," he said, "I've never felt so much love and peace."

Several years later Gerard had his final heart attack and passed on to the God he loved so much. When I heard about his death, I was about to offer Mass. It was a freezing day in February, and the city of Davenport, Iowa, was covered in ice and snow. During the Mass, as I elevated the host after the consecration, a honeybee from out of nowhere landed on my hand. It stayed there until I elevated the chalice, when it flew up and landed on the edge of the cup, remaining for several minutes until it just disappeared. I think my friend the beekeeper was sending a greeting from heaven. The chances are ten to one that you've had a similar experience, and have come to believe like so many Christians that there are no coincidences.

November 19

The Paradox of Life

"Gather to me my consecrated ones, who made a covenant with me by sacrifice." (Psalm 50:5)

Only if we adore something beyond ourselves will we stop adoring ourselves. Pierre Teilhard de Chardin (d. 1955), philosopher and Jesuit priest, said as much when he wrote that we reach moral maturity on the day we realize that we really only have one choice in life: to genuflect before something higher or begin to self-destruct.

Simone Weil (d. 1943), French philosopher, mystic, and social activist, agreed with de Chardin. Despite being a fierce defendant of independence and private conscience, she makes it clear that the deepest need within the human soul is that of being obedient to something beyond ourselves. Without this, she states, we inflate and become absurd, even to ourselves.

We know the truth of this through experience. We feel within ourselves a constant, congenital press toward a healthy self-abnegation and the adoration of something higher than ourselves. We feel good about ourselves only when we don't put ourselves at the center of the world, and we feel right about what we are doing only when we are giving our lives away, when our lives are not about ourselves.

From this, we see that we are built for altruism and, ultimately, for martyrdom. Within the secret of life lies a great paradox—we experience the true meaning of life only when we are dying to ourselves and giving life away.

November 20

Japanese Hell Ship

[A]s servants of God we commend ourselves in every way: in great endurance; in troubles, hardships and distresses; in beatings, imprisonments and riots; in hard work, sleepless nights and hunger. (*2 Corinthians 6:4–5*)

January 1945: Scene: aboard the *Brazil Maru*, one of the Japanese hell ships bringing American POWs from the Philippines to Japan. It was a final move for the soldiers captured three years earlier, having endured the Bataan death march and brutal slave labor. The crowded conditions were horrible. Weakened, emaciated men were rapidly dying of starvation and disease.

Army chaplain Fr. Bill Cummings had stood with his men throughout the ordeal and was greatly loved for his indomitable spirit. So deep and persistent were his daily devotions with the men that even unbelievers stood in respect as he spoke. In Bataan, Father Bill was credited with the line, "There are no atheists in fox holes." Each evening in the ship's stifling hold there was stillness and quiet as he began "Our Father, who art in heaven. . . ." Many joined the prayer, having been convinced by him that God would listen.

As long as his strength lasted, the chaplain moved among the prisoners, offering the last rites and prayers for the dying. Their particular creeds were unimportant to him. When he became too weak to move about, his voice could still be heard praying for his fellow prisoners.

Standing in place, with the support of a friend on each side, he offered morning and evening prayers for the men. Finally, unable to rise at all, with his back braced against a fellow prisoner, he died with the words, "Give us this day . . ." on his lips. Years later, a book with that phrase for a title was written by Sidney Stewart, a witness to the scene.

November 21

The Presentation of Mary

Some of his disciples were remarking about how the temple was adorned with beautiful stones and with gifts dedicated to God. (Luke 21:5a)

The following is a very personal reflection on today's feast day by Pope John XXIII given at a public audience in St. Peter's Square on February 2, 1960.

> Today's celebration of Mary's Presentation in the Temple reminds me of an incident in my childhood when I was taken by my mother to visit a small shrine dedicated to Mary, built on land belonging to my native village, where the Mother of God is honored with special devotion on this feast day. The little sanctuary, called *alle Caneve*, is set among trees at the end of a country lane.
>
> When I arrived with my mother at the tiny chapel, we could not go in because it was so full of people, and so the only way to see the revered statue of Our Lady was through one of the two windows, both high up and barred, on either side of the entrance door. So my loving mother lifted me in her arms, saying, "Look, Angelo, look at Our Lady! It's Our Lady's Feast Day, November twenty-first—Holy Mary presented at the temple."
>
> This is my first clear and most vivid memory of my childhood and of my mother. What sweet and profound joy I feel in the thought that it is a memory of an act of devotion to our heavenly Mother!

November 22

Pius VIII and the Rosary

But I will sing of your strength,
in the morning I will sing of your love;
for you are my fortress,
my refuge in times of trouble.
(Psalm 59:16)

One day, in a simpler age when popes could walk unguarded, Pius VIII was on his way from one wing of the Vatican to another. As he passed through the Vatican art gallery, there was the inevitable knot of tourists gazing at the glowing masterpieces and Grecian marbles. The pontiff paused and smiled. "Beautiful, aren't they?" he asked. "Oh, Holy Father, they're magnificent!" "Would you like to see the greatest treasure of the Vatican?" "Oh yes, of course!"

Pius VIII shrugged his old shoulders and smiled. "I'm a simple man, and to me the most precious treasure in all these gilded halls is right here." And then he opened his palm, and there lay a worn wooden rosary that he had been praying on his way through the long corridors. He may have remembered how often, burdened with the anxieties of Church and state, he would slip into his private chapel and let these beads slowly slip through his fingers, and somehow the wisdom and strength he needed was given in abundance.

November 23

The Passions

At one time we too were foolish, disobedient, deceived and enslaved by all kinds of passions and pleasures. We lived in malice and envy, being hated and hating one another. (Titus 3:3)

In spiritual literature, the term *passions* refers to any powerful or uncontrollable emotion, such as hatred, anger, lust, or vengeance. There is a story that speaks of this:

During the last century a group of young English officers went big-game hunting in East Africa. One of them shot a lioness, and afterward, finding her cubs, took them back to his Norfolk home. He fed them by hand until they could feed themselves, and every day used to romp and play with them. As they grew their play sometimes got a little rough, but still the young man amused himself with his unusual pets.

Then the time came when it was considered wise to have the animals confined in a cage with iron bars, but their owner persisted in going into their cage to play with them as before. He disregarded the warnings of those who feared the lions' strength, until one evening, when the animals were almost full grown, the young man went to visit them as usual. Dusk was falling, and as their owner closed the barred door of the cage behind him, one of the beasts made a spring at him. Before help could reach him, the young man was dead, killed by the pets he had pampered.

Sacred Scripture as well as the church's great spiritual masters tell us that if we do not gain mastery over our passions and keep them under control, they will eventually enslave us. Our freedom is far too precious to surrender to the worst within us.

November 24

Forgiveness

Therefore, my brothers, I want you to know that through Jesus the forgiveness of sins is proclaimed to you. (Acts 13:38)

Because of lingering guilt and perhaps shame, the gift of divine forgiveness can be hard to accept. Often we feel unworthy of it and can't quite believe that the sins of the past are truly forgiven by God. And yet this is the key to the great unburdening and freedom of spirit that Our Lord wants us to experience so that we may be his joyful witnesses.

In this vein, there is a story from the Middle Ages about a mystic who had experienced several apparitions of Christ. After relating this to her confessor, he asked, "Sister, did you talk with him?" She said, "Yes, by his wonderful grace." The priest continued, "The Church is very cautious in such matters. But for the sake of confirmation, ask the Lord this question when he next appears to you: 'What was my confessor's great sin before he became a priest?' " He knew that only God and his own confessor would know.

About three months later, the sister made an appointment to again see the priest. When she came in he asked, "Did you see our Lord again?"

"Yes, I did."

"Did you ask him the question about my sin?"

"Yes, I did."

"And what did he say?"

She smiled and answered, "He said, 'I don't remember.' "

November 25
The Resurgence of Darkness

The idols speak deceit,
diviners see visions that lie;
they tell dreams that are false,
they give comfort in vain.
Therefore the people wander like sheep
oppressed for lack of a shepherd.
(Zechariah 10:2)

In 1996 the Italian bishops expressed their concern over what they saw as a resurgence of Satanism, fortune-telling, witchcraft, and black magic. The Italian bishops' conference, meeting in plenary assembly at the Vatican, explained in an official statement that this new phenomenon is promoted because of its "resonance" in the media, and the "unhealthy interest" it awakens.

Their comments came as they reviewed the Italian translation of the new Ritual of Exorcism. "We are witnessing a rebirth of divinations, fortune telling, witchcraft and black magic, often combined with a superstitious use of religion," the bishops' statement said. They said they were especially worried about the "resurgence of an unhealthy interest in the sphere of the demonic."

The bishops believed that the spread of these ideas leads people to lose confidence in God and to "instrumentalize" God "according to man's immediate interests." "All this offends the dignity and liberty of the person, as man becomes subject to dark, impersonal forces, psychological dependencies and moral degradation."

We should be aware that evil exists and can manifest itself in many ways, from subtle temptations to witchcraft to genocide. Indeed, the reason Christ became man was to defeat Satan, and he says this several times in the Gospels. We, too, are called to defeat darkness in our lives through regular prayer and the sacraments, especially the Eucharist. It is in developing a healthy spiritual life that we shield ourselves from what might hurt or even destroy us.

November 26

The Sari

Give, and it will be given to you. A good measure, pressed down, shaken together and running over, will be poured into your lap. For with the measure you use, it will be measured to you. (Luke 6:38)

In the following story, Mother Teresa speaks of one special lady who wanted to share in her work with the poor. But reading between the lines, we can see that she is also challenging us in our own charity:

> Once a very rich Hindu lady came to see me. She sat down and said, "You know, Mother, I want to share in your work." (More and more people are saying that in India now.) I said that was wonderful. But she admitted a fault and said, "You know, I love beautiful saris." (She was wearing a very expensive sari costing 800 rupees.) "I go every month and buy one."
>
> I prayed a little bit to our Lady to give her the right answer as to how she could share in our work. I said, "I'd better begin with the sari. You know, the next time when you go to buy a sari, instead of buying one for 800 rupees, you can buy a sari for 500 rupees and with the remaining 300 you can buy saris for the poor people."
>
> And so, this generous lady has come down to paying 100 for a sari. I have told her, "Please do not go below 100!" She said it had changed her life. She began to really understand sharing. And she has told me that she has received much more than she has given.

Charity and simplicity of life allow us to concentrate on what is really important in life: faith, family, friends, works of love and other things that bring us fulfillment and not just passing pleasure. It's hard to fight against a consumer culture, but what price can we place on peace of mind?

November 27
War and Peace

Let us therefore make every effort to do what leads to peace and to mutual edification. (Romans 14:19)

The Church often reminds us that peace is the responsibility of each individual—to pray for it, to live it in our lives, and to carry it to others. It is the only way to defeat the violence of our age.

But for those caught in such violence, the God of peace draws especially close even in the midst of it, as this true story from Archbishop Joseph Dimino illustrates.

It was Sunday morning at a Navy chapel in the Pacific. Fr. John Connelly, a chaplain at the post, was offering Mass attended by about 400 soldiers and officers. During his sermon he spoke on the subject of death and eternity.

He told the story of a group of doughboys during World War I who were moving into a dangerous area of the French countryside, passing on their way a roadside shrine—a Pietà, a statue of the Blessed Mother with the crucified Savior in her arms.

Several of the boys could be heard whispering a prayer as they trekked by. For some it would be a last prayer. An enormous explosion was followed by a fierce fireball that lasted several hours. Afterward the carnage was everywhere, and yet several noticed that the Pietà was still standing. But the body of Christ in his mother's arms had been shattered during the battle.

The arms of the Blessed Mother, however, were not empty. For they held the body of a young American soldier . . . blown into the embrace of the Mother of God.

One of the doughboys said, "When I go, I hope she'll be as close. . . ."

"Know that she will be with you always," Fr. Connelly said from the pulpit, "especially in your most dire need." It was about that time when the assembled men heard a distant roar of planes followed by explosive shellfire. It was the morning of December 7, 1941, and for many men in the Pearl Harbor chapel, the story of the Madonna and the fallen soldier would be the last they would hear.

November 28

The Clay and the Rose

But now that you have been set free from sin and have become slaves to God, the benefit you reap leads to holiness, and the result is eternal life.
(Romans 6:22)

One day a man found a piece of clay, which surprisingly had the delightful fragrance of a sweet rose. The man asked: "Piece of clay, tell me what you are. Are you a costly jewel, a rich gem, or some magic stone in disguise?"

"No," laughingly replied the clay, "I am only a poor piece of common clay."

"Then where does your wonderful fragrance come from?"

"Friend," the clay answered, "I will tell you the secret: I have been living near a rose."

Perhaps we can all relate to the adage that faith is not so much taught, but caught, as we remember the people in our lives who had a goodness, love, or tenderness that affected us deeply. We can't help absorbing this goodness, especially when growing up. Now we too, with the grace of God, are affecting others in the same way. This is the primary meaning of that abstract phrase, "building up the kingdom of God," which in reality is a very personal and often unconscious mission.

November 29

A Window to Evil

[An]d the evil spirits came out and went into the pigs. The herd, about two thousand in number, rushed down the steep bank into the lake and were drowned. (Mark 5:13)

As we see, Jesus brings about the healing of the demon-possessed man by commanding the legion of demons to enter the swine. By this action, he revealed his identity as the Son of God, who has authority even over the powers of hell. Later, through his cross and resurrection, he would win the ultimate victory over these powers, but until his kingdom is fully established, we will all battle the power and influence of sin and evil.

New attention has been given to the alarming spread of demonic evil in our time through the publication of *An Exorcist Tells His Story*, by Fr. Gabriel Amorth, the official exorcist for the Diocese of Rome, appointed by John Paul II. He believes that through prayer and discernment, we can often recognize activities in which the demonic is involved. Besides the raw occult, Satan can subtly use a number of channels to influence us, including spiritism, horoscopes, mediums, Ouija boards, the New Age movement, and the like, which open a window to evil. Out of concern and love for her children, the Church has always condemned such practices as contrary to the teaching and spirit of Christ, who alone is the way, the truth, and the life.

November 30

The Contemplative Orders

"Martha, Martha," the Lord answered, "you are worried and upset about many things, but only one thing is needed. Mary has chosen what is better, and it will not be taken away from her." (Luke 10:41–42)

Among the contemplative orders within the Church are the Carmelites, the Poor Clares, and the Trappists. The essential aspect of their mission, according to Thomas Merton, is "kneeling to hold the world before the Most High, and the Most High before the world." They pray for the needs of others, the Church, and the entire world.

These are men and women who consecrate themselves completely to God, taking solemn vows of poverty, chastity, and obedience. In an atmosphere of prayerful silence, they rise at 3:30 AM and gather seven times a day for the Liturgy of the Hours. They combine prayer and study with manual labor; they abstain from television and radio, eat a vegetarian diet, and frequently fast. They seek to maintain a continuous consciousness of Christ and, although it seems implausible in the world's eyes, often experience a peace that is "beyond the world's understanding," as St. Paul put it. All contemplative orders maintain retreat centers for those who seek spiritual renewal, an important part of their mission.

Above all, their prayer and sacrifices are for us, for the salvation of the entire human family, in direct imitation of Christ. They are a great sign to the world, a sacrament, that this God of love is worth devoting your entire life to, radically and joyfully. They are, as Paul VI said, a tremendous gift to mankind.

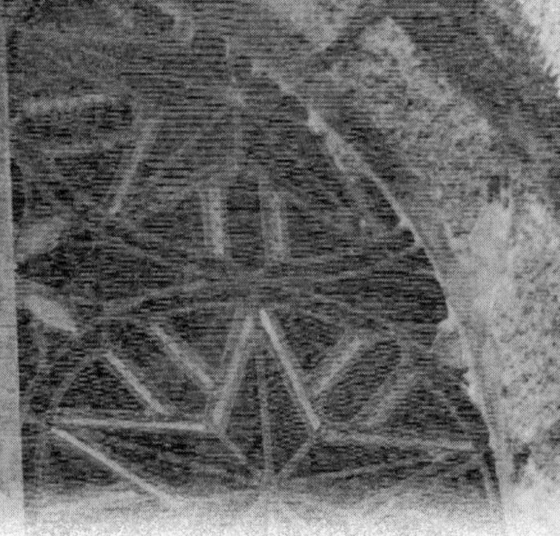

DECEMBER

December 1

John Paul II on Devotion to Mary

And Mary said:
"My soul glorifies the Lord
and my spirit rejoices in God my Savior,
for he has been mindful
of the humble state of his servant.
From now on all generations will call me blessed,
for the Mighty One has done great things for me—
holy is his name."
(Luke 1:46–49)

Authentic Marian devotion is based on Scripture and tradition and leads believers to a closer relationship with Jesus, Pope John Paul II said. True Catholic devotion to Mary "must be far from every form of superstition and hollow credulity," the pope said on September 24, 1992, celebrating the Jubilee of Marian Shrines and closing an international Marian congress.

Apparitions of Mary and other "extraordinary manifestations which the Blessed Virgin often loves to give us for the good of the people of God," he said, must be welcomed "in harmony with ecclesiastical discernment." People who are truly devoted to Mary try to imitate her, "by making their lives a continual journey toward holiness." In addition, "true devotion to Mary should lead people to echo her praise of God the Father, Son and Holy Spirit."

"Although she was the mother of God's only Son and enjoyed a special relationship with God and with the Holy Spirit, she was still human and faced all the hardships of earthly life," he said. "So her spiritual greatness does not place her beyond the reach of modern men and women. She has traveled our path and is in solidarity with us on our pilgrimage of faith."

December 2

The Prayer of Quiet

See, I am setting before you today a blessing and a curse.
(Deuteronomy 11:26)

Fr. Thomas Keating, one of the great spiritual masters of our time, has written that every human being has the amazing potential to become divine, but at the same time each of us has to contend with the historical evolution of our nature from lower forms of consciousness.

There is a tendency in human nature to reach out for more life, more happiness, more of God; but there are also self-destructive tendencies that want to go back to the unconscious and instinctual behavior of our sinful natures. That aspect of the human condition is always lurking within us. Archbishop Fulton Sheen wrote, "Barbarism is not behind us but beneath us." In other words, violence and the other instinctual drives remain as seeds that can develop, if unchecked, into all kinds of evil. We have to come to grips with these tendencies in order for the fullness of grace to flow through us. Prayer, especially the Prayer of Quiet, in which we rest quietly and wordlessly in the presence of God, fosters the healing of these wounds, and allows the peace of God to inundate our entire being, drawing us apart from any evil that lurks within.

December 3

Santa Claus Anonymous

But a poor widow came and put in two very small copper coins, worth only a fraction of a penny. Calling his disciples to him, Jesus said, "I tell you the truth, this poor widow has put more into the treasury than all the others."
(Mark 12:42–43)

Several years ago a thirteen-year-old boy who attended Mohawk Central School at Paines Hollow in New York heard an appeal for contributions to Santa Claus Anonymous, a group that provides gifts for unfortunate children who otherwise would go without Christmas presents. The boy struggled to save a few pennies for this purpose.

On the Friday before Christmas vacation he had fifteen cents and planned to turn in this small treasure at the school that day. But a furious blizzard blasted the area that Friday and the school buses couldn't run. So the boy waded a considerable distance through deep snow to give his fifteen cents to the school principal. The principal found it difficult to control his emotions as he accepted the gift, for the youngster was one of the destitute children listed to receive a Christmas gift from Santa Claus Anonymous.

May this little boy inspire us, as Mother Teresa said, to "give until it hurts." We are then clearly imaging Jesus Christ, who gave everything. We will be surprised to see that whatever we pour out of ourselves, he immediately fills up again, and more besides.

December 4

The Incarnation

In his first letter, Peter speaks of spiritual preparedness:

Therefore, rid yourselves of all malice and all deceit, hypocrisy, envy, and slander of every kind. Like newborn babies, crave pure spiritual milk, so that by it you may grow up in your salvation. (1 Peter 2:1–2)

If we could only understand the awesomeness of the Incarnation," Mother Angelica once said on her television show, "we would at the same time become very, very humble." Advent is essentially a reflection on God's fathomless love, a love that would impel him to take the form of one of his own creatures, emptying himself and, as St. Paul says, "taking the form of a slave." It was the greatest act of humility that creation has ever witnessed. "And try to understand that he would have done this for you alone," Mother continued, "because we are so unimaginably precious to Him."

The awesome event of the Incarnation cannot be understood except through prayerful reflection, in times of quiet that allow us to touch the core of this great mystery. Spiritual reading often leads into this reflective prayer. Since God's love was the sole motivation for the Incarnation, Mother Angelica advised that we give Christ one special gift at Christmas: "Give him yourself. Tell Jesus your gift to him is yourself—your gratitude, your trust, your love. It's what he wants most of all."

December 5

"No One Is More Beautiful"

For God, who said, "Let light shine out of darkness," made his light shine in our hearts to give us the light of the knowledge of the glory of God in the face of Christ. (*2 Corinthians 4:6*)

One cold December morning in Russia in 1849, twenty political prisoners were lined up to be shot by a firing squad. But just before the order was given, an officer rode up, shouting, "Stop! Stop!" It seems Czar Nicholas I had just commuted their sentence to ten years of hard labor in Siberia.

One of the prisoners was a young man named Feodor Dostoevsky. His mother died when he was only sixteen; his father was murdered a few years later. When Dostoevsky got to Siberia, he found a copy of the New Testament and began to read it. By the time he finished it, he was a firm believer. Describing his impression of Christ, he wrote to a friend: "No one is more beautiful or more perfect than Christ. . . . If anyone proved to me that Christ was outside of the truth, I would prefer to remain outside with Christ than inside with the truth."

After his release from prison, Dostoevsky turned to writing novels. In quick succession he wrote such classics as *Crime and Punishment* and *The Brothers Karamazov*. He is celebrated as one of Russia's greatest authors.

December 6

The Dynamic of Conversion

[I]f you confess with your mouth, "Jesus is Lord," and believe in your heart that God raised him from the dead, you will be saved. For it is with your heart that you believe and are justified, and it is with your mouth that you confess and are saved. (*Romans* 10:9–10)

Conversion often takes place when we experience helplessness, the conviction that we can't go on without some kind of divine help. In our desperation we reach out to God, who then has our consent to enter our lives and change everything. The experience can be the result of a personal or family tragedy, alcoholism or addiction, an accident, or any number of things that can bring us to the point of despair, including the experience of war and combat.

During the Second World War, the famous American pilot Captain Eddie Rickenbacker was flying on a special mission to the Pacific Islands. The plane crashed, and Rickenbacker and his crew were lost at sea for three harrowing weeks. He wrote of the experience: "In the beginning many of the men were atheists or agnostics, but at the end of the terrible ordeal each, in his own way, discovered God. Each man found God in the vast, empty loneliness of the ocean. Each man found salvation and strength in prayer, and a community of feeling developed which created a liveliness of human fellowship and worship, and a sense of gentle peace."

Prayer

Lord Jesus, help me to see how you bring good out of evil, how you can use a tragedy, disappointment, or conflict to bear the fruit of conversion or deeper faith in my life. All suffering and pain have meaning and inestimable value when given to you and linked to your cross. Help me to remember this in times of trouble. Amen.

December 7

In God's Underground

Now make confession to the LORD, the God of your fathers, and do his will. (Ezra 10:11a)

In 1964 the Communist government of Romania released a number of political and religious prisoners, one of whom was Fr. Richard Wurmbrand, a parish priest. He had spent fourteen years in prison, three of them in solitary confinement. In his book *In God's Underground*, he describes his experience.

His cell was a dark basement room with no windows; a bare bulb illuminated it twenty-four hours a day. His bed was a rough straw mattress on top of three planks. There were no toilet facilities, and he had to depend on the guards, who sometimes made him wait for hours, laughing at his physical discomfort.

One night Fr. Wurmbrand was startled by a faint tapping on the wall next to his bed. A new prisoner had arrived in the cell next door and was signaling him. Wurmbrand tapped back. This provoked a fury of taps. After a while, Wurmbrand realized that his neighbor was trying to teach him a simple code: one tap is A, two taps is B, three taps is C, and so on. From this crude beginning, his neighbor, who was a radio operator, taught him Morse code.

Fr. Wurmbrand told the radio operator that he himself was a pastor. He then asked the operator if he had a particular faith. There was a long silence. Finally, the radio operator tapped back, "I cannot say so."

Every night the two men spoke through the wall, getting better acquainted. Finally, one night the radio operator tapped out a strange message. It read: "I should like to confess my sins." Fr. Wurmbrand was deeply moved by the request. The confession took a long time, often interrupted by periods of silence, and extended far into the night. When the radio operator finished, Wurmbrand was deeply moved and slowly tapped back the words of absolution. It was a dramatic moment for both men. Then the radio operator tapped through the wall the words: "I am happier at this moment than I have been in many years."

December 8

Shared Joy

When the Gentiles heard this, they were glad and honored the word of the Lord; and all who were appointed for eternal life believed. The word of the Lord spread through the whole region. (Acts 13:48–49)

Of all the qualities that draw others to Christ, it is our inner joy that tends to be the most effective.

I recall one night, soon after my ordination, when I was called to the hospital. As I was walking down the darkened corridor, with no one around, a woman suddenly ran out of one of the patient rooms. She ran up to me—I had never seen her before—and she said joyfully, "He's going to make it. He's better. He's going to make it!" and then made her way on down the hall. I have not seen her since. I'm not sure who she was talking about, but I suspect it was her husband, and that she had just received good news. She couldn't wait to share it. She didn't even have to know the person with whom she shared it; it just flowed from her because she was overjoyed, and joy has to be shared.

It was joy such as this, experienced at the first Pentecost, that allowed the faith to spread like wildfire in the early centuries of the church. Shared joy is by far the greatest catalyst to conversion.

December 9

Always Count on Me

But I am like an olive tree
flourishing in the house of God;
I trust in God's unfailing love
for ever and ever.
(Psalm 52:8)

Love and trust are inseparably linked, and this is why Our Lord implored the French locutionist Gabrielle Bossis to trust him "as though you were blind and I were leading you." At other times he told her:

* Entrust yourself to me constantly. And always give me each moment as it passes. Isn't it better in my hands? Doesn't it say in the gospel, "He laid his hands on them and healed them?" I'll take out of this present moment of yours whatever clings too much to the earth—the selfishness that sullies your intention.

Always trust. Trust more and more—even to the point of expecting a miracle. Don't stop half-way or you will set limits to my love. When you have unfolded your confidence you will unfold it still more without ever being able to exceed what I expect of you.

Always count on me, never on yourself. And you will advance; you will soar with wings like the eagle, my very little girl.

* Trust in me with all your heart since I am your great friend. . . . My help never comes to an end, and I never cease to watch over you. I am infinite and I am love. So lose yourself in me, trusting me to guide you.

* I've taken care of you to the point of dying for you. So you may trust me. . . .

* I am here for you. For your littleness I have my greatness and my power. Above all, don't doubt. Seeing in the dark—there is your victory! Being sure, with the assurance of love.

December 10

Kindness Beyond the Call of Duty

To love [God] with all your heart, with all your understanding and with all your strength, and to love your neighbor as yourself is more important than all burnt offerings and sacrifices. (Mark 12:33)

During the Second World War, at Camp Robinson in Little Rock, Arkansas, a group of Jewish soldiers asked that they be allowed to remain on duty during the Christmas holidays to permit more Catholic and Protestant soldiers to spend the time with their families. From Camp Robinson, the movement spread to camps, navy yards, and hospitals all over the country.

Said Major William Brundick, Catholic chaplain at Fort Dix, New Jersey, to the Jewish soldiers there: "Catholic and Protestant soldiers at Fort Dix are very moved by the gesture of hundreds of Jewish soldiers who have voluntarily decided to forego Christmas furloughs in order to make it possible for a maximum number of Catholics and Protestants to be with their families on Christmas. We are profoundly grateful."

Incidents such as this speak loudly of the indiscriminate love of neighbor that Jesus urges us to show. These incidents even become stories that are remembered and retold, so strong is their message. In our own lives, have we ever attended an ecumenical service just to show solidarity with others? Have we ever donated clothing to a family that was Jewish or Hindu? Sent used books to a prison library? May we look for opportunities to love indiscriminately.

December 11

Peter the Scrooge

For where you have envy and selfish ambition, there you find disorder and every evil practice. (James 3:16)

The life of Peter, a seventh-century tax collector and banker, bears an uncanny resemblance to that of Charles Dickens's Ebenezer Scrooge. Peter was a merciless miser, cruel to the poor, who dubbed him "the stingy one." Once when a baker was delivering bread to Peter at his door, a pauper seeking alms rushed to the doorstep. Out of anger, and to rid himself of the beggar, Peter threw a loaf at the head of the poor man, who received it with delight.

Two days later, Peter fell gravely ill. During this sickness he experienced a terrifying vision of the divine judgment he would face if he did not repent. He saw a balancing scale, on one pan of which a hoard of devils piled his many sins. On the other side were angels who had nothing to place on the opposite pan other than the one loaf Peter had angrily hurled at the pauper.

The vision wrought a total conversion in Peter. Thereafter he donated all his possessions to the poor. After giving his own tunic to a pauper, he experienced a vision of Christ clothed in the same garment. The saint is also credited with the miraculous healing of a deaf and mute man.

Prayer

Lord, as the Christmas season approaches, help me to prepare spiritually. Allow the image of God as a pauper child to move and inspire in me a desire for an ever-deeper conversion.

December 12

Life Is Changed, Not Ended

"And this is the will of him who sent me, that I shall lose none of all that he has given me, but raise them up at the last day. For my Father's will is that everyone who looks to the Son and believes in him shall have eternal life, and I will raise him up at the last day." (John 6:39–40)

If an unborn baby thinks, it is no doubt afraid of birth. To leave the only world it has known seems a kind of death, the entrance into an unknown and foreboding realm. But immediately after birth the child finds itself in loving arms, showered with love and cared for at every moment in a world full of promise.

For Catholics, passing through death is also a birth into a new and beautiful world. Those who are left behind should not grieve as if there were no hope. Life is changed, not ended. Our loved ones live on, in a world beautiful beyond anything we can imagine. With Christ and Our Lady they await the day when they will welcome us with joy. "Do not grieve too much," they say to us. "We are living and we are still with you."

■

December 13

Encountering the Living God

For this reason, since the day we heard about you, we have not stopped praying for you and asking God to fill you with the knowledge of his will through all spiritual wisdom and understanding. (Colossians 1:9)

Prayer is essential to our lives, for it is a direct encounter with the living God. At the same time, we may have so many intentions to pray for (our families, the sick, peace, and more), that it can sometimes be difficult to get them all in. The following suggestions may help:

First, you may wish to write down on an index card the intentions you wish to pray for every day. Place the card in your wallet or purse (or in a prayer book you use each day). Consult it as you pray the Rosary, offering one decade for each intention; this will allow you to pray for five to fifteen intentions each day.

Second, just as a priest normally has an intention for each Mass he offers, so you too can offer the Masses you attend for one or more special intentions. The same can be done for other prayer forms that the church offers us, such as the stations of the cross, litanies, and, of course, novenas.

Another form is conversational prayer with God. Here we simply speak to the Lord about our prayer intention, describing it and lifting it up, so to speak, for him to see and bless. But the most beautiful form of prayer may be that of sheer praise and gratitude, with the Lord himself searching our hearts for our special needs and intentions.

■

December 14
The Arm of Christ

The LORD appeared to us in the past, saying:
"I have loved you with an everlasting love;
I have drawn you with loving-kindness."
(Jeremiah 31:3)

In Pompeii the body of a crippled boy was found with his lame foot. Around his body was a woman's arm, bejeweled. The great stream of ash suddenly issuing from the volcano had driven a terror-stricken crowd to look for refuge. The woman had evidently taken pity on the cripple. The arm outstretched to save was preserved by being imprinted in the ash and discovered by archeologists centuries later.

The arm of the Lord protects his people. He draws us to himself to save all of us. We are never too insignificant for his rescue. It is often said, "If you were the only person left on earth, Christ would die for you alone." Every soul is priceless in the sight of God. Each of us belongs to the Creator: we are his flesh and blood. His salvation is directed to every one of us. No one is left out.

Prayer

Father, may we never cease to praise you for the love and care you show us, even to the point of dying for us. May your praise be ever on our lips. Amen.

■

December 15

The Sheepgate

[A]nd I lay down my life for the sheep. (John 10:15b)

At night, sheep in ancient Israel were gathered into a sheepfold to protect them from thieves, bad weather, or wild animals. The sheepfolds were caves, sheds, or open areas surrounded by low walls made of stones or branches. The shepherd slept in the fold to protect the sheep, often at the entrance. Wild animals could not get in, and the sheep could not get out, without alerting him. He was, literally, the "sheepgate."

Jesus' listeners were aware of the shepherd's role and of his dedication in protecting his flock. In speaking of himself as the Good Shepherd, Christ also evoked the comforting images of Psalm 23, which he and his followers certainly knew by heart.

> The LORD is my shepherd, I shall not be in want.
> He makes me lie down in green pastures,
>   he leads me beside quiet waters,
>   he restores my soul.

Psychiatrists believe one of the deepest needs of the human heart is to be loved and taken care of, for there is still a child in each of us. Reflecting on Jesus as our personal guide and shepherd helps fill that need, but it is not a fantasy. In his eyes we truly are children, and he really is protecting us as his own. May we bring this thought to prayer whenever we feel alone.

■

December 16

"What a Wonderful Feeling"

In those days John the Baptist came, preaching in the Desert of Judea and saying, "Repent, for the kingdom of heaven is near." (*Matthew* 3:1–2)

Babe Ruth was one of the most colorful players baseball has ever known. On a cold December night in 1946, the words of Christ in today's Gospel—"Repent, for the kingdom of heaven is at hand"—took on special meaning for him. Although he had drifted away from the Church, in his New York apartment, overlooking the city lights, he had a big window. Often he would kneel before that window in prayer.

One cold December night he was lying in bed in a New York hospital, seriously ill. Paul Carey, one of his closest friends, was at his side. After a while he turned to Ruth and said, "Babe, they're going to operate in the morning. Don't you think you should see a priest?" Ruth looked into Carey's eyes and said, "Yes, Paul, I'd appreciate your calling a priest."

That night Babe Ruth spent a long time talking to Christ with the priest's help. When he finished, the priest gave him absolution and said he would be back in the morning with Holy Communion before the Babe's scheduled surgery.

After the priest left, Ruth said: "As I lay in bed that evening, I thought to myself what a wonderful feeling to be free from fear and worries. They were all in God's hands now."

December 17

The Hands of Christ

From the fruit of his lips a man is filled with good things as surely as the work of his hands rewards him. (Proverbs 12:14)

Following World War II some German students volunteered to help rebuild a cathedral in England, one that had been badly damaged by the Luftwaffe bombings. As the work progressed, they also began to gather the pieces of the shattered statue of Christ with his arms outstretched and bearing the inscription, "Come unto Me." They were able to repair all the damage except for Christ's hands, which had been completely destroyed. The workers then made the decision to leave the hands off and changed the inscription to read: "We shall be the hands of Christ."

The inscription was inspired by a prayer by St. Teresa of Avila:

Lord Christ,
you have no body on earth but ours,
no hands but ours,
no feet but ours.
Ours are the eyes through which your compassion
must look out on the world.
Ours are the feet by which you may still
go about doing good.
Ours are the hands with which
you bless people now.
Bless our minds and bodies,
that we may be a blessing to others. Amen.

December 18

The Feminine Face of God

The LORD appeared to us in the past, saying:
"I have loved you with an everlasting love;
I have drawn you with loving-kindness."
(Jeremiah 31:3)

The self-giving love of God is expressed uniquely and perfectly in the Blessed Mother, who, in one beautiful analogy, is the "the feminine face of God." She conveys the maternal warmth and beauty of divine love, speaking primarily to the heart.

Some spiritual writers believe that without Mary we cannot fully enter into the mystery of Christ's compassionate love. For instance, sometimes we are apt to speak more about Jesus than to him, and he in effect becomes more of an argument for the moral life than the door to the spiritual life, which is the life of communion with the Father, Son, and Holy Spirit.

But Mary calls us to the heart of her Son. Most conversions are the result of an encounter with his love; very few are wrought through the intellect. The Blessed Virgin keeps nothing for herself but leads us directly to Christ, and every petition we offer to her is passed to her Son, with her own prayer enfolding it. In the end you cannot intellectualize the love of God any more than you can intellectualize a mother's love.

December 19

The Third Prayer

Be strong and courageous. Do not be afraid or terrified because of them, for the LORD your God goes with you; he will never leave you nor forsake you. (Deuteronomy 31:6)

Some day we will learn the full story of the Spanish martyrs of the Civil War in Spain from 1936–39, a confusing and bloody war that included a vicious persecution of the Church. Here is one narrative that was communicated to the press by the Apostolic Delegate to Canada:

Fr. Marcos was a noted preacher. As he stood before the firing squad he asked a favor: that he be allowed to preach one last, brief sermon. The officer in charge consented.

Marcos blessed himself and began. "I have always prayed for three things," he said. "First, that by the grace of God I would save my soul. Secondly, that I would be allowed to give my life for Christ. It seems likely that both these prayers are going to be granted. But whether my third prayer has been granted or not, I still have no idea. The third prayer was that one soul at least would achieve heaven through my preaching."

Suddenly one of the men in the firing squad threw away his rifle, ran up, and knelt at Marcos's feet, asking for absolution. The rest of the militia yelled at him, "Get away! Get away or you'll be shot along with him!"

The priest made the sign of the cross over the soldier and pronounced the words of absolution. There was a crackle of gunfire, and Fr. Marcos and his militiaman fell together.

December 20

The District Nurse

Jesus went through all the towns and villages, teaching in their synagogues, preaching the good news of the kingdom and healing every disease and sickness. (Matthew 9:35)

A J. Cronin tells of a district nurse he knew when he was in practice as a doctor. For twenty years, single-handed, she had served a ten-mile district. "I marveled," he says, "at her patience, her fortitude and her cheerfulness. She was never too tired at night to rise for an urgent call. Her salary was too low, and late one night, after a particularly strenuous day, I ventured to ask her, 'Nurse, why don't you make them pay you more? God knows you're worth it.' 'If God knows I'm worth it,' she answered, 'that's all that matters to me.' "

She was working, not for human approval, but for God. And when we work for God, riches and prestige should be the last things that enter into our mind.

December 21

Peter's Net

Then Jesus came to them and said, "All authority in heaven and on earth has been given to me. Therefore go and make disciples of all nations, baptizing them in the name of the Father and of the Son and of the Holy Spirit, and teaching them to obey everything I have commanded you. And surely I am with you always, to the very end of the age." (Matthew 28:18–20)

A priest was fond of the technique of dividing his sermon into several major points. For example, he'd begin by referring to the "five smooth stones" that David used to defeat Goliath. Then he'd divide his sermon into five points. Or he'd begin by referring to the "seven days of creation" and then divide his sermon into seven points.

One day his congregation nearly had heart failure when he began referring to the "153 fish" that Peter caught in his net. Actually the individual fish weren't important to the preacher, or to Peter for that matter, but the symbolism of 153 was.

Scholars suggest that the 153 fish stand for the number of nations of the world, which ancient historians placed at 153. Peter's net stands for the church, which is able to embrace all the nations of the world without breaking. In fact, the word "catholic" means "universal," and the church's primary mission is to pass down to each generation the message and teachings of Christ, often referred to as "the Good News," or the gospel. This, indeed, is part of the mission of every Catholic.

■

December 22

St. John Nepomucene, Confessor

Then I acknowledged my sin to you
and did not cover up my iniquity.
I said, "I will confess
my transgressions to the LORD"—
and you forgave
the guilt of my sin.
(Psalm 32:5)

Over five hundred years ago (1419), St. John Nepomucene was appointed by King Wenceslaus IV of Bohemia (in the modern-day Czech Republic) to be court preacher; later Queen Johanna, the wife of the king, chose him as her confessor.

One day the king, who was mad with jealousy over his wife, sent for Fr. Nepomucene and ordered him to reveal what the queen had said in her confessions. The priest tried to explain what an evil thing he was asking, but he persisted with bribes of wealth and position, but finding this of no avail, he reverted to threats.

Still the priest remained silent, and he was finally imprisoned and tortured with fire and the rack. But he remained steadfast. Finally, in a rage, the king summoned the executioners and gave orders for the priest's death. They waited until nightfall for secrecy, and then with feet bound back to his neck and a wooden gag in his mouth, St. John was cast into the River Vltava.

But as the body floated down the river, five bright lights shone over the lifeless form, bringing the townspeople to the riverbank, where they drew the martyr's body out of the water and ultimately discovered the truth behind the murder.

Wenceslaus IV fled, fearing the anger of the people. He subsequently lost the Czech throne and reportedly died a miserable death.

Three hundred years later, at the opening of the confessor's tomb in 1719, the body was found as only bones and dust, with one exception. The tongue that had absolved so many penitents and had kept its silence to the point of martyrdom was found to be incorrupt, perfectly preserved. It is honored to this day as the most precious relic of the Cathedral of Prague.

In the end, I think, it is a special grace from Christ that keeps the seal of the confessional so inviolate. He puts a guard over the lips of priests, as the psalmist writes, and normally gives us the memory of a sieve—at least in confessional matters. In the lives of priests it's one of the little persistent miracles for which each of us is profoundly grateful.

■

December 23

A Miracle Beneath the Sea

May the LORD *answer you when you are in distress; may the name of the God of Jacob protect you. (Psalm 20:1)*

On Sunday afternoon, June 1, 1975, Barrel Dore was on an oilrig in the Gulf of Mexico. Suddenly it wobbled, tipped to one side, and crashed into the sea. He was trapped inside a room on the rig, and as it sank deeper and deeper into the sea, the lights in the room went out and it began to fill with water.

Thrashing about in the darkness, Dore accidentally found a huge air bubble that was forming in the corner of the room, and thrust his head inside it. Then a horrifying thought, "I'm buried alive," sent a shiver down his spine. He began to pray out loud, and as he did, something remarkable happened. He said later:

"I found myself actually talking to Someone. Jesus was there with me. There was no illumination, nothing physical. But I sensed him, a comforting Presence. He was real. He was there."

For the next twenty-two hours that Presence continued to comfort Dore. But now the oxygen supply inside the bubble was giving out and it seemed death was inevitable within a short time. Then a second remarkable thing happened. Darrel saw a tiny star of light shimmering in the pitch-black water. Was it real, or after twenty-two hours, was he beginning to hallucinate? Dore squinted. The light seemed to grow brighter. He squinted again. He wasn't hallucinating; the light was real, coming from a diver's helmet. He had been found. His twenty-two-hour nightmare was over.

It's been said that for those who don't believe in miracles, no proof is enough, and for those who believe, no proof is necessary. As a hospital chaplain I am no longer amazed when I see or hear of a miracle from the people I minister to, and I believe that miracles are much more common than most people realize. Especially in the realm of the spirit, miracles should be expected. May this encourage us to pray even for the impossible.

December 24

Silent Night

All the lands are at rest and at peace; they break into singing. (*Isaiah* 14:7)

High up in the Austrian Alps, in an area called Tyrol, lived a young Austrian priest, Fr. Joseph Mohr. On Christmas Eve in 1818, he sat in his study and looked out at the hushed stillness of the night that had settled over the snow-clad beauty of the mountains. The prayer in his heart was transformed into poetry as he put the words together at his desk. Thus "Silent Night, Holy Night" was written.

On Christmas morning he took the lyrics to the home of his good friend, Franz Gruber, a musician and church organist. In the next few hours he composed an exquisite melody for the beautiful words. The two men played and sang the hymn together at the Christmas Mass that evening.

For over a year the composition rested in Mr. Gruber's desk, but in 1819 an organ repairman saw the music, asked to hear it, and subsequently transmitted the hymn from village to village in the course of his work. Twenty-three years later it was published under the title of "The Tyrolese Song," and eventually made its way into the hearts of the faithful around the world.

Like Fr. Joseph, do we have gifts that we can share with others? Whether it's poetry, a good singing voice, a listening ear, cooking, woodworking, or whatever other gifts God has given us, the coming year may be the time to put them to good use, in the spirit of Christmas, for the benefit of others and for the good God who gave them to us.

December 25

Long Walk, Much Love

I have told you this so that my joy may be in you and that your joy may be complete. (John 15:11)

At a Catholic mission school in Namibia, an African boy listened carefully as his teacher explained why Christians give presents to each other on Christmas Day. "The gift is an expression of our joy and gratitude over the birth of Christ and the desire to give to those we love," she said.

When Christmas Day came, the boy brought the teacher a seashell of lustrous beauty. "Where did you ever find such a beautiful shell?" the teacher asked.

The youth told her that there was only one spot where such extraordinary shells could be found—a certain bay a few miles away.

"Why . . . why, it's so beautiful," said the teacher. "But you shouldn't have gone all that way to get a gift for me."

His eyes brightening, the boy answered, "Long walk part of gift."

December 26

Christmas Light

[They] asked, "Where is the one who has been born king of the Jews? We saw his star in the east and have come to worship him." (Matthew 2:2)

Christmas is a season of light—the light of angels among shepherds, the light of a great star beckoning wise men, and in our own day the multicolored lights of Christmas trees, outdoor decorations, and the bright glow from the windows of homes where families are gathered to celebrate.

The image of light applies to each of us as well, commissioned at our confirmation to spread the light of God's love to family, friends, and the community we live in. We don't have to rely on our own resources for this, since the whole purpose of the Incarnation was to fill us with the light of Christ himself. He is always the source of power that infuses us with the energy and gifts we may need, if we but ask.

Although our characters differ and our personalities are unique, yet our many colors form a harmony of love, just as Christmas lights do on an evergreen. In the darkness of a cold world, the glow of the shining lights is truly beautiful.

December 27

Reckless Generosity

Then they opened their treasures and presented him with gifts of gold and of incense and of myrrh. (Matthew 2:11)

As our reading illustrates today, Christmas is the great season of love and giving. The Magi, awed by the miracle of God's coming into the world as a helpless infant, responded by offering him their most precious gifts.

The spirit of giving is captured in this passage from Frank O'Connor's *An Only Child*:

> One Christmas, Santa Claus brought me a toy engine. I took it with me to the convent, and played with it while mother and the nuns discussed old times. But it was a young nun who brought us in to see the crib. When I saw the holy child in the manger, I was distressed because little as I had, he had nothing at all. For me it was fresh proof of the incompetence of Santa Claus.
>
> I asked the young nun politely if the holy child didn't like toys, and she replied composedly enough, "Oh, he does, but his mother is too poor to afford them." That settled it. My mother was poor too, but at Christmas she at least managed to buy me something even if it was only a box of crayons.

I distinctly remember getting into the crib and putting the engine between his outstretched arms. I probably showed him how to wind it as well, because a small baby like that would not be clever enough to know. I remember too the tearful feeling of reckless generosity with which I left him there in the nightly darkness of the chapel, clutching my toy to his chest.

December 28

St. Francis and the First Crèche

This will be a sign to you: You will find a baby wrapped in cloths and lying in a manger. (*Luke* 2:12)

In the year 1223, St. Francis of Assisi celebrated Christmas in a way that the world had never seen before. He said to a friend of his: "I would like to celebrate Christmas Eve with you, but now listen to my thoughts. In the woods you will find a cave, and there I would like you to arrange a manger filled with hay. There should also be an ox and a mule, just as at Bethlehem. I want for once to celebrate seriously the coming of the Son of God upon earth and to see with my own eyes how poor he wished to be for our sakes."

His friend attended to all of Francis's wishes, and at midnight on Christmas Eve the brothers came together to celebrate the festival of Christmas. All carried lighted torches, and they stood around the manger with their candles, so that it was as light as day within the cave.

The Mass was offered with the manger as the altar, so that the divine child, under the forms of bread and wine, should himself come to the place, as really present as he had been in the stable at Bethlehem. May we reflect on this Real Presence as we celebrate Christmas Mass this year, for the Christ child is present there in his very flesh and blood.

December 29

The Spider's Web

When they had gone, an angel of the Lord appeared to Joseph in a dream. "Get up," he said, "take the child and his mother and escape to Egypt. Stay there until I tell you, for Herod is going to search for the child to kill him."
(Matthew 2:13)

After the birth of Jesus, the story is told, when Joseph and Mary were on their way to Egypt, they sought refuge in a cave after a grueling day of travel. It was very cold, so cold that the ground was white with hoar frost. A little spider saw the infant Jesus and was inspired to do something to keep him warm in the cold night. She decided to do the only thing she could, and spun a web across the entrance of the cave, to make, as it were, a curtain.

Along the path came a detachment of Herod's soldiers, seeking more children to kill in obedience to Herod's bloodthirsty order. When they approached the cave, they were about to burst in to search it, but their captain noticed the spider's web, covered with the white hoar frost and stretched across the entrance to the cave. "Look at the spider's web here," he said. "It's not broken, so there can't be anyone in there." So the soldiers passed on, and they left the Holy Family in peace.

And that, so they say, is why to this day we put tinsel on our Christmas trees, for the glittering tinsel streamers stand for the spider's web, white with hoar frost, stretched across the entrance of the cave on the way to Egypt. It is a lovely story, and this much, at least, is true: no gift that Jesus receives is forgotten.

December 30

The Flanders Miracle

But I tell you who hear me: Love your enemies, do good to those who hate you, bless those who curse you, pray for those who mistreat you. (*Luke* 6:27–28)

There is just one season in the year when men seem able to realize for a moment what the Incarnation means, and never was this so evident as in the Flanders trenches at Christmas, 1917.

Just before Christmas there had been some attacks and counterattacks here and there, and many casualties, but as the holy season drew closer the firing seemed to die down by a general instinct. On Christmas Eve in some sectors the German parapet was decorated with candles, and the singing of carols was heard. In the morning greetings were shouted from trench to trench and all along the line soldiers began walking into no-man's land for a talk with their equally adventurous enemies. Even officers entered into the spirit of the season, and as the day went on a good part of both armies had left their trenches and were fraternizing in crowds between the lines, exchanging cigarettes and chocolate from their Christmas parcels. It was an extraordinary event, never before seen in the annals of war.

The spirit of Christmas—divine Love coming into the world—can move us as well to reconciliation and forgiveness. All we need is the will to forgive, for the sake of Jesus, and he will supply all the rest to make it really happen.

December 31

The Temple Bells

May the God of hope fill you with all joy and peace as you trust in him, so that you may overflow with hope by the power of the Holy Spirit.
(Romans 15:13)

A Carmelite priest in Japan speaks of a unique New Year's Eve tradition in his homeland in which the worst of the old year is discarded and the hope and resolutions of the new year are born. "For centuries," he says, "the Japanese have understood this to be the message of the Temple Bell. But at no time of the year is this so clear as New Year's Eve, when the temple bells of Japan are sounded 108 times during the last moments of the passing year."

While in many lands people attend parties to see out the old year and welcome the new, in Japan the custom of many is to head for the temple—one of the huge, famous ones if you can brave the crowds, or a local one if not—to make resolutions and follow the ceremony of the bells.

Many people were taught to think of the 108 strokes as signifying the 108 evil passions. "To those of us who grew up in this sort of society, the process symbolizes casting off, one by one, the evils of the past year. And indeed, somehow with each boom I feel as if my heart were being purified of the old and filled with hope for the coming year."

Tonight, may we feel all the old sins of the past year fade away in God's forgiveness and love. It is a bright, new beginning, as God wishes.

■

Notes

January 11: This anonymous poem is from Richard Beyer's *Blessed Art Thou* (Notre Dame, IN: Ave Maria Press, 1996), 177.

January 13: The story of Tony Melendez is from Steven Barrie's "The Miracle of Tony Melendez," *Los Angeles Times*, 25 December 1987, C4.

January 14: The story told by Mother Teresa is from *Mother Teresa: In My Own Words*, compiled by José Luis González-Balado (New York: Random House, 1997), 101.

January 16: The quotation from Aleksandr Solzhenitsyn is from *The Gulag Archipelago 1918–1956: An Experiment in Literary Investigation* (Boulder, CO: Westview Press, 1997), 462, and is used with permission.

January 18: Mother Teresa's words from the 1979 Nobel Peace Prize awards are from *Mother Teresa: In My Own Words*, 177.
The anonymous poem is from *2000 Years of Prayer*, Michael Counsell, compiler (Harrisburg, PA: Morehouse Publishing, 1999), 316.

January 19: The words written by Gabrielle Bossis are from *He and I* (Sherbrooke, Québec, Canada: Mediaspaul, 1985), 196.

January 20: The poem "Embracing Love" is by the author.

January 22: This prayer appeared in Beyer, *Blessed Art Thou*, 180.

January 23: The quotation from St. Therese of Lisieux is from T.N. Taylor, ed., *The Story of a Soul: The Autobiography of St. Therese of Lisieux* (Teddington, UK: Echo Library, 2006), 43.

January 24: The message for the World Day of the Sick is from John Paul II, *Letter for World Day of the Sick* (2001), paragraph 3.
The quotation from an apostolic letter by John Paul II is from *Salvifici Doloris* (February 11, 1984), paragraph 30.

January 26: The quotation from Fr. Slavko Barbaric is from a sermon given at St. James Church, Medjugorje, Bosnia-Herzegovina, November 20, 1998, and is used with the permission of the Order of Franciscans, Siroki Brijeg, Bosnia-Herzegovina.

January 27: The words written by Gabrielle Bossis are from *He and I*, 281.

January 28: The quotations from Henri Nouwen are from *Clowning in Rome* (Garden City, NY: Doubleday Image, 1979), 116.

January 30: The quotation from Mother Teresa is from her address at the National Prayer Breakfast, Washington, DC, February 3, 1994.
The quotation from Dietrich Bonhoeffer is from *Ethics* (New York: Macmillan, 1965), 175–76.

February 1: The quotation from Frederick Buechner is from *Now and Then* (New York: Harper & Row, 1983), 83, and is used with permission.

February 2: Pope John XXIII's poem "For Peace" is from Beyer, *Blessed Art Thou*, 137.

February 3: Pope Leo XIII's poem "It Is Sweet Music" is from Beyer, *Blessed Art Thou*, 132–33.

February 4: The quotation from St. Vincent de Paul is from F.A. Forbes, *St. Vincent de Paul* (Rockford, IL: TAN Books, 1999), 76.

The quotation from St. John of the Cross is from Kieran Kavanaugh, *John of the Cross: Selected Writings* (New York: Paulist Press, 1987), 211.

February 9: The quotation from Dr. von Bodelschwingh is from Hans-Walter Schmuhl, *Friedrich von Bodelschwingh* (Hamburg, Germany: Rowohlt Taschenbuch Verlag, 2005), 144. Note: The quotation was given to the author by Janya Martin, a professor of German at Baylor University in Waco, Texas, in the course of a conversation. Later I asked her for the source, which was written in German. There is no English translation.
The quotation from Eleanor Roosevelt is from the daily quotation of 14 March 2007 on <http://quotationspage.com/quote/2558>.

February 13: The poem "In Time of Worry" is from Beyer, *Blessed Art Thou*, 192–93.

February 16: The official Congressional Medal of Honor citation for "Joseph Timothy O'Callahan" is from the entry of 22 April 2006 at <http://www.history.army.mil/html/moh/wwII-m-s.html>.

February 20: Pope Pius XII's prayer "Mary Our Strength" is from Beyer, *Blessed Art Thou*, 136.

February 21: The words of Carol Houselander are from *The Reed of God* (New York: 1st Arena Letters, 1978), 31.

February 24: The poem by James Dillet Freeman is from *Prayer, the Master Key* (Garden City, NY: Doubleday, 1968), 56, and is used with permission.

March 2: The words written by Gabrielle Bossis are from *He and I*, 116.

March 5: The quotation from Mother Teresa is from *My Life for the Poor: Mother Teresa of Calcutta*, José Luis González-Balado and Janet

Playfoot, editors (New York: Ballantine Books, 1987), 39, and is used with permission.

March 7: Pope John Paul II's prayer "Our Lady of the Millennium" is from Beyer, *Blessed Art Thou,* 145.

March 14: The story is from H. von Schroeder's "The Hands of Christ," *The Journal of Hand Surgery,* 13 March 1998, 32–36.

March 17: *Open Mind, Open Heart* (New York: Continuum International Publishing Group, 2006); *Invitation to Love* (New York: Continuum International Publishing Group, 1994); *The Mystery of Christ* (New York: Continuum International Publishing Group, 2004).

March 22: The story and quotation are from Emilie Griffin's *Turning: Reflections on the Experience of Conversion* (New York: Doubleday, 1980), 76.

March 24: The prayer by James of Sarug is from Beyer, *Blessed Art Thou*, 149.

April 4: The story and quotation are from G. Gordon Liddy's *Will: The Autobiography of G. Gordon Liddy* (New York: St. Martin's Press, 1996), 122.

April 6: The citation for Fr. Eugene P. O'Grady is from *Medal of Honor Recipients: 1863–1979* (Washington, DC: Government Printing Office, 1979), 285.

April 11: The story is from Raymond Jones's "Stories of Faith," *Pulpit*, 4 November 2002, 12.

April 14: The words written by Gabrielle Bossis are from *He and I,* 168.

April 15: The excerpt from John Paul II is taken from *Crossing the Threshold of Hope* (New York: Knopf Publishing, 1995), 24.

April 16: The quotation from Mother Teresa is from González-Balado and Playfoot, editors, *My Life for the Poor: Mother Teresa of Calcutta*, 81.

April 23: The prayer by Paul Claudel is from Beyer, *Blessed Art Thou*, 160–61.

April 24: The poem is from B.G. Skinner's *Henry Francis Lyte: Brixham's Poet and Priest* (Exeter, UK: The University of Exeter, 1974), 141.

April 25: The verses are from Harry Edward Piggot's *My Song Is Love Unknown: The Words of Samuel Crossman* (Oxford, UK: Oxford University Press, 1949), 84.

April 26: The quotation from John Vannorsdall is taken from *The Best of John Vannorsdall: 1976–1990* (Minneapolis: Augsburg Fortress, 1989), 95.

April 28: The quotation by Victor Hugo is from and John Chambers' *Conversations With Eternity: The Forgotten Masterpiece of Victor Hugo* (New York: New Paradigm Books, 1998), 154.

April 29: The prayer is taken from Suzanne Noffke, ed., *Catherine of Siena: The Dialogue* (Mahwah, NJ: Paulist Press, 1980), 216.

May 1: The quotation from John Paul II is from the papal audience on 25 April 2001, reprinted on the Vatican website: <http://www.Vatican.va/holy_father/john_paul_ii/audiences/2001/documents/hf_jp-ii_aud__20010425_en.html>.

May 8: The information is from Viktor E. Frankl's *Man's Search for Meaning* (Boston: Beacon Press, 2000), 92.

May 10: The prayer by Mother Teresa is taken from Beyer, *Blessed Art Thou*, 165–66.

May 11: The excerpt is from Thomas Keating's *Open Mind, Open Heart: The Contemplative Dimension of the Gospel* (New York:Continuum International Publishing Group, 2006), 112.

May 14: The story by Mother Teresa is from González-Balado and Playfoot, editors, *My Life for the Poor: Mother Teresa of Calcutta*, 127.

May 15: The quotation is from Jean-Baptiste Chautard's *The Soul of the Apostolate* (Rockford, IL: Tan Books & Publishers, 1977), 211.

May 16: The quotation is from Edward Leen's *Progress Through Mental Prayer* (Hartford, CT: Catholic Authors Press, 2006), 188.

May 21: The excerpt is from Eugene Vandeur's *Pledge of Glory: Meditations on the Eucharist and the Trinity* (Westminster, MD: Newman Press, 1958), 193.

May 23: The poem by Dallan Forgaill is from Edward Alfred Alton's *History of Ireland: From the Earliest Times to the Present Day* (Boston: Adamant Media Corporation, 2005), 113.

May 26: The quotation is from Antonio Gallonio's *The Life of St. Philip Neri* (Ft. Collins, CO: Ignatius Press, 2006), 94.

May 27: The poem is from Beyer, *Blessed Art Thou*, 170–71.

May 30: The story is from Joseph Manton's *Straws from the Crib* (Boston: Pauline Books and Media, 1964), 131.

June 3: The anonymous poem "Creation" is from Counsell, *2000 Years of Prayer*, 133.

June 9: The lyrics by Charlie Daniels are from the webpage <http://wisdomquotes.com/quote/charliedaniels>.

June 11: The story is taken from Sholem Asch's *The Apostle* (New York: Carrol and Graf Publishers, 1985), 133.

June 12: The excerpt is from Raniero Cantalamessa's *Loving the Church: Scriptural Meditations for the Papal Household* (Cincinnati, OH: Servant Publications, 2005), 151.

June 14: The anonymous poem is from Counsell, *2000 Years of Prayer*, 142.

June 15: The prayer by Blessed Charles Eugène de Foucauld is from Counsell, *2000 Years of Prayer*, 254.

June 19: The material on Medjugorje is from Fr. Richard Beyer's *Medjugorje Day by Day* (Notre Dame: Ave Maria Press, 1993), 3–8. Websites devoted to Medjugorje include <http://Medjugorje.org> and <http://medjugorje.net>.

June 20: The letter by Dr. Tom Dooley is from Theodore Martin Hesburgh and Jerry Reedy's *God, Country, Notre Dame* (Notre Dame, IN: University of Notre Dame Press, 1990), 211.

June 21: The quotation is from Henri Nouwen, *Life of the Beloved: Spiritual Living in a Secular World* (New York: Crossroad Publishing, 2002), 116.

June 24: The prose by this anonymous author is from Counsell, *2000 Years of Prayer*, 181.

June 25: The prayer "God's Joy" is from Counsell, *2000 Years of Prayer*, 96.

June 28: The interview is from James S. Hewett's *Illustrations Unlimited* (Wheaton, IL: Tyndale House Publishers, 1988), 282.

June 30: The excerpt from *Lumen Gentium* (21 November 1964) is from the Vatican website: <http://www. Vatican. va/archive/hist_councils/ii_vatican_council/documents/vat-ii_const_19641121_lumen-gentium_en.html>.

July 1: *Newsweek* poll conducted by Princeton Survey Research Associates, Princeton, NJ, 14 April 2001.

July 4: The story of Corrie ten Boom is from her book *The Hiding Place* (New York: Bantam, 1984).

July 6: The prayer by St. Thomas à Kempis is from Counsell, *2000 Years of Prayer*, 143.

July 8: The quotation is from Elie Wiesel's *Night* (New York: Penguin Books, 1981), 65.

July 13: The quotation from Tertullian is from Geoffrey D. Dunn's *Tertullian* (New York: Routledge, 2004), 232.

July 17: The prayer is from an article by Jonathan Bates, "Dietrich Bonhoeffer—Integrity, Faith, and Suffering," *Stanley News & Press*, 2 February 1984, 12.

July 22: The words of Mother Teresa are from *No Greater Love* (Novato, CA: New World Library, 1997), 87.
The words of John Paul II are from "Fides et Ratio," 15 September 1998, at the Vatican website:<www.vatican.va/holy_father/john_paul_ii/encyclicals/documents/hf_jp-ii_enc_15101998_fides-et-ratio_en.html>.

July 25: The statement is from John Cardinal O'Connor's "Abortion: Questions and Answers," July 1990, at the Priests for Life website: www.priestsforlife.org/magisterium/cardocqanda.html.

July 27: This excerpt is from William Abbot, ed., *The Documents of Vatican II* (New York: America Press, 1966), 233.

July 28: The prayer is from Howard Hong's *The Essential Kierkegaard* (Princeton: Princeton University Press, 2000), 134.

August 1: The excerpt is from Dorothy Herrmann's *Helen Keller: A Life* (Chicago: University of Chicago Press, 1998), 155.

August 5: The words of John Paul II are from his address "Jubilee of the Agricultural World," 11 November 2000, at the Vatican website: <http://www.vatican.va/holy_father/john_paulii/speeches/documents/hf_jp-ii_spe_2000111 ljubilagric_en.html>.

August 7: The quotation is from Judith Halperin's *Mickey Marcus: The Story of Colonel David Marcus* (Jacksonville, FL: Bloch Publishing Company, 1949), 191.

August 8: The prayer is from Counsell, 2000 *Years of Prayer*, 87.

August 13: The story and quotation are from Margaret Reeson's *No Fixed Address: The Story of Noreen Towers* (Sydney, Australia: Albatross Books, 1992), 66.

August 15: The prayer by James Ryman is from Beyer, *Blessed Art Thou*, 273–74.

August 17: The story is from Dr. David Elkind's *Child Development and Education: A Piagetian Perspective* (New York: Oxford University Press, 1976), 188.

August 19: The prayer is from Elizabeth Roberts, *Life Prayers: From Around the World* (New York: Harper Collins, 1996), 34.

August 20: The quotation from Pope John XXIII is from *Journey of a Soul: The Autobiography of Pope John XXIII* (New York: Image Books, 1999), 155.

August 23: The story is from Cathy Collins, "A Last Assignment," *Catholic Mother Magazine,* Lent, 2004, 5. Note: *Catholic Mother Magazine* "invites mothers to create a Catholic culture in the home. Our aim is to inspire, entertain, and inform Catholic mothers as we raise our children in the faith." Their website is <www.catholicmother.ca>.

August 24: The story is from Ron Steinman's *The Soldiers' Story* (New York: Barnes & Noble, 2000), 131.

August 25: The excerpt is from Abbot, *The Documents of Vatican II*, 274.

August 30: The prayer is from Roberts, *Life Prayers: From Around the World*, 163.

September 4: The story is from *Cagney by Cagney* (New York: Random House, 1975), 49.

September 10: The prayer "You Are God" is from Roberts, *Life Prayers: From Around the World*, 121.

September 12: The excerpt is from Fr. Slavko Barbaric, *Pray With the Heart* (Steubenville, OH: Franciscan University Press, 1988), 108.

September 14: The excerpt is from Evelyn Bence, ed., *Mornings With Henri Nouwen* (Ann Arbor, MI: Servant Publications, 1997), 28.

September 15: The poem is from Roberts, *Life Prayers: From Around the World*, 65.

September 16: The excerpts are from Bossis, *He and I*, 173.

September 17: The letter is from Counsell, 2000 *Years of Prayer*, 112.

September 18: The excerpt is from Gerald M. Costello, *Our Sunday Visitor's Treasury of Catholic Stories* (Huntington, IN: Our Sunday Visitor, 1999), 65.

September 21: The prayer is from Etienne Gilson, *The Philosophy of St. Bonaventure* (Quincy, IL: Franciscan Press, 1965), 166.

September 22: The excerpt is from Kent M. Keith and Spencer Johnson's *Anyway: The Paradoxical Commandments* (New York: G.P. Putnam's Sons, 2001), 12. Used with permission.

September 23: The quotation is from *The Teachings of Pope Paul VI* (Washington, DC: United States Catholic Conference Publications Office, 1975), 56.

September 24: The story is from Mother Teresa, *No Greater Love*, 64.

October 1: The quotation is from John Clark, ed., *Story of a Soul: The Autobiography of St. Therese of Lisieux* (Washington, DC: ICS Publications, 1996), 144.

October 2: The prayer is from Beyer, *Blessed Art Thou*, 116.

October 5: The story is from John Farrow's *Damien the Leper* (New York: Image Books, 1998), 117.

October 6: The quotations are from M. Scott Peck, *People of the Lie: Hope for Healing Human Evil* (New York: Touchstone, 1993), 198.

October 7: The words of the anonymous author are from Beyer, *Medjugorje Day by Day*, 127.

October 12: The story is from Graham Greene's *The Power and the Glory* (New York: Penguin Books, 2003), 49.

October 13: The prayer is from Michael John Bernard, "I Want to Love You," *The Little Chronicle*, March 2005, 9.

October 14: The quotation is from Fr. Albert Shamon's *The Power of the Rosary* (Oak Lawn, IL: CMJ Publisher, 1992), 9.

October 16: The excerpt is taken from John-Paul II's *Pope John Paul II: In My Own Words* (New York: Gramercy Books, 2002), 135.

October 18: The story is from Bishop Johannes Neuhausler, *What Was It Like in the Concentration Camp at Dachau?* (Stuttgart, Germany: Verlagsgruppe Georg von Holtzbrinck, 1979), 6.

October 22: The story by Dale Francis is from "Return to the Priesthood," *Columbia*, September 1989, 6.

October 23: The quotations are from Bence, *Mornings With Henri Nouwen*, 27.

October 24: The prayer is from Roberts, *Life Prayers: From Around the World*, 46.

October 25: The quotation by Charles de Foucauld is from Jean-Jacques Antier's *Charles de Foucauld* (San Francisco: Ignatius Press, 1999), 133.

October 29: The words by Raymond J. de Souza are from "Buckley's Catholic Legacy," *National Catholic Register*, March 9, 2008, 14.

The words by Richard John Neuhaus are from "Religious Freedom Upside Down (and a word on William F. Buckley Jr.)," 29 February 2008, at CatholicBlogs.com, a Division of Sacred Heart Media LLC, <http://proecclesia.blogspot.com/2008/02/fr-richard-john-neuhaus-religious.html>.

November 3: The excerpt is from Frances Beer's *Julian of Norwich: Revelations of Divine Love and The Motherhood of God* (Cambridge, UK: D.S. Brewer, 1999), 94.

November 6: The story is from F.H. Drinkwater, *Catechism Stories* (Hartford, CT: Catholic Authors Press, 2007), 113.

November 8: The poem by Tennyson is from "Poetry: Ulysses," at <http://home.att.net/~tennysonpoetry/uly.htm>.

November 13: The prayer is from Silvana Borruso, trans., *St. Augustine LifeGuide: Words to Live by From the Great Christian Saint* (South Bend, IN: St. Augustine Press, 2006), 133.

November 15: The story is from Carlo Carretto's *Letters from the Desert*, anniversary edition (Maryknoll, NY: Orbis Books, 2002), 87.

November 21: The quotation is from Pope John XXIII, *Journey of a Soul*, 109.

November 26: The story is from González-Balado, *Mother Teresa: In My Own Words*, 54.

November 27: The story is from the private sermon file of Archbishop Joseph Dimino, former Ordinary of the Archdiocese for Military Affairs.

November 29: See Gabriel Amorth's *An Exorcist Tells His Story* (San Francisco: Ignatius Press, 1999).

December 4: The quotation is from the television program "Mother Angelica Live," Irondale, AL: Eternal Word Television Network, 7 December 2001.

December 6: The story and quotation are from Lind Swarthout, *Captain Eddie Rickenbacker: God Still Answers Prayers* (Whitefish, MT: Kessenger Publishing, 2007), 43.

December 7: The story is from Richard Wurmbrand's *In God's Underground* (London, UK: Hodder & Stoughton, 1969).

December 9: The excerpts are from Bossis, *He and I*, 134–35.

December 16: The story is from Leigh Montville's *The Big Bam: The Life and Times of Babe Ruth* (New York: Random House, 2007), 154.

December 17: The prayer is from Kieran Kavanaugh, ed., *The Collected Words of Teresa of Avila* (Washington, DC: ICS Publications, 1976), 155.

December 19: The story is included in Frances Lannon's *The Spanish Civil War* (Oxford, UK: Osprey Publishing, 2002), 224.

December 20: The quotation is from A.J. Cronin's *Three Loves* (Boynton Beach, FL: Pyramid Books, 1967), 86.

December 27: The passage is from Frank O'Connor's *An Only Child* (Syracuse, NY: Syracuse University Press, 1997), 67.

About Paraclete Press

Who We Are

Paraclete Press is an ecumenical publisher of books and recordings on Christian spirituality. Our publishing represents a full expression of Christian belief and practice—from Catholic to Evangelical, from Protestant to Orthodox.

Paraclete Press is the publishing arm of the Community of Jesus, an ecumenical monastic community in the Benedictine tradition. As such, we are uniquely positioned in the marketplace without connection to a large corporation and with informal relationships to many branches and denominations of faith.

We like it best when people buy our books from booksellers, our partners in successfully reaching as wide an audience as possible.

What We Are Doing

Books

Paraclete Press publishes books that show the richness and depth of what it means to be Christian. Although Benedictine spirituality is at the heart of all that we do, we publish books that reflect the Christian experience across many cultures, time periods, and houses of worship.

We publish books that nourish the vibrant life of the church and its people—books about spiritual practice, formation, history, ideas, and customs.

We have several different series of books within Paraclete Press, including the best-selling Living Library series of modernized classic texts; A Voice from the Monastery—giving voice to men and women monastics about what it means to live a spiritual life today; award-winning literary faith fiction; and books that explore Judaism and Islam and discover how these faiths inform Christian thought and practice.

Recordings

From Gregorian chant to contemporary American choral works, our music recordings celebrate the richness of sacred choral music through the centuries. Paraclete is proud to distribute the recordings of the internationally acclaimed choir Gloriæ Dei Cantores, who have been praised for their "rapt and fathomless spiritual intensity" by American Record Guide, and the Gloriæ Dei Cantores Schola, which specializes in the study and performance of Gregorian chant. Paraclete is also the exclusive North American distributor of the recordings of the Monastic Choir of St. Peter's Abbey in Solesmes, France, long considered to be a leading authority on Gregorian chant performance.

Learn more about us at our website:
www.paracletepress.com,
or call us toll-free at
1-800-451-5006.

You might also enjoy...

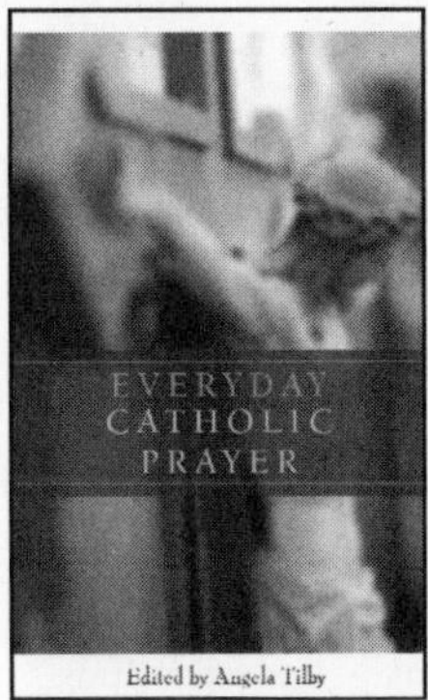

Everyday Catholic Prayer

Edited by Angela Tilby
ISBN: 978-1-55725-510-5
$14.95, Hardcover

Too busy to pray?

This book is for you. Designed for busy lives and everyday people, *Everyday Catholic Prayer* provides psalms and Scripture readings for each day of the week, patterned on the liturgy of the hours.

The St. Francis Prayer Book

By Jon M. Sweeney
ISBN: 978-1-55725-352-1
$14.95, Paperback with French flaps

This warm-hearted little book is a window into the soul of St. Francis, one of the most passionate and inspiring followers of Jesus. With this guide, readers will:

- Pray the words that Francis taught his spiritual brothers and sisters to pray.
- Explore Francis's time and place and feel the joy and earnestness of the first Franciscans.
- Experience how it is possible to live a contemplative and active life, at the same time.

Available from most booksellers or through Paraclete Press
www.paracletepress.com; 1-800-451-5006
Try your local bookstore first.

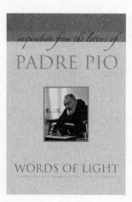